Femininity to Feminism
*Women and Literature
in the Nineteenth Century*

TWAYNE'S WOMEN AND
LITERATURE SERIES

_____

Kinley E. Roby, General Editor

Femininity to Feminism

Women and Literature
in the Nineteenth Century

SUSAN RUBINOW GORSKY

Twayne Publishers • New York
Maxwell Macmillan Canada • Toronto
Maxwell Macmillan International • New York Oxford Singapore Sydney

Twayne Publishers	Maxwell Macmillan Canada, Inc.
Macmillan Publishing Company	1200 Eglinton Avenue East
866 Third Avenue	Suite 200
New York, New York 10022	Don Mills, Ontario M3C 3N1

Macmillan Publishing Company is part of the Maxwell Communication Group of Companies.

LIBRARY OF CONGRESS CATALOGING-IN-PUBLICATION DATA

Gorsky, Susan Rubinow.
　　Femininity to feminism : women and literature in the nineteenth century / Susan Rubinow Gorsky.
　　　　p.　　cm. — (Twayne's women and literature series)
　　Includes bibliographical references (p.　　　　) and index.
　　ISBN 0-8057-8975-8 (hc : alk. paper) : $22.95. — ISBN
0-8057-8978-2 (pb : alk. paper) : $13.95
　　　　1. Women and literature—Great Britain—History—19th century.
　　2. Women and literature—United States—History—19th century.
　　3. American literature—Women authors—History and criticism.
　　4. English literature—Women authors—History and criticism.
　　5. American literature—19th century—History and criticism.
　　6. English literature—19th century—History and criticism.
　　7. Feminism and literature—History—19th century.　8. Femininity
(Psychology) in literature.　I. Title.　II. Series.
PR115.G67　1992
820.9'9287'09034—dc20　　　　　　　　　　　　　　　　　92-5277
　　　　　　　　　　　　　　　　　　　　　　　　　　　　　　CIP

The paper used in this publication meets the minimum requirements of American National Standard for Information Sciences—Permanence of Paper for Printed Library Materials. ANSI Z3948-1984. ∞™

10 9 8 7 6 5 4 3 2 1

PRINTED IN THE UNITED STATES OF AMERICA

Contents

General Editor's Note

The Twayne's Women and Literature Series seeks to provide a critical history of British and American women writers from the Anglo-Saxon age to the modern era and to present women as the subject as well as the creators of literature and to say something about how these dual roles have helped to shape our societies. It is often a record of struggle by women to write, to be published, and to find a sympathetic audience for their work. Each of the volumes examines the cultural influences at work shaping women's roles during a particular period and the attendant consequences for them as women and writers. The Series also presents a chronological account of women's efforts to find and develop their own voices in environments frequently hostile to their being heard at all.

Foreword

No other segment of English and American literature has recently been subject to more reassessment and reinterpretation than nineteenth-century fiction by and about women. Until the 1970s, the conventional understanding of nineteenth-century American literature, presented in literary histories and college classrooms, was that the great intellectual flowering of the early decades of the century—generally termed the "American Renaissance" and featuring the work of Emerson, Melville, Poe, Thoreau, and Hawthorne—gave way by the 1870s to less "artistic" literary movements such as local color and ultimately realism, with its emphasis on ordinary people rather than dramatic extremes such as Ishmael and Hester Prynne, and its undercurrent of social critique. That women writers on both sides of the Atlantic were at least as numerous as men during the century—and that their work was popular with readers—was known at the time, as witness Hawthorne's famous remark about the "mob of scribbling women." But the subsequent privileging of "elite" over "popular" literature, the devaluing of literature by women and literature about domestic issues (including the work of Charles Dickens), and an increasingly rigid distinction between history and literature as disciplines left such fiction outside the mainstream of nineteenth-century literary history.

Two quite separate intellectual movements have made possible new evaluations of nineteenth-century fiction such as this book by Susan Gorsky and others. Beginning in the 1950s, the American Studies movement in academia provided models for studying culture by observing the relationships among art, social and political history, philosophy, and technology. Instead, for example, of regarding novels such as *The Scarlet Letter* and *David Copperfield* as works of literature that existed as entities in and of themselves, interdisciplinary scholars viewed them as arising from and responding to cultural realities and values that could be ascertained with some accuracy. Further, this movement toward interdisciplinary study, which has had wide-ranging effects on the humanities and social sciences, blurred the distinction between "elite" or "high" culture and "popular" or "mass" culture, recognizing that such cultural products as films and other popular entertainments, mass-circulation periodicals, and even physical artifacts such as quilts, toys, and advertising slogans can be significant clues to understanding shifts in ideology that may in turn be reflected in "serious" art. Widely read novels, even if formulaic, are among the best vehicles for assessing the taste, values, and expectations of ordinary readers at various social levels.

By the 1970s, the women's movement had begun to have a dramatic effect on the content and modes of inquiry of many academic disciplines, including literary study. Just as the leaders of the women's movement of the 1960s recognized that theirs was but one episode in a long-fought battle for political and social equality, so scholars sought a heritage of women authors and characters, and in the process made clear the kinds of biases that had informed earlier editors, scholars, and critics—biases that had forged a canon of American and English literature dominated by white male authors. While the canon issue continues to be hotly debated, the efforts of feminist scholars have had several unignorable effects on the study of literature. One of these is the rediscovery of numerous women authors such as Kate Chopin, Fanny Fern (Sara Willis Parton), and Zora Neale Hurston. Closely related is the reconsideration of the value of types and genres of literature traditionally considered peripheral. Thus, regional literature frequently designated with the label "local color" can now be seen as the beginning of the movement toward realism of the late nineteenth century rather than the nostalgic, picturesque scribblings of (largely female) authors; and what has been called the "sentimental" or "domestic" novel has value for understanding the socioeconomic history of women and family life.

Concurrently, the study of women's history has enriched both historical methodology and our ability to understand the forces that had produced both a partial sense of history and a partial literary canon. Historians such as Gerda Lerner, Anne Firor Scott, Lillian Schlissel, Anne Douglas, and Mary Kelley have highlighted in their own research the fact that most women have not left behind the kinds of public documents represented by novels, political speeches, and records of business transactions, but must instead be understood through their private expressions: letters, diaries, memoirs, and even physical artifacts such as needlework and recipes. As Susan Glaspell's play *Trifles* makes clear, such apparently insignificant records are frequently rich in meaning.

The truism that the novel as a form arose in response to the emergence of a large middle class of literate people is currently under considerable attack by scholars who trace the form back to such poems as the *Iliad* and groups of stories such as *Tales of the Arabian Nights*. Nonetheless, it is true that during the late eighteenth and the nineteenth centuries fiction became increasingly popular in both England and America, with novels serialized in mass-circulation periodicals, sold by subscription services, and passed from one reader to another within families and groups of friends. In addition to serving as entertainment, fiction communicated moral and ethical values, and for women readers in particular, as Rachel Brownstein argues in *Becoming a Heroine*, fiction proposes models for how their lives might be lived—their options and possibilities, or, as Brownstein puts it, "structures they use to organize and interpret their feelings and prospects" (xviii). With women as both writers and readers of novels, both constrained by options for their future in terms of relationships, education, and employment, the novel of this period serves more often to reinforce than to challenge the values of the culture that produced it. Just as the chief goal of most women was marriage, for example, popular nineteenth-century novels, whether written by men or women, tended to feature what Brownstein terms the "marriage plot," ending when the heroine has achieved this objective.

Even when, as was frequently the case, these novels featured melodramatic or sensational elements and depended heavily on coincidence to drive the plot, they still reflected certain realities of nineteenth-century culture, and often embodied the author's critique of these realities. In Fanny Fern's highly melodramatic and coincidental novel *Rose Clark* (1856), for example, the author explores the deplorable conditions at a boarding school for orphans, and denounces as unfair the fact that men have legal protection for abusing their wives. A couple of decades later, Marietta Holley, in *My Opinions and Betsey Bobbet's* (1872), an amusingly dialectical and overtly feminist novel, presents the stereotype of the husband-hunting spinster, but makes it clear that such behavior on the part of a woman was motivated by economic necessity. The authors' prefaces to these two novels—one straightforward, the other satiric—are instructive for their assumptions about readership. In the preface of the book, Fanny Fern describes the ideal reader of *Rose Clark* as located in a family setting:

When the frost curtains the windows, when the wind whistles fiercely at the key-hole, when the bright fire glows, and the tea-tray is removed, and father in his slippered feet lolls in his arm-chair; and mother with her nimble needle "makes auld claes look amaist as weel as new," and grandmamma draws closer to the chimney-corner, and Tommy with his plate of chestnuts nestles contentedly at her feet; . . . For such an hour, for such an audience, was it written.

In the preface to her book, Marietta Holley, in her guise as folksy narrator Samantha Allen, assumes her reader's familiarity with novels like *Rose Clark* as she, with tongue in cheek, announces her inability to write such a novel: "I cant write a book, I don't know no underground dungeons, I haint acquainted with no haunted houses, I never see a hero suspended over a abyss by his gallusses, I never beheld a heroine swoon away, I never see a Injun tommy hawked, nor a ghost; I never had any of these advantages; I cant write a book" (v–vi). Despite the differences in tone, both authors presupposed readers for whom novels were normal fare, those who were accustomed to gaining some of their understanding of life from fiction.

Feminist critics of the past twenty years have tended to take two approaches to the nineteenth-century novel. One of these approaches—the earlier one—focuses on female characters as they emerge from the lens of a male author: to investigate, for example, how Hawthorne assessed Hester Prynne, or what significance Penelope Lapham had for William Dean Howells. Such is the approach taken by Judith Fryer in *The Faces of Eve: Women in the Nineteenth Century Novel*. Critics such as Fryer and others have demonstrated how cultural beliefs and values have influenced the depictions of women in fiction, perpetuating stereotypes of women as, variously, passive, weak, seductive, shrewish, and occasionally strong and self-determining. A second major approach, complementing the first, is that which considers women's fiction as distinct from that of men—arising from separate needs, goals, and experiences. An early contribution to this approach was Helen Waite Papashvily's *All the Happy Endings*; more recent and more influential is Nina Baym's 1978 book *Woman's Fiction*, which deals with the period from 1820 to 1870 in American literature. A central concern of recent scholars of women's fiction of the nineteenth century has been to rescue it from the oblivion occasioned by such critics as Fred Lewis Pattee, who, in *The Feminine Fifties*, emphasized the sentimental and melodramatic aspects of this fiction rather than its existence as an art form responding to specific values and conventions. The effort to recover and reconsider women's fiction has also resulted in the creation of two journals devoted to such work: *Legacy* and *Turn-of-the-Century Women*.

The process of taking seriously a tradition of women's novels has led to such books as Susan K. Harris's *Nineteenth Century American Women's Novels: Interpretive Strategies*, and it has also led to the most recent development in this field of literary study: going beyond the novels themselves to the authors and the culture that produced them and their fiction. Why did nineteenth-century women write? Why did they write the kind of fiction that they did? What did it mean for them to publish their work? These and other questions are explored in Mary Kelley's *Private Woman, Public Stage*:

Literary Domesticity in Nineteenth-Century America and Susan Coultrap-McQuin's *Doing Literary Business: American Women Writers in the Nineteenth Century*. Most women wrote as a matter of economic necessity, to support themselves and/or their children. That they depended upon income from their writing meant in turn that they had to respond to their readers' tastes and values. What Pattee derided as sentimentality, such as the frequent association of female characters with flowers and birds, was, as Susan K. Harris points out, a system of codes that had meaning for the nineteenth-century reader: a character so identified was to be regarded sympathetically, no matter what the turns of plot would expose her to.

Fanny Fern provides such codes for her title character Ruth Hall, but because the novel itself includes several satiric portraits of characters later revealed to be Fanny Fern's own relatives, the author herself was described as "unwomanly" and the novel was denounced by many critics. It is the tension between public and private that Mary Kelley identifies as a source of much discomfort for women writers, and that is part of the reason for the use of pseudonyms (Fanny Fern, George Eliot). In other words, authors were as subject to the constraints of cultural convention as the characters they created; just as a character who deviated too sharply from the piety and passivity associated with "true womanhood" risked controversy, so women writers had to create carefully their public personas or risk severe criticism for stepping into the man's realm. Hawthorne's comment about the "scribbling women" had less to do with literary taste than it did with competition in the marketplace.

Yet despite various barriers to freedom of invention and full selfhood, nineteenth-century fiction by both women and men provides remarkable insights into actual expectations for women's lives in the areas of education, marriage, social interaction, and behavior. To read autobiographies by women of the period as well as advice manuals and etiquette books is to observe assumptions about women's abilities and inclinations that also inform the fiction—whether or not the author is in sympathy with them—and that underlay opposition to the movement for female suffrage and other kinds of equality. The stories of female characters in nineteenth-century fiction, whether melodramatically or realistically rendered, reveal the anxieties and adjustments of a rapidly changing social order in which the cultural ideology looked to women to provide domestic stability even as growing numbers of women protested against the status quo and gradually won for themselves a more significant voice in the public life of England and America.

Nancy A. Walker
VANDERBILT UNIVERSITY

Susan B. Anthony and Elizabeth Cady Stanton

Courtesy of the Library of Congress

Preface

The women's movement of the nineteenth century changed contemporary life by redefining women's sense of themselves, their relationships with others, and their role in the state. The story of that transformation, often reflected and sometimes foreshadowed in literature, is the subject of this book. After an introduction to nineteenth-century life and literature, separate chapters explore the areas of marriage and family life, education, and jobs. The reform movement, addressed directly in the final chapter, provides background throughout.

Social historians and literary critics often use literature as a source of information about women's lives. Since history traditionally tended to ignore women, this makes sense, especially in the nineteenth century, whose literature bears an unusually close relationship to social reality. But this approach also presents a danger: it must not be forgotten that literature is art, not history, and thus may not faithfully describe women's roles. Artists make decisions and shape their material for reasons far removed from the desire to present society accurately.

One of the ways in which I explore literary portrayals of women's roles is rather unusual in that it involves statistics. For more than 250 of the novels that I read, I not only considered the usual literary concerns but also collected data about key issues in women's lives during five time periods between 1800 and 1920. I enumerated facts about family life, education, and work, such as the numbers of women who attend secondary school or become doctors or marry at a given age or get divorced or have more than five children. Assisted by a computer, I then compared these data with appropriate and reliable historical facts. Although this approach cannot offer infallible information about all Victorian literature, it does provide a unique insight. The actual figures rarely appear in the book, but when they do they serve as a reminder that literature necessarily skews reality, whether unconsciously or for some artistic or thematic purpose. Literature does not always attempt to present accurate historical portraits; rather, it addresses the contemporary debate about women in fascinating and often subtle ways.

While literature forms the basis of this study, fact and fiction work together as sources, each with its own relevance. Understanding society enhances interpretation of individual works and literary trends. Popular literature, often directly mirroring current ideas, also reaches the widest audience. For the sake of breadth, accuracy, and completeness, little-known works appear side by side with major literature, and men's writings complement women's. Some works receive detailed comment; others simply demonstrate a pattern or support a point. To make reading easier in a book that cites hundreds of works, and to make references more readily available, page numbers for literary quotations occur in the text with bibliographic data in the list of "Primary Sources: Literature." Citations of secondary sources appear first in the notes.

In one sense, this book began twenty years ago, when my research led to several articles on women in Victorian literature. But in another sense it began after the editors at Twayne, who had kindly invited me to write another book for them, expressed interest in a study of women in literature and society. Gradually the idea of a single book evolved into the current series, to my great delight.

My thanks to Lewis DeSimone of Twayne Publishers and Kinley E. Roby, the series editor, for their initial encouragement and continuing enthusiastic commitment. A grant from Cleveland State University supported an assistant for my preliminary research: I am very grateful to Diane Kendig, former graduate student and current friend, who spent long hours checking bibliographies and preparing lists of authors and texts. Most of all, I thank my husband, Buzz, who wrote the computer programs that allowed me to collate and graph data. For years he has listened with interest to stories about women writers, changing laws and attitudes. This book would not exist in its present form without him, and it would not have been as much fun to write. For his love and support, I dedicate the book to him.

Femininity to Feminism
*Women and Literature
in the Nineteenth Century*

Louisa May Alcott

Courtesy of the Library of Congress

CHAPTER
1

Introduction: Literature and Society

> Toward the end of the eighteenth century a change
> came about which, if I were rewriting history, I
> should describe more fully and think of greater
> importance than the Crusades or the War of the
> Roses. The middle-class woman began to write.
> —Virginia Woolf, A *Room of One's Own*[1]

Exploring the role of women during the nineteenth century means considering the evolution of feminism, a loaded word that implies a variety of ideas and arouses conflicting reactions. Feminism suggests a practical determination to alter unjust laws, whether about divorce, property, or voting rights. But it also implies a philosophical questioning of traditional values and ideas, from women's intellectual and emotional capacities to male-female relationships to the ways women and men think, act, and feel. A lot happened to women's roles and the women's movement during this period of ferment. The greatest visible changes occurred in family life, education, and jobs, areas that affect all aspects of human existence.

England and America share a heritage of culture, assumptions, laws, and beliefs. American law has its origins in British common law, American literature has often imitated England's and America's dominant religions

1

came over with the pilgrims. Until the nineteenth century, philosophical and artistic movements tended to cross the Atlantic from east to west. In the 1800s, however, America found that unique political, economic, and social realities in the New World required new attitudes, laws, and literature. Through war and economic expansion, the American territory spread from sea to sea and beyond. Westward pioneers pursued dreams of land, freedom, and wealth, and the creation of canals and roads suggested that the vast land could become one nation. Sectional differences threatened the fragile alliance, painfully reasserted through the Civil War. An earlier war separated the American colonies from England, but by the nineteenth century the British Empire stretched from Africa to Asia, from the Indian Ocean to the Caribbean. It included more than fifty colonies—areas as diverse as today's New Zealand, Sierra Leone, India, and Jamaica.

The nineteenth century is often seen as a time of relative stability, when people shared the values of family, progress, patriotism, and God; but it was truly an era of change. Cities and industries erupted in the countryside. Social reform, new educational opportunities and jobs, and writings like Darwin's *Origin of Species* challenged the established order of the universe and the position of humankind. Romanticism legitimized individuality, imaginative expression, and freedom, fostering an atmosphere in which to explore feminist ideas. In this era of search, change, and retreat, familiar patterns seemed sometimes a comforting sanctuary, sometimes a trap to destroy. Accepted values and behaviors sanctified by lip service could mask a reality quite different from the myth. The impact of change is especially obvious in women's lives.

Women's position at the end of the eighteenth century was little changed from the Middle Ages. According to British common law and thus American law, women were essentially men's property: before marriage, a woman's life was determined by her father; after marriage, by her husband; the unmarried woman was considered somehow unnatural. A woman's social status and economic well-being depended on the man in her life, and, to a very large degree, her happiness depended on his goodwill. She had almost no opportunity for education, no chance to develop special interests or choose a career other than wife and mother.

In establishing its constitution, the United States made it clear that neither slaves nor women deserved the full rights of citizenship. A few years after emancipation, male former slaves were granted the right to vote, but it took another half century for women of any color, born slave or not, to earn the same right in the United States and in England. Symbolically and actually, women were seen as less than fully human.

The roots of this attitude lie deep in Western culture. Laws codified attitudes dating back at least to the Old Testament, reinforced by Christian writings. The Book of Genesis states that the first woman was created from man, thus establishing a hierarchy that persists in church doctrine and practice to this day. Anne Bradstreet underscores the positions of God, man, and woman in her poem "To My Dear and Loving Husband" (1678): "Thy love is such I can no way repay / The heavens reward thee manifold I pray."

The Bible defines woman as saint *and* sinner, mother of the human race, source of suffering and source of salvation. Eve, tempted by the devil, in turn tempts Adam to sin, and thus sorrow and death enter the world. Mary, untouched by sexuality, gives birth to the son of God and thereby offers a path out of sin and suffering. The Old Testament God is a patriarch; the New Testament offers God the Father *and* God the Son. The most significant women in the Judeo-Christian tradition appear only in relationship to male figures, as wife or mother. So women were defined for centuries.

Women who maintain socially acceptable relationships with men are "good" women; those who defy the norms are "bad." The archetypal good woman starts as a virtuous, obedient daughter and ends as a submissive wife and nurturing mother. If, through fate or accident, she remains unmarried, she can become a saint, devoting her life to religion, good works, her parents, or perhaps her orphaned nieces and nephews. The archetypal bad woman undercuts the role and power of men: if married, she becomes a shrew or nag; if unmarried, she might be seductive, perhaps bearing a child out of wedlock, or mannish, perhaps seeking an education or career. Even her unintentional defiance of the norm disturbs society's equanimity.

In time the social norm, inherently destructive of women's individuality and rights, had to change. Recognizing the opportunity provided by the new nation's birth, Abigail Adams warned her husband: "remember the ladies and be more generous and favorable to them than your ancestors. Do not put such unlimited power into the hands of the husbands. Remember, all men would be tyrants if they could. If particular care and attention is not paid to the ladies, we are determined to foment a rebellion, and will not hold ourselves bound by any laws in which we have no voice or representation."[2] While John Adams responded, "I cannot but laugh," women—and some men—soon took such ideas quite seriously.

The early feminist movement, from late in the eighteenth century through the first decades of the twentieth, addressed both practical and theoretical issues. Feminists sought to change marriage laws, control their own property, and obtain jobs and education. They wanted political power, the "voice or representation" to make laws themselves. But they also attempted

3

to change their second-class status in another sense, desiring recognition as independent people defined by their actions and valued in and for themselves. These philosophical issues lay beneath the surface of pragmatic actions and goals. By the early twentieth century, feminists made many practical gains, but women's position did not yet equal men's. The nineteenth-century feminists left a legacy of change, but also a legacy of work yet to be done: they sought—as today's feminists still seek—true equality.

Literature in a Time of Change

Literature both influences and reflects the times in which it is written, sometimes prefiguring events in society and sometimes supporting an earlier reality by suggesting that it still exists. In the nineteenth century, poetry tended to be stylized, formal, and often dissociated from social reality; an exception is Elizabeth Barrett Browning's poem about child labor, "Cry of the Children" (1844). In part because of Victorian censorship, the theater largely degenerated into imitations and revivals of eighteenth-century comedies, presentations of Shakespeare's plays suitably purged to fit new sensibilities, and banal or melodramatic contemporary works: Mark Twain's "Royal Nonesuch" parody is more apt and less exaggerated than many modern readers of *Huckleberry Finn* (1844) realize.

Fiction dominated the literary scene. The chosen vehicle for many great writers, the novel reached the widest and most varied audience and most directly revealed social change. Because it was women who most often read and wrote novels, changing attitudes toward women's roles are most reflected in and perhaps influenced by fiction. Finally, as Virginia Woolf suggests in the words heading this chapter, many women wrote about and for themselves. Thus, the best literary source for considering women's changing roles is fiction, especially the realistic novel.

But how real is the realistic novel? Some historians use fiction as a source, arguing that since history tends to ignore women, novels provide more useful information about their lives; theorists may even challenge the objectivity of history itself, suggesting that it, too, is fiction. Further complicating matters, some literary critics argue that the author is also a kind of fiction. Yet clearly literature has an author, a human being influenced by the beliefs and events of the time and whose writings are likewise colored; clearly, regardless of bias, historians use facts differently from novelists.

Novels use details of external reality to establish a character, describe a setting, or suggest a theme. They use social data not necessarily to provide an accurate picture of society at a given time and place but to enhance some element of fiction. Given that purpose, they distort fact, whether consciously or unconsciously. To expect fiction to serve as a literal source of history is to ignore what makes it art. Yet, while not social documents, novels are closer to reality than most other genres.

The fictional use of realistic detail derives from and affirms an aesthetic theory and philosophical stance with these premises: the world "out there" is objectively definable; it is separate from the perceiver; it is "real" and significant in itself, not just in relation to the perceiver. When these ideas lost their widespread acceptance around 1900, the nature of the novel began to change.

Nineteenth-century fiction presents a fairly consistent picture of daily life: Husband and wife live comfortably with one or two children and at least one servant in a fairly large private house. Each day except Sunday, the man goes to work in one of the professions or in business. The woman spends her days close to home, visiting neighbors, performing charitable acts, sewing, reading, or subtly forwarding her daughters' chances of marriage. The boys attend school and perhaps college, while the girls receive little education but acquire a few graceful arts. Marriages almost never end in divorce, men are nearly always faithful, and women virtually never work outside the home. But social reality did not always match this picture, for a variety of reasons.

Because even the most realistic novel is still art, it reflects literary convention as much as social reality. Understanding how writers define women's changing roles and the evolution of feminist thought requires recognizing the interrelationship between literature and reality and knowing something about literary heritage.

The Realistic Novel

Early in the eighteenth century, the novel developed both the parameters that loosely demarcate the genre and the constant bending of those parameters that gives the genre its characteristic flexibility. Defoe explored the boundaries between fiction and nonfiction; Richardson tried various modes of narration; Fielding struggled tongue-in-cheek to connect the new genre to the old ones, suggesting that *Joseph Andrews* (1774) might be either a biography or a "comic epic-poem in prose" (7). As early as 1767, Laurence Sterne could challenge the barely established conventions with the outrageous, great, and experimental *Tristram Shandy*. The genre's versatility appears not only in the work of these masters but also in a proliferation of variants. Sterne's exploration of psychological theory and human nature found followers; Walpole, Radcliffe, and others introduced the Gothic novel; Fanny Burney's *Evelina* (1778) prefigured Jane Austen's more important novels of manners, and all of these authors had uncounted imitators.

By the early nineteenth century, the novel was established as the genre that most directly represented real life. True, Sir Walter Scott's historical romance, designed to reflect the imagination of the author more than the reality of ordinary life, had many followers who met the universal need to escape from the ordinary and to savor the enchantment of other worlds. Romanticism dominated America's extraordinary midcentury literary flowering, but even Melville and Hawthorne adhered to the fundamental rule of allowing their audience to identify with their characters and situations. England's "penny dreadfuls" and America's "dime novels" spawned a plethora of adventure tales with contemporary references, bloodshed, and violence; Dickens adapted this popular genre to his purposes. Gothic fiction also remained, to find major exponents such as Edgar Allan Poe and Mary Shelley, to sneak into the works of Scott and the Brontës, and to be satirized in Austen's *Northanger Abbey* (1803). But every variant of the novel has some realistic portrayal of human nature if not of ordinary human life; literature would hold little interest if it lacked connection with its readers' real concerns.

The dominant form in the nineteenth century had a far more direct connection with the real world: through variations such as the novel of manners, the problem novel, and the psychological novel, the genre consistently attempts to portray reality in fiction—to use ordinary language to show ordinary people doing ordinary things. Regional fiction, such as the short story collections *A New England Nun* (1891) by Mary E. Wilkins Freeman and *The Country of the Pointed Firs* (1896) by Sarah Orne Jewett, set its characters' situations in the context of a specific culture—thus revealing social history, especially women's daily lives. Among these local colorists were other poets and novelists of the American south and west: Kate Chopin, Mary Murfree, Grace Elizabeth King, and Constance Fenimore Woolson, sometimes described as the first realistic writer. The romantic love story of Jackson's *Ramona* (1884) depends upon the actual struggle for land and power among Indians, Mexicans, and whites in California. So, too, propagandistic fiction like Stowe's *Uncle Tom's Cabin* (1852) or historical romances like Hawthorne's *The Scarlet Letter* (1859) let us ask what the Victorians considered "the question of supreme interest in art, the question

6

upon which depends our whole interest in art": namely, "what are its relations to life?"[3]

Mimesis—the notion that art imitates the world outside itself—is an ancient aesthetic theory. Devoted to truthful representation, realistic novels are designed to reflect the authors' understanding of the world immediately around them, a world whose attributes can be determined through direct experience, and in which the consequences of actions can be discerned. Authors deal not with absolute truths but with relative ones, not an ideal sought through transcendence but a reality found in experience. Such a theory of art pretty much demands a representational mode: thus, realists strive to present a world very much like the one they perceive, and they struggle to make their perception widely accepted rather than esoteric.

Most practitioners of the realistic novel tend to see themselves partly as teachers or moral guides. Realistic novels display an unusual degree of social consciousness, attempting to address the conscience and redress the ignorance of their readers. The most trivial plot may work toward this end. Decrying the sentimentality and escapism they see in romantic fiction, and usually avoiding overt moralizing, realists present a picture of ordinary life designed to inculcate in the reader an understanding of some truth, to enhance a sense of morality or reveal essential human bonds. Moralizing or propagandizing novels necessarily assert a fairly direct relationship between art and life: if art did not imitate life, it could not hope to influence it. Early nineteenth-century novelists, more comfortable with the assumptions of their age, tend to speak for them, whereas later writers tend, however subtly, to criticize their society, as is obvious when they deal with the transformation of women's roles.

Concerned with presenting an immediately significant world with which their readers can sympathize, realists focus on character, the external and psychological effects of action, the outcome of moral decisions or ethical positions, and, above all, the everyday details of normal life in ordinary middle-class society. Because of the realistic novel's social setting and educational or moral purpose, its plot often revolves around a social problem. The heroic adventures and misadventures of the romance and the distancing effect of the historical novel give way to the mundane events and issues relevant to men and women supposedly very much like the men and women reading about them. The point is verisimilitude, though not simply for its own sake. The small truths should lead to greater ones.

Victorian novelists and critics questioned how imagination affects writing and how a novel relates to the world it reflects. Defending *Oliver Twist* (1841) as realistic, Dickens, in his preface, claimed to present degraded figures "as they really are," without the "allurements and fascinations" used by less realistic writers, because truthfulness is artistically and morally justified (ix). Many authors insist on the veracity of the most romantic tales: Hawthorne may call *The Scarlet Letter* a "romance," distinguishing it from a "novel"; yet even in the pretense of finding tantalizing historical records in the "Custom House" introduction, he symbolically reminds us of what Thackeray, in the "Preface" to *Pendennis* (1850) calls "the advantage of a certain truth and honesty." Charlotte Brontë argues that a book in which "Nature and Truth" are the sole guides would probably lack an audience and would wrongly ignore that "strong, restless faculty," the imagination.[4] Bored by popular realistic fiction, one critic proclaimed, "We may hope that the next fashion in fiction will take us to something more exciting and poetical than the domestic sorrows of brewers' wives."[5] Some argue against restrictions of topic or language, others say realism limits the place of ideas in fiction. George Eliot is not alone in objecting that those writers who claim to be most realistic are often the least, for they base their characters on convention rather than life. Literature is not life: literature selects, organizes, unifies, and transforms what exists outside it. Still, the predominant form of prose fiction, most popular at midcentury but flourishing to the end, had at least a pretense of realism, for both literary and philosophical reasons.

The forms and devices of eighteenth-century fiction, like the values and beliefs of the Enlightenment, lingered only briefly into the new century. Novels with tighter structures replaced the episodic picaresque. *David Copperfield* (1850), *Ruth* (1853), *Adam Bede* (1859), and even *The Adventures of Huckleberry Finn*, though literary descendants of *Tom Jones* (1749) and *Moll Flanders* (1722), bring the adventures nearer to home and present characters with more ordinary lives, interests, and problems. Character and realism take center stage. While Dickens and Twain may echo the "comic epic-poem" in their hyperbole and symbolic stock figures, they more honestly merit *Joseph Andrews*'s name of "biography" than does the original.

Dickens and Twain use aspects of melodrama and low comedy; Eliot, Gaskell, and Hawthorne, psychological fiction and symbolism; Alcott, sentimentality; the Brontës, Gothic romance. Yet all of their novels are more or less faithful to the society they describe, more or less designed to call attention to human nature as revealed through social interaction. Prison reform, slavery, sexual double standards, the poor laws, contemporary religious practice, jobs for women, education, or class distinctions—the most popular novels confront such issues directly and with thematic purpose.

The realistic novel may or may not be propagandistic or well formed; it may or may not make use of symbolism, melodrama, mythic patterns, or traditional plots. This variety makes it more difficult to determine whether a realistic novel accurately reflects society or skews its analysis of a given social issue, either intentionally or unintentionally. To complicate matters, society underwent fundamental redefinition on both sides of the Atlantic during these years.

The Society Reflected in Literature

Nineteenth-century life in England and America was extremely diverse. To identify the "typical" reader or character, one must consider a variety of issues, including place, time, and social class.

As America grew from a strip of land along the Atlantic Ocean to a nation stretching beyond continental bounds, *where* one lived implied differences in citizenship (state or territory?), economics, and life-style (factory owner or mill-hand? plantation owner or slave?). While social distinctions outweighed regional ones in England, agriculture dominated the south, factories the midlands and the north. A London home could be a slum tenement, a fine urban residence, or a house in a garden suburb. Each variation profoundly affected daily life, from religion to education to attitudes about women.

The extent of change in social reality and in attitudes in the nineteenth century was so great that it is very difficult to determine *when* our typical person lived. The first years of the century were a time of optimism during which many people believed that science and technology could resolve all of society's problems. In contrast, by the end of the century, the overall picture was one of agricultural depression, labor unrest, and increasing political, economic, and ideologic tensions. Thus life in 1895 barely resembled life in 1855 or 1805.

Much of the new hope derived from technological and attitudinal changes. In 1825, the new Erie Canal symbolized America's growth, and in 1832 the First Reform Bill ushered in an era of English social reform. In these early decades, Manifest Destiny seemed natural, economic prosperity and expansion seemed assured. In 1851, American literature flourished, and England celebrated the Great Exhibition of the Works of Industry of All Nations, better known as the Crystal Palace. From 1851 to 1881, Britain's gross national product doubled; Britain became the world's wealthiest country, London the greatest city. Cities and railroads multiplied, the middle class expanded and moved upward, and the working classes also reaped some financial rewards.

Yet the seeds of disillusion were always present: from the beginning of the period, reformers pointed to miserable conditions in slums and factories, even worse on plantations. By mid-century, events ranging from the publication of Darwin's *Origin of Species* to the Crimean War had rocked the Western world. The United States experienced a bloody, demoralizing Civil War; the closing of the frontier by the 1890s further undercut the American dream. As the English argued over new laws like the Second Reform Bill (1857) which gave town workers the vote and suggested that political and social power might slip from traditional aristocratic leaders to the "masses," similar fears emerged in the postwar American South when freed black slaves sometimes outnumbered former masters. And in England, Prince Albert's death led Queen Victoria into a period of seclusion suggesting to many the end of the monarchy.

Still, the Queen's Jubilee in 1887 showed that Victoria was both alive and beloved, whatever the state of the monarchy. She outlived the period that bears her name, dying long after the halcyon era of progress and certainty gave way to the incipient doubts inherent in the transition to modernism. The derogatory sense of the term "Victorianism," used since the 1890s, aptly suggests a conservative tendency in manners and mores. Victorianism remains a complex and loaded term, increasing the difficulty of defining a "typically" Victorian time period.

Once we have identified *when* and *where*, we still need to decide *who* best represents nineteenth-century life. Despite stunning diversity in society and culture, two significant and related features are the rise of the middle class and the rise of the realistic novel, which was written largely about and for that middle class.

In *Sybil* (1845), Disraeli made popular the idea of England as "two nations . . . the rich and the poor . . . between whom there is no intercourse and no sympathy; who are as ignorant of each other's habits, thoughts, and feelings, as if they were dwellers in different zones, or inhabitants of different planets; who are formed by a different breeding, are fed by a different food, are ordered by different manners, and are not governed by the same laws" (74). Was it two nations, as Disraeli says (a sufficiently startling idea), or three—the traditional "upper," "middle," and "lower" (or "working") classes—or five, or ten, or more classes, each distinguishable by some economist or social historian? Important distinctions existed, based on objective factors such as income, housing, occupation, and education, and unquantifiable factors such as the status and power traditionally associated with a particular occupation or school, a set of manners or beliefs. Despite professions of egalitarianism, America shared some of England's emphasis on class.

Believing in the rightness of a preordained social hierarchy, the English also felt that worthy individuals could rise "above their station," an idea intrinsic to the American dream. Yet antagonism between classes and jockeying for position within a given class characterized both nations, and often appear as literary themes, with special relevance for women.

The once-stable British society became frankly pluralistic. Urban laborers differed from farm laborers; both opposed mill operators; all three differed from aristocrats, some of whom maintained a traditional feudal relationship with tenant farmers while others, discovering coal on their land, became great mine owners. In the United States, such distinctions were most obvious in the South, where white plantation owners outranked rural "poor whites," who maintained a sense of superiority by forming the backbone of the Ku Klux Klan to harass and terrorize former slaves. Slaves and American Indians stood outside the social stratification defined by property, education, religion, and background. Yet as a nation of immigrants, America more easily defined people through individual achievement rather than group identity.

In England, where birth normally establishes status, the hereditary nobility remained far more than a titled and leisured class. They were the nation's acknowledged leaders, whose attitudes and values had profound influence. While others struggled to acquire the attributes of gentility, birth and training gave the aristocrat style, grace, courage, and nobility of manners. When aristocrats bought up much of the "commons" (commonly used meadowlands) early in the century, they increased their tangible power along with their acreage. Feudal landlords on immense holdings, they might invite tenants to agricultural fairs or coming-of-age feasts or evict them from modest family homes; tenants were wooed for their votes—and the secret ballot was unknown until 1872.

Next came the gentry, the country families, younger sons of peers, the baronets, squires, and "gentlemen." Law and tradition gave them power in local government and society. Land conferred status, financial clout, and the right to play landlord, sportsman, or country host. The impact of both the gentry and the aristocracy spread as the middle class tried to emulate if not enter higher social circles.

The burgeoning middle class (or classes) came next, defined by jobs, living conditions, and attitudes. According to the *Oxford English Diction-*

ary, the term *middle class* was first used as early as 1812. The Industrial Revolution added commercial men and manufacturers to the original shop-keepers and professionals. As they gained wealth, acumen, and polish, the new members increased their upward mobility. Each level imitated the manners and mores of the group immediately above, with tremendous impact on women.

The desire for gentility supported the traditional social hierarchy. The title of "gentleman" might accrue to a village shopkeeper, doctor, or small landowner. The size, location, stock, and clientele of a shop determined the status of the owner and his wife. Manufacturers and industrialists purchased land and sent their sons to the right schools in order to approximate membership in the gentry. Through his efforts, a man could become a gentleman; a woman could become a lady by marrying a gentleman.

Theoretically, anyone could obtain the moral ideal of respectability, honor, industry, courage, and self-control, and in that sense be genteel. Respectability, the most important of these qualities, reflected the power of absolutes derived more or less directly from the Bible, variously interpreted by different religious groups. The implication that individuals could redeem themselves through faith and good works supported the idea of labor as ennobling and the value of deferring immediate gratification in favor of higher but ultimately attainable goals. Yet this same theory led to restrictive codes of behavior, censorship, unwavering assertions of moral propriety, and the fervor to convert a whole populace, which in turn contributed to both hypocrisy and psychological confusion.

While opinions varied about the propriety of card-playing or dancing, respectability always connoted decorous dress and manners, honesty, chastity, a serious attitude toward family and work, cleanliness, tidiness, and an earnest avoidance of mere frivolity. Although interpretation of the rules might be more or less liberal or sanctimonious, it was always sufficiently strict to support the status quo. True, some people flaunted their rebellion by gambling, maintaining a mistress, or succumbing to a bohemian artist's life. Against such behavior, the middle class strove through example and preaching to make real an image half borrowed from the gentry and half derived from its own sense of moral and social propriety. From this, and against it, developed the realistic and social-problem novels. Though not always representative, the "respectable" were vocal, and they read realistic fiction.

In all social classes and almost without exception, women earned their status from their fathers and husbands. Middle-class men demonstrated financial success by giving wives and daughters lives of leisure, and genteel ladies did not work outside the home or for pay. These families had to ensure women an idle respectability in which feminine pursuits replaced useful activity unless related to charity or family life. The devaluation of women's jobs from pre-Industrial times to the middle of the century, a devaluation based largely on economics, was handily supported by the fundamental belief that women were men's physical, moral, and mental inferiors. In turn, the belief in women's innate inferiority fostered the view of women's work as socially undesirable. This vicious circle caused profound differences in education, expectations, responsibilities, and opportunities for girls and boys.

In contrast, lower-class men and women worked together in fields and factories, and women were exploited rather than sheltered. As the middle class became increasingly aware of the poor people crowded into mews and alleys just behind the fashionable city streets, reform movements grew. The objects of attention included farmers, semiskilled or unskilled workers, servants, slaves, craftsmen dispossessed by machines, and country laborers dispossessed as small farms merged into large ones. The urge for reform fit middle-class ideas of social and moral responsibility, but it also resulted from labor agitation and publicity exposing the workers' plight. Fearing that slums bred not just physical but moral disease, reformers looked first at the obvious misery of factory workers and slum dwellers. The smoke rising from new factories became symptom and symbol of the Industrial Revolution.

Artisans might aspire to rise in status by emulating middle-class virtues, but most laborers merely sought to survive the long hours and poor conditions of mines or factories, if they even found work. By 1900, reform efforts eradicated the worst conditions—five-year-olds working in mines, fifty-hour work weeks for nine-year-olds in the cotton industry, pregnant women (cheaper than horses) strapped to coal carts, mining towns without water, urban slums with one privy for half a dozen families.

Literature about slum life and industrialization became popular, especially during times of agitation for reform. Yet even that literature was directed at the middle class, who might do something to help. Throughout the century, the middle class formed both subject and audience of the most important literature.

The Novel and the Middle Class

The phenomenon of a mass reading public began in the nineteenth century.[6] Poems appeared in magazines and in slim books that might grace a parlor table. But the most popular reading material was fiction, whether published in one volume or three, serialized in newspapers or magazines, bought or borrowed from libraries. As inexpensive editions of popular works proliferated to meet the new literacy and interest of the middle and working classes, the ability to own books spread downward. Still, most middle-class readers subscribed to circulating libraries or patronized "free" libraries designed to give workers access to books.

Opening a package from the circulating library was a family occasion. Like advertising today, a subscription library such as Charles Edward Mudie's "Select Circulating Library" in England could determine a book's success through large orders and a seal of approval. Circulating libraries, assuming they knew the public's taste and morals, supported the prevalent censorship. Moral rather than literary merit often determined a book's availability and popularity.

For the upper classes, reading was not a new interest or skill. Although workers' literacy increased, reading for pleasure differs greatly from signing your name or deciphering a job application. Poor lighting, crowded living conditions, and exhaustion made theaters, parks, railway excursions, and other forms of cheap entertainment more popular than reading. Still, workers whiled away long train rides with books, sought advancement through tracts and moral tales from public reading rooms and libraries, or relaxed over a penny dreadful or dime novel, an easy-to-read adventure tale or sentimental story, a newspaper or tabloid, a broadside featuring grisly or sensational stories, or even a condensed Shakespeare play or Scott novel.

The middle class had more money, time, and literacy than the lower classes, and more interest in education and advancement than the upper classes. Even in recreation, they sought the useful and uplifting as well as the entertaining. They connected moral and social improvement, ideas fostered by the American Puritan heritage and the English Evangelicals and Utilitarians. If reading for fun might injure rising and righteous members of the middle class, wholesome literature with a moral purpose could benefit them. Reading became the dominant form of entertainment as well as a way to enforce morality and family unity: each evening, families would gather into the famous reading circle with the latest newspapers, magazines, or novels.

That image influenced publishers, libraries, and writers, and censorship was a fact of literary production. In 1818, Thomas Bowdler published *The Family Shakespeare,* containing oddly expurgated versions of the plays, changing words and altering scenes to protect the innocence of daughters in the reading circle. Bowdler gives his name as well as his practice to many "bowdlerized" books. With the innocent young girl as touchstone, editors cut and altered words in contemporary and earlier works. First to go were unorthodox opinions and hints of sexuality—references to the body, passion, or pregnancy. The editors' purpose and defense lay overtly in the desire to uphold the contemporary moral ideal and covertly in the desire to avoid offending readers.

One observer, evaluating the books found in miners' houses, suggests laborers are "backward to attempt anything that requires steady thinking": miners "had rather read any popular work, such as The Christian Philosopher, the Pilgrim's Progress, or Walter Scott's novels, choosing fiction, history, geography, and books about British warfare rather than logic, mathematics, economics, and grammar."[7] Modern readers hardly judge the selection as frivolous, but Victorians read sermons, biographies, essays, scientific texts, religious tracts, inspiring tales with overt morals, and self-help books. Weeklies and monthlies carrying serious literature, art criticism, debates on social, moral, and religious issues matched papers devoted to sports, humor, adventurous exploits, and household hints. And always there was a market for fiction.

Determining the popularity of a given book would require knowing both sales and library circulation figures. Even that information falls short, for a dozen people might hear a book in the family circle, and a whole neighborhood might share a single newspaper. Inflated advertisements and manipulated sales figures create further inaccuracies. Attempts to outline the story of nineteenth-century readership rely on such data plus trade rumors and comments in private diaries or letters.

We cannot know for sure which novels were most popular, or which best represent contemporary life. Given the sheer volume of literature produced and the fact that some is unavailable, we cannot read exactly what Victorians read. But we know that fiction was the most popular genre, and within that genre, the most popular was the realistic novel dealing with and read by the middle class. We also know that a fair representation must include novels that, though now unread, were once popular enough to leave a mark on literature and society. Remembering Woolf's words at the head of the chapter, we know that women were central, as both writers and readers. Women both influenced and were influenced by social change, and they both influenced and were influenced by literature. Novels written by, about, and for the middle class reveal a great deal about women's roles, people's reactions to those roles, and the evolution of feminism.

George Eliot

Courtesy of the National Portrait Gallery, London

Marriage and Family: Gentle Ladies and New Women

> This history is chiefly concerned with the private lot
> of a few men and women; but there is no private life
> which has not been determined by a wider public life.
> —George Eliot, *Felix Holt, the Radical* ([1866], 45)

Love and marriage constitute the traditional themes of nineteenth-century literature, as they did of women's lives. The idea that women reigned in the home is part truth, part myth, part lie; but the literature of the day implies that it is virtually all truth. In battling to enlarge women's sphere, feminists had to cut through a great deal of myth along with more palpable kinds of resistance. Through the years, literature both maintained and undercut the myth. The outer world of marriage described in documents—when people married, when they had children, how many children they had, how much it cost to furnish a home or live "genteelly"—appears in literature, especially fiction. And decades before modern psychological literature, authors also wrote about the inner world of feelings—what it's like to fall in love, why people marry. If we believe the majority of authors, both worlds contented most women.

Nineteenth-century literature reflects an ideal of marriage and family life. All the realistic details of houses and servants and carriages cannot mask that fact. The problems faced by couples serve to complicate plot, but ulti-mately the novels sanction the glory of marriage. With rare exceptions, problems occur before the wedding, not after. Once the pair has persuaded reluctant parents to approve the marriage, once the future husband has found a suitable job or disproved the nasty rumors about himself, once the woman has outgrown her misguided desire to attend college or fulfilled her honorable desire to care for her aged parents, then all is well: husband and wife settle happily ever after into a comfortably patriarchal domesticity, and the door closes on their lives. The family and its home, a symbol of isolated unity, create the natural center of life. Even literature that unlocks the door to a couple's sacred home normally idealizes marriage, so that unfaithful husbands and unhappy wives, let alone divorce, are the rarest exceptions. Sometimes a man seeks a second wife when the first dies, perhaps in child-birth, but most marriages last forever. Society's rapid change and resulting dislocations generally go unmentioned, or, if present, form an implicit part of the backdrop. Literature shows young women learning to love, young men finding ways to win the heroines, and marriages if not made in heaven then sealed there.

Yet from the earliest days, there is a counterbalance of questioning, re-fining, seeking new truths. Several women writers and a few men offer an occasional problem marriage, an occasional woman who seeks an educa-tion for fulfillment or who wants—not just needs—to work. These are the gentle doubters. More ardent reformers directly address the need to revise the emphasis on and the definitions of marriage, attacking the unhealthy realities and insisting on the unacknowledged *un*realities of the supposed norm.

The Idealization of Family Life

Arguing that contemporary women were little better off than slaves, the English philosopher John Stuart Mill, in *The Subjection of Women* (1869), predicted new freedoms and opportunities in an era of change. Decades ahead of her time, the American feminist and abolitionist Sarah Grimké asserted that "human rights are *not* based upon sex, color, capacity or con-dition" and insisted that only "despots will deny to woman that supreme sovereignty over her own person and conduct which Law concedes to man."[1]

Some of the early feminists who, like Grimké, lectured, petitioned, attended women's rights conventions, and braved the scorn of their country-men and women, insisted their cause would make women better wives and mothers. Grimké believed absolute equality between husband and wife would lead to a "true relation" free of "difficulties"; yet if a marriage proved "uncongenial," she rejected both divorce and "free love." Rather, the "un-happy couple" must "bear in quiet home seclusion, the heart withering consequences of your own mistakes": "You owe this to yourselves, to your children, to society" (Lerner, 92–93).

More radical feminists evaluated not only marriage but other options. Early in the period, the ideal of the Perfect Lady, the genteel ornament of feminine innocence, gave way to the Perfect Woman, the genteel upholder of moral virtue, symbolic goddess of the very small universe of the private home. Later still, the Perfect Woman was challenged if not supplanted by the New Woman, the independent but still feminine being who hesitantly opened the door to the world outside of marriage.

Very few of Grimké's or Mill's contemporaries, male or female, Ameri-can or English, shared their views. Most saw marriage as the center of a woman's life, an institution unquestioned in significance or structure. A woman's real life began when she entered into marriage, an indissoluble relationship that made her invisible under the law. Literature generally ac-cepted and supported this situation: marriage was the most desirable goal of virtually every woman's life and a natural part of nearly every man's. The fact that the rules of marriage differed for men and women did not limit this idealization, but it strongly influenced the development of feminist attitudes about womanhood and marriage.

The poetry of the day, lacking the immediate, concrete contact with reality that marks drama and especially fiction, idealizes and spiritualizes love and family life. Exceptions exist, such as "The Battle Hymn of the Republic" (1862) by Julia Ward Howe, but far more characteristic is Lydia Maria Child's Thanksgiving poem, "Over the River and through the Woods" (1844–46), celebrating the return to "grandmother's house." Much popular poetry sentimentalizes marriage: often written by women, poems in newspapers and women's magazines describe love as the gentle flame warm-ing the hearth that lights the center of the home. Many of these poems read like the parody Mark Twain provides through Emmeline Grangerford's maudlin verse in *Huckleberry Finn*. The Byronic hero and the free spirit of this age of romanticism and revolution rarely touch women in literature. In Elizabeth Barrett Browning's melodramatic narrative poem *Aurora Leigh* (1857), the poet Aurora first rejects the traditional life of feminine gentility and marriage for her vocation but later marries the blind Romney. He will fulfill their romantic vision of a revolutionary society of freedom and truth; she will serve as helpmate and assistant.

Poe's "To Helen" (1831) offers the stereotype of the saint or good woman, representing the ethereal muse or the goddess who guides men safely home. In contrast, Dante Gabriel Rossetti offers Lilith, the symbolic bad woman, who "draws men to watch the bright web she can weave"; this poem about the archetypal temptress bears the apt title, "Body's Beauty" (from *The House of Life* [1870]). Neither Helen nor Lilith is the marrying type.

Emily Dickinson's poems reevaluate traditional expectations of marriage. Reading these biographically, one senses that Dickinson, like Aurora Leigh, considered the options of marriage and art, but, given the realities of contemporary wedded life as well as her personality, chose the latter. The poems reflect a tortured ambivalence about the value of marriage and women's roles. She writes, "I'm 'wife'—I've finished that / That other state" (1860); and she suggests that marriage, the only way to become a woman, is akin to death.

Even such remarkable poems by an exceptional author assume that marriage defines a woman's life. The impact of that norm on a sensitive, talented woman is suggested by the number of artist-heroines and the painful lives their creators describe. Yet in virtually all literature, love is supposed to lead to marriage. Gradually, as society struggled to redefine the relationship between the sexes, so literature struggled to come to grips with this redefinition. Sometimes the more obviously feminist literature attempted to influence the pace and nature of change.

Women in literature expect to marry and do marry, unless prevented by the kinds of complications that lead to extended plots and, not so incidentally, underscore the desirability of marriage. Marriage is so clearly the norm that women almost never voluntarily consider alternatives. Men talk less about marriage and do not spend their days waiting to change their state from incomplete singleness to blessed union; nevertheless, they, too, regard marriage as the norm for themselves and unquestionably for women.

In the real world, many single women and men lived useful, interesting lives. Nor did people fail to marry only because parents or fate intervened to create the sudden complications in which authors revel; some simply *chose* not to marry. Still, single women were considered abnormal, objects of pity or scorn.

When they did marry, real people had large families, a fact literature seldom reflects. Heroes and heroines come from families in which childbirth, if it occurs at all, occurs offstage. During courtship and early in marriage, couples rarely mention children; at most, they might indirectly refer to a wished-for heir to appear in the vague, distant future. Widespread censorship helps explain why authors hesitate to discuss characters' family planning, in any sense of that term. But perhaps society's belief that marriage obviously leads to childbearing meant that children need not be discussed; they are simply assumed. These explanations do not fully justify fiction's small families—three or two or even one offspring when society expected double or triple that number. Perhaps too many characters would be artistically unnecessary—difficult for authors or confusing for readers. Or perhaps some authors tried to make a point by limiting family size.

All literature, even the realistic novel, idealizes society in some way, just as it displays the impact of current ideas and past literary conventions. The fragile Victorian heroine mirrors the delicate blonde of the sentimental novel as much as she embodies social reality or the ideal. Illness, suffering, and death function thematically in a moral design with a long literary heritage. Orphans and prodigal sons, fallen women and patient Griseldas maintain their traditional impact when transplanted into nineteenth-century literature. Fiction designed to proselytize or enlighten uses hyperbole to stress a problem or to create a dystopian or utopian vision revealing the evils of contemporary society or invoking a better one. Such literature can readily introduce a poor family with too many mouths to feed, or a single woman dedicating her life to helping others. But most literature, designed primarily to entertain, avoids controversy by accepting its audience's prejudices. For years, literature supported a myth of the perfect family, a myth against which feminists fought overtly in the real world and covertly through literature.

Love and Marriage

Nineteenth-century literature makes it clear: young women marry; young men find suitable jobs that provide position, respectability, identity, and the chance to marry. Heroines discuss what makes a good match, when and whom they will marry. Heroes talk less about these subjects but still expect to marry. Parents worry about a suitor's eligibility in terms of social and financial status, age, and sometimes morality, though almost never compatibility. Some wonder about the right reasons to marry and some recognize that not all people should marry, but the norm is simple: virtually every woman and most men wish to settle down with the right spouse and make a home together.

This accurately reflects the exalted vision of marriage, symbolized by the matriarch Queen Victoria. The ideal family, in reality and in literature, consisted of a father whose employment provided a comfortable social standing; a mother who was her husband's inferior in all ways except her femininity, the indefinable quality that enabled her to make their home a well-run refuge from the outside world; and mannerly children and servants whose demeanor reflected the virtuous atmosphere of home and mistress. The upper classes sometimes mocked this ideal; families struggling for economic survival had no hope to reach it. Yet the stereotype penetrated the lower classes, reinforcing its power: the genteel lady could hardly exist in a family working in a factory or on a farm, but exist she did—as an ideal. This image of the family fit the religious beliefs and the notion of respectability that characterized the middle class, and the model became a goal.

Christina Rossetti was one woman for whom such a life did not occur, although she had several love affairs and was once engaged. A talented poet, she poured her emotions into her verse, producing erotic, painful poems of longing and renunciation. The titles of "Shut Out" and "Dead before Death" reveal their meaning; poems like "Goblin Market" warn of the dangers of sexuality (1862). "Venus's Looking Glass" (1875) imagines a world where women rule through the traditional power of love: as Venus tempts the harvesters from their labor, each "laughed and hoped and was content."

Novels emphasize marriage more directly. As Edwards says in *Susan Fielding* (1864): "custom . . . exact[s] that lovers, marriage, and again lovers should fill nine-tenths of every three volumes" (18). Most novels end when lovers become spouses, but a few go further. In Black's romance *A Princess of Thule* (1873), and even more in Eden's domestic novel *The Semi-Attached Couple* (1860), characters learn that problems develop when a couple doesn't truly know each other. Eden suggests leaving newlyweds alone to foster in private "that complete dependence on each other, which insures habits of confidence and forbearance" after the initial disorder of "tastes and tempers" (94–95). Since the typical brief courtship allowed the merest acquaintance, such issues must have been more important than fiction admits. Literature assumes that marriage, the natural state, will naturally succeed.

In *Felix Holt*, Eliot acknowledges that "in the ages since Adam's marriage, it has been good for some men to be alone, and for some women also." But quickly, perhaps defensively, she adds that her heroine, Esther, "was not one of these women; she was intensely of the feminine type, verging neither towards the saint nor the angel" (397). Oliphant in *Agnes* (1865) observes that the "common fate" for those who are neither saints nor angels is "marriage and motherhood, a love, a wedding, a new household" (1:31). The home symbolizes the marriage within. Although novels occasionally suggest that moral values outweigh material ones (Eliot's *Adam Bede*, Guyton's *Married Life* [1863]), most assert the importance of a house, especially to the woman. Gaskell's title character in *Sylvia's Lovers* (1863) is unusual in failing to "show the bright shy curiosity about her future dwelling that is common enough with girls who are going to be married" (358). Almost inevitably, one of the first rooms furnished is the nursery, as authors—perhaps unconsciously—reinforce the norm. Men provide the house and support the family, women decorate the house and care for the children, and both recognize the value of home and family.

Although many male characters would support the man in Carey's *Herb of Grace* (1901) who says marriage is "his haven and comfort . . . his dearest Rest" (440), most authors insist that marriage matters more to women, or at least matters differently. In Trollope's *Dr. Thorne* (1858), Frank enjoys his normal occupations "quite as vehemently as though he were not in love at all," while "Mary sat there at her window, thinking of her love, and thinking of nothing else. It was all in all to her now" (389). True, a man must consider his job even to get married; but Frank's occupations are his horses and dogs, neither practical nor essential. In *The Landlord at Lion's Head* (1897), Howells satirically suggests that Jeff wants to linger "in the abandon" of love, "to give himself solely up to it, to think and to talk of nothing else, after a man's fashion. But a woman's love is no such mere delight. It is serious, practical. For her it is all future, and she cannot give herself wholly up to any present moment of it, as a man does" (113). Though Howells implies this holds true generally, Jeff's impractical immaturity justifies his fiancée's reactions. However universal the idea, however innate the desire, society's assumption that women will marry inculcates the expectation. Only saints, angels, and evil women fail to care about marriage.

Using society's rules as well as the literary stereotypes of light and dark heroines—Eve before and after the Fall, or the Virgin Mary and Mary Magdalene—James Fenimore Cooper divides women into categories based on their marriageability. Cora, the dark heroine of *The Last of the Mohicans* (1826), is not the stereotyped temptress; physical darkness, inherited from her part-African mother, makes her unmarriageable. Alice is the typical blond heroine, prone to fainting and raised to a feminine helplessness that seems especially silly on the American plain. Requiring care and love, Alice is a "precious burden," the pure, gentle, passive woman whose background and behavior merit marriage. Society's rules make Hetty and Judith Hutter, the fair and dark ladies of *The Deerslayer* (1841), unmarriageable: they are illegitimate children, reared by an outcast man. Hetty, passive and feminine, is also feebleminded; Judith carries strong-mindedness to the point of rebellion and illicit sex, accepting her role outside the norm. The details vary little within immutable stereotypes: saint and sinner, blond and brunette, marriageable and unmarriageable.

Marriage is the "ordinary destiny," as Caroline says in Charlotte Brontë's *Shirley* (1849): "Till lately I had reckoned securely on the duties and affections of wife and mother to occupy my existence. I considered, somehow, as a matter of course, that I was growing up to the ordinary destiny" (158). With the title character, she defines girls' lives: "The great wish—the sole aim of every one of them is to be married. . . . They scheme, they plot, they dress to ensnare husbands" (348). Gaskell likewise acknowledges the normalcy, the essentiality, of the "ordinary destiny." In *North and South* (1855) one character explains, "as I have neither husband nor child to give me natural duties, I must make myself some, in addition to ordering my gowns" (417). A woman's "natural" life is a family.

Even the flirt and the independent woman outgrow these ideas, with rare (usually tragic) exceptions. In Carey's *Lover or Friend* (1890) love so alters the heroine that, unsurprisingly, she no longer desires freedom. A woman who persists in flirting, jilting, or ignoring men may end up chastised by friends, shunned by society, and even unmarriageable, like Cynthia in Gaskell's *Wives and Daughters* (1866). James transports the innocently flirtatious title character of *Daisy Miller* (1879) to Europe to avoid the limitations of American naïveté. Daisy's behavior implies that she doesn't care about appearances. But she maintains her essential innocence to her death: by flirting as society suggests only married women can, she mocks hypocrisy, not personal virtue. Audacious and self-reliant, she brings American values to a European community that cannot handle them. Society prevents her marrying and, significantly, the story ends with her death.

This emphasis on marriage remains even as real society and its laws changed, altering assumptions about marriage. Linton's *Autobiography of Christopher Kirkland* (1885) asserts that ideas of marriage suiting an old society do not fit the modern world: not "a complex and widely differentiated society like ours—where men cannot marry when young, and women cannot marry where they would; where the highly developed nervous organization of the race makes compatibility difficult to find and incompatibility impossible to bear; where woman's domestic life is cramping and dissatisfaction is fatally common for both men and women alike" (206–7). Yet decades later, even such unconventional novels as Lawrence's *The Rainbow* (1915) and *Women in Love* (1920) and Charles Bellamy's

Experiment in Marriage (1899) present marriage as the norm. Ursula ex-emplifies the traditional female situation when facing "that empty period between school and possible marriage" (*Rainbow*, 352). While the main characters in *Women in Love* ask whether marriage is a fulfillment or a trap and struggle to redefine relationships in and beyond marriage, they also insist that an intense union enriches and completes life. Bellamy's book establishes a utopia where women are economically independent and chil-dren are wards of the state; with the traditional sex roles revised, marriage and divorce result from personal feelings. This vision was a long way from reality in the 1800s.

Husbands and Wives

The changes in men's and women's roles came slowly and painfully, in literature as in reality. While a new bride among laborers or farmers might dwell with several generations of her husband's family in a tenement or on a farm, the nuclear family dominated the middle class. Even elderly parents usually stayed in their own homes, maintaining privacy and independence for both families. A contemporary comment on the 1851 census in England emphasizes the symbolism: "It is so much the order of nature that a family should live in a separate house, that 'house' is often used for 'family' in many languages."[2] Owning a house became a significant goal, and the physical boundaries of the home demarcated the family safely united within. To enhance laborers' homes and lives, the middle and upper classes promulgated schemes ranging from the patronizing (reforming morality to suit the reformers) to the practical (improving sanitation in New York's tene-ments or building model cottages like those Prince Albert commissioned for the Crystal Palace Exhibition).

Virtually any man's home was his castle, where law and custom let him rule with nearly absolute power. His wife reigned not as queen but as that pure, charming, sympathetic, domestic, self-sacrificing, subservient, self-less creature that Woolf called the "Angel of the House."[3] This symbol of the Perfect Woman comes from Coventry Patmore's verse series (1892) in which the heavenly heroine lacks individual desire or mind, leads an ordi-nary life, but guides her man to greatness. For many feminists like Woolf, the Angel of the House, a demon internalized from the social ideal, must be killed before women can achieve identity, independence, and the chance to fulfill their talents.

The law reinforced society's comforting view of the Angel of the House.

With no legal existence separate from her husband, a woman could not sign contracts, own property, or sue for divorce, and had no rights over her children. Queen Victoria had so much influence partly because she provided an exalted model of domesticity: even the proud queen acknowledged her husband's superiority, deferred to him in ways that distressed statesmen, and for decades concentrated on the domestic sphere, bearing a large—but not unusually large—family of nine children. Her marriage and later endless mourning epitomized the cult of pure womanhood.

The patriarchal nature of marriage seemed unaffected by the fact that men and women tended to marry at about the same age. American women normally had more freedom than their English sisters: some colonies initially offered land and even voting rights to potential female settlers. Once the shortage of women eased, women frequently lost these rights. Still, frontier and farm families necessarily maintained a practical equality between the sexes, regardless of the laws.

John Stuart Mill insisted in *The Subjection of Women* that women's subordination to men was a kind of political oppression, but most disagreed with him, seeing it as natural. Blackstone's *Commentaries on the Laws of England* (1765) described the legal situation in force through most of the century: "By marriage, the very being or legal existence of a woman is suspended, or at least it is incorporated or consolidated into that of the husband, under whose wing, protection, or cover she performs everything."[4] The law maintained, and society believed, that the husband's will was supreme, his word absolute. Until well past midcentury, the wife stood before the law as a child, her word only a wish. Sarah Grimké observes the "terrible effect" of the laws on "noble minded women even where the husbands did all in their power to annul them": such women are demeaned, knowing "that they enjoyed the privileges they had, not by right, but by courtesy" (Lerner, 97).

Motivated by society's valuing work as a virtue and by the traditional male role, the husband had to ensure his family's comfort. Homes displayed visible signs of upward mobility in a parlor rug, some pictures on the wall, or books from the circulating library displayed with casual prominence. Leisure also marked status, and the uses of leisure varied by class and time period. Having at least one servant very nearly defined middle-class status.

The wife's role in the household reflected profound ambivalence toward women. Women's magazines and housekeeping manuals offered advice on budgeting, marketing, cooking, and cleaning, as well as child rearing—all essential information for the bride. They often addressed the "servant problem": having trained a new servant—often a country girl innocent of basic cleanliness and housekeeping skills—the wife had to govern her work, keep her satisfied but not cheeky, and probably soon find her replacement. Concerned about status, many parents educated their daughters above their station, so that the bride could sing or embroider but not order a meal or keep a budget. Yet, unprepared as she was, she planned the budget, ran a large and complex household, ordered food and arranged meals, nursed the ill, supervised her children's early education, and guided the moral development of children and servants. She needed the skills of a restaurant manager, dietitian, nurse, teacher, cleric, bookkeeper, and housekeeper, and the strength of all these combined. Yet she was considered her husband's inferior in virtually all ways. Common knowledge, reinforced by manuals and magazines, lectures, sermons, and "scientific" studies, said women lacked men's physical, intellectual, and moral strength. Ironically, this morally weak creature served as priestess of the home, moral guide to the household, and creator of a sanctified refuge from the pressures of the outside world. This daughter of Eve was considered at great risk should she awaken from her sexual innocence: many commentators saw women as free of any inconvenient sexual desires; Eve the temptress, however popular in myth and literature, lived outside the ideal. The woman was the angel who could help a man control his sexual urges. The young girl's parents and later her husband helped her to spin a delicate cocoon in which to live, but unlike the butterfly, she was to remain forever chrysalis.

This was the ideal—or the myth; and, like all myths, it draws strength from its links to reality. As myth and as reflection of society, it permeates literature. Exaggerating only slightly, Trollope satirically compares women to ivy, the "delicate creeper" and "parasite" that winds around the "strong wall": such plants "were not created to stretch forth their branches alone, and endure without protection the summer's sun and the winter's storm," but "when they have found their firm supporters, how wonderful is their beauty, how all pervading and victorious!" (*Barchester Towers*, [1857], 479).

Male supremacy is simply assumed; defying convention risks destruction. One man explains that a woman needs a father to control her until "her natural and legitimate master," her husband, assumes the job. Although the woman finds the "patient Grizzel" contemptible, her miserable death reinforces the norm (Broughton, "*Goodbye Sweetheart*" [1872], 17–18). At the extreme, the heroines of Dumaurier's *Trilby* (1893), MacDonald's *David Elginbrod* (1863), and Howells's *The Undiscovered Country* (1880) are controlled by male hypnotists or spiritualists: the mesmerist's victim and spiritualist's medium are invariably female and usually doomed. Howells brings his exploration of the spirit world, the "undiscovered country," to a rare happy ending when Egeria's father dies, freeing her to fall under another man's "spell," the acceptable spell of love.

Because of their supremacy, men who fail to educate their wives may "wreck" the household (Grand, *Heavenly Twins* [1893], 550). One man claims ever-increasing love, then warns his future wife that disobeying his "commands" or opposing his "wishes" equals betraying him and "acting in an underhand way," causing her to "forfeit" his "respect" (Carey, *Mrs. Romney* [1894], 147). By right and responsibility, the husband teaches his wife obedience; to fail means to neglect his quasi-parental duty. To avoid the "calamitous," a woman must "subordinate her opinions" to her husband's (Ward, *The Testing of Diana Mallory* [1907], 91). Or, as one husband warns, "you must take my word about what is proper for you. . . . What do *you* know about the world? You have married *me*, and must be guided by my opinion" (Eliot, *Daniel Deronda* [1876], 655).

Why? Because an endless circle, beginning with the feminine ideal and upbringing that forced women to remain in the position of children, ensured that men would be better educated, more aware of the world, less innocent. Even Twain's uneducated hero in *Huckleberry Finn* has the ingenuity and superiority to contrive a plan Mary Jane and her sisters follow to outwit the Duke and King. One woman who insists her husband has no right to guide and chastise her would delight no feminist, since her reason is that her father still lives (Trollope, *Towers*, 290).

Social reality plus literature's emphasis on women's fragility lead to frequent invoking of the Sleeping Beauty motif. The symbol appears overtly in Gaskell's *Cousin Phillis* (1865), where a young man leaving for Canada prays God will keep his "sleeping beauty" pure and at peace until he returns like "a prince" to "waken her to my love" (93).

It is typical that Gaskell's young man hesitates to marry until he can provide a home to meet the standards of bride and family, even though this necessitates leaving his beloved for two years while he forwards his career. In Craik's *John Halifax*, a man won't encourage a woman's love unless he can match her parents' status, and similar worries haunt other class-conscious English novels such as Trollope's *Framley Parsonage* (1861) and Eden's *The Semi-Attached Couple*. The idea also occurs in American novels; one reason Natty Bumppo of Cooper's Leatherstocking Tales can't find a suitable wife is that his life precludes marrying a girl raised in "decent" society.

Charlotte Brontë's presentation of this problem in *The Professor* (1857) is unusually moving, perhaps because it reflects her experience. She solves the hero's tremendous difficulties in providing for the heroine by having both husband and wife work, but this requires some delicate negotiation and unusual openness as the spouses defy society's rule. A hero's worry about supporting his future wife can become an obstacle to make plots more intricate and delay the happy ending. If love conquers the man's pride, he may ask the woman to wait until he has enough money. Considering the desire for gentility and the need to support large families, the man had quite a responsibility.

Yet the norm of the superior male was mocked, and not always gently. Perhaps women mimicked a "seeming submission" in which men are handled like a sulky horse, as in Mary Mitford's *Our Village* (1832). A female character explains that if women realize the horse will return home "by sunset," they can let him choose his own pace; like "all his sex," he might willingly "abandon" his "dominion" once it is "undisputed." The speaker makes the analogy overt: "Two-thirds of the most discreet wives of my acquaintance contrive to manage their husbands sufficiently with no better secret than this seeming submission," an especially apt approach since "we have no possible way of helping ourselves" (213–14).

In fact, until late in the period, women realistically had "no possible way" to deal with unreasonable or even criminal husbands other than using the traditional feminine wiles of fake submission and quiet management. Law and tradition placed women under men's control. The man provided material property for his wife and family, but he also had the right to regard them as his property. The language in Meredith's *Diana of the Crossways* (1885) offends the modern reader with a once-standard idea: a man sympathizes with another about how sad it is to be the "owner of such a woman, and to lose her!" (95). When Edna Pontellier, the emerging new woman of Chopin's stunning *The Awakening* (1899), asserts her independence, she instinctively knows she must "put away her husband's bounty in casting off her allegiance" (208). Shocking a potential lover, she proclaims, "I am no longer one of Mr. Pontellier's possessions to dispose of or not. I give myself where I choose" (282). Her hesitant awakening from the dream—or nightmare—of traditional marriage could come only after years of feminist awareness.

Marriage settlements helped solve women's economic dependence, but fictional parents who speak of such settlements rarely address the true problems. Rather, literature defines a settlement as a source of "pin-money" (Gore, *Progress and Prejudice* [1854], 2:76). A heroine's guardian trivializes the issue, explaining that a settlement tells wives "what they ought to spend," makes their "little charities . . . fruits of their own self-denial," and prevents their husbands' complaints of extravagant clothing bills (Eden, *Semi-Detached House* [1859], 114).

A few works seriously confront women's economic powerlessness. In Clay's *Heiress of Hilldrop* (1885), the naive honesty that prevents a family from seeing the need for a settlement causes pain for their daughter and complications for the plot. A character who argues for the protection of a settlement reflects women's insecurity by observing, "we can none of us say what we shall be" in the future (Bury, *Separation* [1830], 2:49).

In *The Portrait of a Lady* (1881), James solves the problem of financial dependence by making Isabel Archer wealthy. Yet even transported from the innocence of America to the relative liberty of Europe, the beautiful Isabel truly has little freedom. Essentially, all she can choose is whom she will marry. She selects Gilbert Osmond, although another suitor, Ralph Touchett, warns, "you're going to be put into a cage" (340). Accepting Osmond's proposal, she feels "the slipping of a fine bolt—backward, forward, she couldn't have said which" (309).

Why marry at all? And why Osmond? Another suitor, Caspar Goodwood, suggests that marriage offers a chance for freedom: "An unmarried woman—a girl of your age—isn't independent" (160). Isabel rejects Caspar because she fears his strength, passion, and sexuality, knowing that to marry him is to succumb to him; she selects the apparently weak Osmond, hoping to maintain her independence. Ironically, Osmond is the more stultifying, as everyone except Isabel realizes before the wedding, and as she soon learns. Their stillborn child symbolizes their empty lives; their gardenless house proves a moldy dungeon. Isabel later rejects a new chance at love with Caspar, perhaps still fearing his sexuality, and the book ends with her future in question. She achieves some freedom and perhaps maturity, but hers may not be a fortunate fall, as the echoes of Milton's *Paradise Lost* suggest.

Her rare economic freedom gives Isabel more choice than most women, yet she truly has no choice, for both she and her creator accept the norm. Job, social rank, family background, and finally marital status define a man; her husband defines a woman: she is his wife and mother to his children, she takes his social standing, and his job determines her daily life. Most women accept this position: even estranged from her husband, a woman exclaims, "I could not live away from you and my children" (Wood, *East Lynne* [1866], 634). Edna in Chopin's *The Awakening* questions the rightness of married life and rejects her traditional role, then commits suicide.

And, even in 1899, this story of a believable woman who dares to fight the norm and her own demons, dying in the process, shocked its readers.

Evaluating women's limited choices, Portia tells her friend Susan that some birds like to live in cages, but "there are birds and birds . . . and I am not a bullfinch. I was not born for a cage"; Susan can't understand why a woman should "want anything who has got home—home and some one to love her and take care of her" (Edwards, *Susan*, 88). Although Portia jokes that Susan draws her feelings from sentimental romances, she ultimately marries and presumably lives happily ever after in her bullfinch's cage, proving her friend correct.

A woman ideally serves as "help-meet," as the preface of Guyton's *Married Life* makes overt. The best woman provides man with "a real, true love to depend on" (Eden, *Couple*, 237). Harold Frederick's naturalistic *The Damnation of Theron Ware* (1896) explores a man's downfall, or perhaps his awakening (the novel was published in England as *The Illumination*). Light-haired Alice models the perfect wife, "the crowning blessedness" of Theron's life (20); she dresses well, reads, sympathizes with her husband, plays the piano without the dangerous talent of Theron's passionate dark lady, Celia. When he begins to awaken—or fall—Theron mourns the time "Alice had been one with him" (38) and scolds that a wife should "understand, and make allowances, and not intrude trifles" (173). Since Theron deserts his job, tries to write a book for which he lacks intelligence and background, and becomes intellectually and sexually infatuated by Celia, Alice is hardly intruding "trifles." Neither character is attractive, but Alice earns sympathy when Theron insists the ideal helpmate is obedient, dependent, submissive, and unquestioningly loyal, yet treats her as if she "had absolutely no mind at all" (241).

Brontë's *The Professor* offers a very different view of the helpmate. The wife so respects her husband that she calls him "Monsieur," but she also helps him found and run a school, to earn money and prevent boredom. She successfully fulfills and keeps separate her careers as teacher and loving homemaker: to her husband she is "lady directress" each day, and "my own little lace-mender . . . magically restored to my arms" each night (223).

Woman also serves as a mystical source of life and renewal in literature. Her archetypal role as spiritual guide occurs frequently, often with a strongly moralistic tone. When Grace's fiancé says he has been bad, she promises to be his mentor (Oliphant, *Oliver's Bride* [1885]). Thackeray's *Pendennis* blames a woman for allowing a man to fall: "If Laura had spoken as Helen hoped, who knows what temptations Arthur Pendennis might have been spared" (278). Brontë's Jane Eyre can accept marriage with Rochester when he is helpless, because she can be his nurse. And *Theron Ware* concludes with Alice helping her sickly husband prepare for a new life.

But this female role ironically conflicts with the ideal of the innocent child-wife. Men praise obedient, submissive, helpless, innocent women: "You have been a good child"; "[your] pretty little head" has "plenty of sense" (Carey, *Romney*, 146–47); admitting his brutishness, a husband apologizes for frightening his "poor child out of her sense" (Eden, *Couple*, 227). Sometimes characters realize that this uneven relationship cannot work: in Eden's novel, ultimately the wife grows from "a foolish spoiled child" to "a happy woman" (237). In *David Copperfield* Dickens solves the problem of the appealing child-wife who fails to grow up by allowing delicate little Dora to die, thus giving David a chance to find his mature partner, Agnes. No child could manage a real wife's role, running a house and raising children. This may be one reason that novels so often end by closing the door on the ingenue's marriage.

Failure to run a house properly usually occurs because a woman is unprepared for marriage, but sometimes she rejects responsibility. One future bride needs help furnishing a kitchen: she rightly asks, "How can I know about pots and pans, and how many are necessary, without practical knowledge supplied by recent experience?" (Oliphant, *Bride*, 90). Early in their marriage, Theron and Alice laugh at their domestic innocence: "Alice in a quandary over the complications of her cooking stove; Alice boiling her potatoes all day, and her eggs for half an hour; Alice ordering twenty pounds of steak and half a pound of sugar, and striving to extract a breakfast beverage from the unground coffee-bean" (*Theron Ware*, 22). More seriously, the impoverished Reverend Barton's good wife in Eliot's *Scenes of Clerical Life* (1858) rapidly learns all she must, and even when pregnant she "salted bacon, ironed shirts and cravats, put patches on patches, and re-darned darns" (90). The American woman on a pre–Civil War plantation had special responsibilities, for slaves were regarded as children. While observing the irony that masters may legally separate families, proving "we care for no tie, no duty, no relation, however sacred, compared with money," Mrs. Shelby in Stowe's *Uncle Tom's Cabin* "tried most faithfully, as a Christian woman should—to do my duty to these poor, simple, dependent creatures," caring for them, teaching them "the duties of the family, of parent and child, and husband and wife" (43).

In contrast, Mrs. Hofland's moralizing *Daughter of a Genius* (1824) observes that a woman who takes inadequate care of house and family gains the "ill will of all her neighbors" and loses her social position and her husband's respect (17). Wilkie Collins in *Poor Miss Finch* (1872) describes a household where the maidservant is "slovenly" and the children run about "in dirty frocks," because the mother, with disarrayed hair and "lace cap . . . all on one side," prefers reading novels to accounting for the housekeeping money, soap, candles, or food (12–13). This would not happen if women were properly trained, according to Guyton's *Married Life*: "Little girls may very early be taught the secret of making home the happiest, cosiest, bonniest place in all the world; and that not by making them small cooks, and precocious kitchen-maids—though every woman ought to count cooking and the tasteful arrangement of rooms among her accomplishments; but by training them to be industrious, thoughtful, quick, and yet gentle in action, and, above all, unselfish." Guyton complains that the "grandmothers" of current heroines learned about housekeeping and studied the "cookery-book," while their granddaughters learn to "dance, and dress, and draw in every possible style," which would be fine if they simultaneously attended to their households. But when they do not, "the servants hold a perpetual Saturnalia in the kitchen" as "stores diminish," shirts lose their buttons, socks grow holes, and the "husband grumbles" and "looks reproachfully at the sweet fairy-like creature" who sits across a table laden with "watery soups, tough stews and hashes, and under-done joints." Guyton insists that proper education can prepare women to be "good housewives, and at the same time elegant scholars and accomplished members of society" (29–31).

This diatribe against the way society prepared (or failed to prepare) women for marriage reinforces the ideal of the Perfect Woman—virtuous, domestic, selfless, and giving. It omits only one feature for a complete picture of women's role: maternity.

Children and Child Rearing

In reality, children formed the center of the family and were the direct, daily responsibility of women. Some families employed governesses, far fewer employed nurses, and even fewer used wet nurses. Mothers tended their children from birth at least until school age, and often educated their daughters. High infant mortality, minimal preparation for motherhood, and a strong sense of duty caused much anxiety as women tried to raise virtuous, obedient, respectful, healthy children.

Important as children were in reality, literature focuses on them only in adventure tales like *Tom Sawyer* (1875) and *Huckleberry Finn*; bildungsromane like *The Mill on the Floss* (1860) and *David Copperfield*; school stories like Farrar's *Eric* (1858) and Hughes's *Tom Brown's Schooldays* (1857); or sentimental successes like Alcott's *Little Women* (1868), Dickens's *The Old Curiosity Shop* (1841), and Yonge's *Daisy Chain* (1856). Although *Huckleberry Finn* grimly details child abuse and violence, most literature depicts school days, toys and tea parties, afternoons of berry picking, quiet evenings of reading and games, and minor punishments for such naughtiness as cutting one's own hair. Since most heroines are between 17 and 25, heroes a few years older, they are not children; since their stories end at marriage, they don't have children. Still, literature acknowledges that families expect and desire children.

Describing the impact of an infant's birth, Oliphant's *Heart and Cross* (1863) typifies the idea that children enrich family life. The parents realize that this "new living, loving creature, with all the possibilities of life burning upon his fresh horizon," links them "to the other generations of the world; belonging not to ourselves, but to the past and the future" (10–11).

A few writers, and more as time passed, defy this glowing view of automatic maternal love and enhanced family joy. When a woman dares state that she doesn't like children, a man chastises, "Don't say that—it is unwomanly!" She "sarcastically" comments, "to a man they may be imps of Satan, but to the ideal woman they must always be cherubs—biting, kicking, scratching cherubs, but *cherubs* always" (Broughton, *Good-bye*, 96). Another character admits that the "general supposition" that a baby can heal a faltering marriage "ought" to be true, but notes, "I have oftener seen the child of such parents become a bone of contention between them and the cause of greater estrangement than otherwise" (Marryatt, *Too Good for Him* [1865], 6).

In *The Emancipated* (1890), after piously acknowledging that "the average woman" finds maternity "absorbing," Gissing undercuts the ideal: "the average woman is incapable of poetical passion, and only too glad to find something that occupies her thoughts from morning to night." The new mother learns her baby has "somehow altered, modified" her love for her husband and ended "the time of passionate reveries." Contrary to her expectations, her "mother's love" cannot replace, "destroy, nor even keep in long abeyance, those intellectual energies which characterized her" (270). The child has changed the modern mother's life, not necessarily for the better.

Edna Pontellier's "awakening" includes her realizing that she is no "mother-woman . . . fluttering about with extended, protecting wings when any harm, real or imaginary, threatened [her] precious brood." Idolizing neither husband nor children, she sees no "holy privilege" in joining the women who "efface themselves as individuals and grow wings as ministering angels," such as Adèle Ratignolle, "the embodiment of every womanly grace and charm," whose husband must "adore her" unless he is a "brute" (19). While Edna learns that she wrongly assumed her husband to share her tastes and values, she wants to be a good wife and mother, since he is a good husband by current standards. Though accepting responsibility for her children, "she would sometimes gather them passionately to her heart; she would sometimes forget them." Separated from them, she feels "a sort of relief, though she did not admit this, even to herself" (47–48). To her foil Adèle, she says, "I would give up the unessential; I would give my money, I would give my life for my children; but I wouldn't give myself" (122)— suggesting that to be herself precludes being a "mother-woman."

Gradually awakening, Edna rejects her husband's claims, first defying him by remaining outside against his will, later refusing him her bed, still later moving into her own house. Her husband frets that she is "not herself," failing to see "that she was becoming herself" by shedding the costume of the false self society had dressed her in (147–48). Although Edna "resolved never again to belong to another than herself" (208) and says before her fatal swim that she will not be "forced into doing things" (291), she may die for her children. Despondent, confused, unsure of herself, she murmurs "nobody has any right—except children, perhaps—and even then . . ." (291). Fearing the children may compel her into "the soul's slavery," she chooses "to elude them" (300). The sea seductively calls her as passion called earlier, but her suicide may be a final ironic acknowledgment of the power of children in women's lives. Failing to be a "mother-woman" may leave no alternative.

A solution Edna found inadequate is to limit the mother's role. Women like Barbara in Wood's *East Lynne* accept their role as models of virtue and instillers of "Christian and moral duties," but turn over "the rest" of the child care to nurses and governesses. (410–11) But abandoning a child to a nurse's care can be deadly: in Yonge's *Daisy Chain*, for example, Flora learns how a young mother should behave when a nurse fatally overdoses her baby with opium. Most women accept the responsibility of child rearing, selecting and supervising governesses and nurses if not becoming more actively involved.

Women are to raise their children, then let them go. Thus pride overwhelms fear when a mother sees her son in uniform: "she had accomplished her woman's work—she had brought him up to the man's estate; and that was her sufficient reward" (Moore, *Esther Waters* [1894], 441). Yet child rearing was so central that some authors recognized what modern writers call the "empty-nest syndrome." Since women "have a self larger than their maternity," when their children leave home for college or business, they have "wide spaces of their time which are not filled with praying for their boys, reading old letters, and envying yet blessing those who are attending to their shirt-buttons" (Eliot, *Felix*, 102–3).

Long before Freud, it seemed obvious to society that biology is destiny; given their reproductive capacity, women are assumed to have the emotional capacity for motherhood. Authors ask whether a "fallen woman" can be a good mother, since she should serve as her children's moral guide; in both Gaskell's *Ruth* and Hawthorne's *The Scarlet Letter*, kind characters suggest the child might help keep the woman from further sin. But a basic irony escapes literature as it does society: how could child-wives, incapable of making moral decisions or governing their money, be entrusted to raise children? Exalted descriptions insist on a chain of influence from mother to child to grandchild and beyond, ultimately affecting all of society. As Edith in Guyton's *Married Life* says, "How much depends on us mothers! It seems to me that we are the instruments that make and mar the world. . . . Men, I believe, have not half the responsibility committed to them by God that we have, for it is we who train the men in the years when the disposition is most plastic" (266–67).

Echoing reality, fatherhood is considered less important in literature. Authors rarely explore men's feelings about children or show them engaging in child care. Oliphant's *Agnes* is exceptional in describing a father's obsessive desire to keep his daughter "always young, always delicate, virginal, a thing apart." He "shrank from the thought" that she would want to marry: "It was not only that he thought as a doting father might, nobody good enough for his beautiful child—but that the idea itself was profane, a kind of desecration" (31–32). Much more typically, when Mrs. Lapham suggests the family move to "do the best we can for the children," her husband Silas accepts her wisdom (Howells, *Silas Lapham* [1885], 27). The father provides his wife sheltered and conspicuous leisure and gives his children the social and financial position to ensure them a good future—for girls, a good match; the mother does the rest.

As one character suggests, "every child belongs to the mother in a far profounder sense than to the father" (Ward, *Marriage*, 194). Unlike a man, a childless woman is somehow lost. Men who witness the title character of Grand's *Ideala* (1888) gather children about her see "something wrong in the world when such a woman misses her vocation, and has to scatter her love to the four winds of heaven, for want of an object upon which to concentrate it in all its strength" (90). A bad marriage produced this life of "martyrdom."

As women owe unquestioned obedience to their husbands, so children submit to their parents' wishes. Carey flamboyantly emphasizes this: although Malcolm's home was "a house of bondage" with no "sympathy" between him and his mother, he still gives her, "at least outwardly, the *obedience and honor* that were *due* to her" (*Herb*, 27). Most fictional parents support, educate, and care for children. James's exceptional bad mothers rightly earn readers' distaste and resentment. Ralph Touchett's mother in *The Portrait of a Lady* at least does minimal harm. Far more objectionable is the neglectful Ida Farange, who ignores her daughter for days on end in *What Maisie Knew* (1897). Caught between her parents, Maisie cannot win, astute as she is: knowing her mother does not love her, she has no self-esteem, no sense of self-love.

Late in the period, sometimes ahead of society and sometimes more slowly, literary ideas of marriage and family life begin to change, as women start to insist on a life "apart from that imposed . . . by the duties of wedlock" (Gissing, *Odd Women* [1892], 167). But even radical proposals tend to accept both the importance of children and the inherent differences between men's and women's roles. Linton's *Christopher Kirkland* exemplifies these ideas while rejecting the traditional hierarchy of God, man, and woman. Arguing that women deserve an education different from men's but "as good in its own way," and that men and women should have equal rights over their property and children, she insists: "I was, and am, among those who hold that women, though helpmates, should not be slaves to men; that duties do not exclude rights; and that 'He to God, she to God through him,' though pretty enough in poetry, makes but a mighty poor kind of life for her in practice, and reduces co-partnership to serfdom" (1–3).

Asking for a new balance, like most authors Linton accepts the biological and philosophical basis of the traditional female role. Gilman's feminist fantasy, *Herland* (1915), creates a matriarchy in which women give birth through parthenogenesis. Only in such an exceptional way does literature escape the tradition. Otherwise, the essential values remain unchanged: biology is destiny, the family is central, the woman is helpmate, sex roles do and should differ.

Pregnancy, Birth, and Family Size

An already high birth rate in 1800 peaked at nearly 36 births per thousand between the 1850s and 1870s, then declined steadily and quite rapidly, reaching 30 per thousand at the end of the century and 22 per thousand two decades later.[5] The decrease resulted from and caused changes in daily life and attitudes, especially regarding women.

Historians speculate that birth rates rose as children became more economically useful and fell as social change diminished that usefulness. This may explain the large families of farmers, but not those of unskilled laborers, for whom children offered no economic blessing, nor does it fit other economic factors. Even the number of illegitimate births rose sharply at midcentury in England.[6] Better health probably meant fewer miscarriages and certainly led to more years of childbearing. Since the proportion of people married during those years remained relatively stable, fertility within marriage changed dramatically.

Married couples had children almost immediately, and continued having children at fairly close intervals for fifteen or twenty years. In a study of more than 50,000 upper-class and professional families, which tended to have fewer children, over 80 percent had a child in the first year of marriage.[7] Family size increased to an average of five to six children at midcentury, decreasing to about half that number before World War I.

In 1860 only one-fourth of English families had three or fewer children, nearly one-third had five, six, or seven children, and families of eight, nine, ten, or more accounted for another third of the population. By 1920, 80 percent had either one to three children or no children at all (*Population: Report*, 24–26).

This startling change can largely be explained by new attitudes toward childbearing and child rearing. The prime economic factor was probably the desire to achieve a higher standard of living for parents and children. Many new conveniences enhanced middle-class existence, but they cost money: a coal-burning cast-iron range replaced the open fireplace and portable oven; piped water and bathtubs were introduced; sewing machines, washing machines, and carpets came to seem necessities, though items such as pianos remained luxuries. As the cost of living rose, food absorbed half the middle-class budget, while rents more than doubled. The material advantages of a small family became obvious.

Large families diluted the mother's attention and energies. Accepting child rearing as a serious, long-term responsibility, parents wanted to pay more attention to their children and offer them a secure social and financial start—a very difficult goal in a household of eight or nine children. This increased tensions, leading Edward Gibbon Wakefield to describe the middle class as the "distressed" or even the "anxious, vexed, or harassed class."[8] Margaret Sanger, the famous American advocate of birth control, associated family size and economic status, observing that large families and poverty coexisted in the slums she visited. More personally, she notes in her auto-biography that her mother, who had eleven children, died thirty years before her father.[9] Women confronted the very real possibility of death in childbirth or through the exhaustion of bearing many children; pregnancy was more a time of dread and anxiety than of happy anticipation. Perhaps the famous Victorian prudery derives in part from a very practical desire to limit pregnancies.[10]

The increased accessibility of birth control played a less significant role than many claim. Virtually all methods of birth control known after 1875 had existed many decades earlier: abstinence, the rhythm method, and coitus interruptus required no special equipment, and manuals outlined these methods along with the sheath or condom for men and the sponge for women. Moreover, in most American states in 1800 abortion, at worst a misdemeanor, was advertised in newspapers, although by 1900 politics and economics led to almost total restriction of abortion. At midcentury, advertisements for condoms appeared in respectable newspapers; the ads described the products in detail, including a reusable "French safe." But while birth control was *available* to prospective parents in 1825, it was their grandchildren who eventually began to *use* it.

As early as 1822, advocates of contraception discussed its benefits.[11] Reinforcing the importance of new ideas over economics, the birth rate decreased most rapidly for members of the "modern" professions such as engineering and medicine, declining later and more slowly among families in traditional middle-class occupations, such as religion and business. Some people considered books on birth control obscene, but others bought and presumably read such sources as Dr. George Drysdale's text, *The Elements of Social Science; or, Physical, Sexual, and Natural Religion: An Exposition of the True Cause and Only Cure of the Three Primary Evils: Poverty, Prostitution, and Celibacy.*[12] Dr. Drysdale warns people to consider whether "Preventive Sexual Intercourse" causes "moral and physical harm." But he also discusses sexual pleasure in analyzing the advantages of each contraceptive method. Thus he recommends the sponge over either condoms or coitus interruptus not only because the last may produce "nervous disorder and sexual enfeeblement and congestion," but because both methods detract from men's *and* women's pleasure. He considers contraception more natural than abstinence, one of the "three primary evils" of his title.

While books such as Drysdale's appeared sporadically, the English trial of Charles Bradlaugh and Mrs. Annie Besant in 1877 for reprinting and selling an American book that advocated birth control caught the public's attention. The trial concerned freedom of the press as much as birth control, but many described the book—Dr. Charles Knowlton's *Fruits of Philosophy*—as obscene. Published first in America, then reprinted in England in 1834, the book became a best-seller after the trial. Between 1877 and 1891, readers bought hundreds of thousands of copies of Knowlton's work and even more pamphlets advocating and explaining contraception, and they began to practice what they read about. By the 1870s, books overtly advocated smaller families for the sake of maternal health, child rearing, and population control. It was not contraception, but new attitudes toward family life and women's roles that doomed the family as it once was and as it is nostalgically evoked.

Literature sharply disagrees with reality in describing childbearing and family size. A study of representative novels reveals that typical families in fiction are far smaller than those in society. Between 1850 and 1880, when real families averaged five to six children, the average for fictional families was just over two children, and that remained the norm throughout the period. The only exceptions are that fictional families tended to be slightly but not significantly larger just past midcentury and more families were childless at the end of the period than at the beginning. Three times as many fictional families as real families had three or fewer children, although almost none are childless. In contrast, seven times as many real families had eight or more children, and literature very nearly excludes large families. Failing to reflect social change, literature generally ignores the issue of family size, undoubtedly influenced more by artistic concerns. But some later novels do address the issue, and perhaps readers who contrasted their large families with literature's small ones thought about the advantages of each.

Authors have sound artistic and thematic reasons to limit family size. Extra siblings would be unnecessary complications in a story about two sisters' rivalry over a young man or a young man's growing up. Orphans make good heroes and heroines, as in *Bleak House* (1853), *Oliver Twist*, and *Huckleberry Finn*; siblings would detract from the intent by making the orphans seem less alone. Premarital sex nearly always leads to pregnancy, but since the fallen woman either learns from her experience or dies, she has just one child (*Adam Bede, Ruth, The Scarlet Letter*). Many novels end with a prophetic vision of the newlyweds after a year or two, with one child. A glimpse further into the future might disclose more children, but they are irrelevant to the assertion that all is now well, and they might even raise undesirable complications. Characters must be named, they must be kept active or their absence explained, their lives must be significant: if they don't fit the plot, there is little point in introducing them, and that alone could explain literature's small families.

But novels do mimic reality in the speed with which couples become parents, normally within a year of marriage. Typical in pace if not in number, a family in Trollope's *Three Clerks* (1858) has two children in 36 months of marriage, while one in Gore's *Mothers and Daughters* (1830) bears four children in six years.

The one-child family is so rare in fiction that writers offer justification for it: Gaskell explains in *Sylvia's Lover* that her heroine's parents married late in life and so had only one daughter; often single children are orphans. More surprisingly, authors also explain large families, common in society, but defined in literature as unusual.

A daughter of a large family whose children "came very improbably close together" comments that "a Frenchman might well hold up his hands in astonished horror at the insane prolificness—the foolhardy fertility—of British households" (Broughton, *Nancy* [1874], 3). Such a family usually serves a literary purpose: the novel might focus on the children, perhaps discussing the effect of their parents' death, or it might proselytize, showing the impact of family size on financial or social position or on women's lives. If a book has one large family, it usually has more: families of three, six, seven, and eight inhabit Marryat's *Too Good for Him*. But children tend to be treated simply as a part of life—rarely numerous, rarely the center of attention. Even if essential, as in *The Awakening*, they may lack identities, serving merely as abstractions.

Trollope reflects a real concern when he notes Reverend Quiverful's "impossible task of bringing up as ladies and gentlemen fourteen children on an income which was insufficient to give them with decency the common necessities of life" (*Towers*, 220). Eliot's *Scenes from Clerical Life* shows a woman's struggle to survive a life of penury and child rearing: she cannot regain her health after childbirth because she never stops working for her numerous offspring. Thus Eliot deliberately connects birth control, family size, and women's stultifying roles.

As common as childbirth is, prudery and censorship preclude discussing pregnancy. In Eliot's *Adam Bede*, Hetty's pregnancy is acknowledged only after the birth of her illegitimate child; in *The Scarlet Letter*, Hester Prynne steps out of prison and into the novel carrying the infant Pearl. Veiled references to pregnancy include an "interesting state of health" (Eden, *House*) and a woman's being told to rest and avoid dinner parties (Carey,

Lover). Even a late, radical novel detailing a pregnant woman's edginess, jealousy, and tears, has the character say, "I'm in the family way" (Moore, *A Mummer's Wife* [1888], 265).

When mentioned at all, births occur at home or in lodgings, rarely in a lying-in hospital or similar facility. Most unusually, Moore's *Esther Waters* deals directly with childbirth and with miserable hospital conditions. Twice rejected by hospitals because she is unmarried, Esther is mistreated when finally admitted. Callous nurses gossip with dirty, brusque student doctors who prefer jokes and flirtation to patient care. "Overcome with pain and shame," Esther is terrified of death: "how long the time, how fearful the place!" In a graphic portrayal, Esther screams as "it seemed to her that she was being torn asunder." After betting on the length of Esther's labor, a nurse and student finally summon the doctor: "He placed a small wire case over her mouth and nose. The sickly odour which she breathed from the cotton wool filled her brain with nausea; it seemed to choke her." Emerging from the chloroform, she hears "a tiny cry." Her son may look like "a pulp of red flesh rolled up in flannel," and she knows how difficult life will be after her three week hospital stay, but birth arouses her maternal love: "she thought she must die of happiness"; "her personal self seemed entirely withdrawn" (146–49).

Moore's focus on childbirth is unusual, but Esther's reactions are not. Feminists agitating for reform in contraception, childbirth, and the treatment of unwed mothers often insisted upon the sanctity of a mother's love. A divorced man thinks of his former wife "with longing and tenderness" when he remembers her "lying white and exhausted after child-birth, with the little dark head beside her": this memory "melted him" (Ward, *Marriage*, 212). His loss is most poignant when he thinks about the center of woman's role—childbearing and child rearing. Realistic about that emotion, the novel also rightly acknowledges the odds of dying in childbirth, a part of real life and a reason for feminist concern.

Death and Dying

Death, very much a normal part of nineteenth-century life, held special meaning for women. Rather than disappearing to nursing homes and hospitals, the elderly and terminally ill died at home, with the woman as nurse and comforter. With little medicine and no training, she took responsibility for nursing a sick child, husband, housemaid, or, in an epidemic, an entire village. She faced death in each of her many pregnancies and when her children took ill. Compared to reality, literature reflects the *changing* death rates with fair accuracy, exaggerates the *numbers* of dead, and alters the *causes* of death.

Probably as a result of better living conditions, health, and medicine, the death rate declined during the eighteenth and nineteenth centuries. Although death rates rose in periods such as England's cholera epidemic in the 1830s and the American Civil War, the rate steadily declined from the 1880s through the 1920s. In England, the annual death rate of about 22 per thousand through midcentury dropped by about one-third in the first decade of the twentieth century.[13]

Changing mortality rates among infants and small children are especially noteworthy. Pneumonia, scarlet fever, smallpox, and measles claimed many infant lives, but so did overdoses of the various opium-containing formulas used to quiet children or ease the pain of teething. The mortality rates for children between ages one and four decreased by about 90 percent in the century after the 1840s, but the story for infant mortality was less positive: while many more children survived their first year in 1940 than in 1840, the death rate actually increased in the 1890s to a rate very nearly matching the start of the period (*Population: Report*, 18; Branca, 96). The lack of progress in maternal mortality was equally discouraging: in 1838 five Englishwomen out of every thousand could expect to die in childbirth; in 1892 the figures were essentially unchanged (Branca, 81). Feminists were frustrated by the lack of progress, which probably resulted from a typical lag between a medical discovery and public acceptance or use of that discovery. By midcentury, health professionals knew how to prevent puerperal fever, then the greatest single cause of maternal mortality, yet a major epidemic of puerperal fever occurred as late as 1872 (Branca, 88–89). The death rate generally remained higher in urban areas, probably because overcrowding and slums facilitated the spread of disease. The late-century influx of immigrants less able to assimilate than earlier ones enhanced these problems in America, and in both countries rapid urbanization strained the resources of small towns suddenly transformed into big cities.

Since authors tend to reflect current issues, concern for the high death rate could have led to an early focus on death (the death rate in novels is as much as 10 times that in reality in novels taking place prior to 1850), although the kinds of deaths occurring in literature argue against that explanation. Later novels, exaggerating the real social progress by a marked decline in the death rate of characters, might have been celebrating health gains. Changing women's roles might be another cause: as death less frequently occurred at home, it became less a part of daily life for authors or their readers. But literature is more interested in the impact of death than the facts about death. Thus, more characters die from unrequited or lost love than from war, childbirth, cholera, and all other diseases combined.

Cholera, typhoid, smallpox, scarlet fever, and unidentified "fevers" rarely kill major characters. The horrors of a cholera epidemic are merely implied in Lever's *St. Patrick's Eve* (1845). More graphically, Gore's *Women as They Are* (1830) notes that in three weeks, "forty-seven persons out of a population of two hundred were swept away" (2:26); an epidemic kills 36 villagers in one day in Edward's *Susan Fielding*. Typhoid fever kills two boys in Gaskell's *Mary Barton* (1848), and two more die of an unspecified fever in Hofland's *Daughter of a Genius*. Traveling held special dangers: in Yonge's best-selling *Heir of Redcliffe* (1853), the hero dies of a fever contracted in Europe, while in Meredith's *Diana of the Crossways*, a woman who once lived in India experiences general weakness, then dies.

But the causes of death lie close to home, as feminist reformers often observed. A cholera epidemic points to the problems of overcrowding and poor sanitation: "It is hard to human nature to make all the humiliating confessions which must precede sanitary repentance; to say, 'I have been a very nasty, dirty fellow [and may be] the cause of half my own illnesses, and of three-fourths of the illness of my children'" (Kingsley, *Two Years Ago* [1857], 238–39). Yet these "confessions" are the necessary first step to change, as real women on sanitary commissions or in nursing said.

Consumption, a major cause of death, normally occurs in working-class literature like Moore's *Esther Waters*; but in Alcott's *Little Women*, Beth, an "angel in the house," fades away in a typical representation of death—sentimental, domestic, and religious. Helping a poor family, she catches scarlet fever, then becomes consumptive. Jo sees in her thin face "a strange, transparent look . . . as if the mortal was being slowly refined away, and the immortal shining through the frail flesh with an indescribably pathetic beauty" (409). At first "miserable" about her condition, Beth learns "it isn't hard to think of or to bear" (411). She describes life ebbing in an image Alcott recalls at the moment of death: "It's like the tide, Jo, when it turns, it goes slowly, but it can't be stopped" (412). Accepting the truth, the family gains strength from "the increased affection which comes to bind households tenderly together in times of trouble." Surrounded by flowers, pictures, and family, Beth becomes "a household saint in its shrine." At last, unable to work and in great pain, she feels a "natural rebellion" against death; but peace returns and "with the wreck of her frail body, Beth's soul grew strong." When the "tide went out," the women in the family "made her ready for the long sleep that pain would never mar again" (454–59).

A young clergyman who dies from consumption experiences similar stages. At first angry—"he was so young, and the love of life was so strong within him, and the thought of disease and death so terrible"—David gradually becomes "more resigned and peaceful," accepting death and feeling "a strange calm" (Carey, *Herb*, 349, 353).

Characters die of other realistic causes, too, from battle wounds to stroke, heart conditions, and aging (Kingsley, *The Hillyars and the Burtons* [1865]; Oliphant, *Perpetual Curate* [1864]; Gaskell, *Barton*; Eliot, *Middlemarch* [1871]; Bennett, *Old Wives' Tale* [1908]). Soldiers and sailors die in battle (Kingsley, *Two Years*) or when their ships sink (Crowe, *Susan Hopley* [1861]; Meredith, *Beauchamp's Career* [1876]). Sinclair's *Holiday House* [1839] reflects the real state of medicine when Frank returns from the navy with a fever resulting from a wound.

Accidents occur more frequently in literature than in reality. Characters drown (Oliphant, *The Doctor's Family* [1863], fall off cliffs (a 13-year-old boy in Farrar's *Eric*), have carriage accidents (the mother in Yonge's *Daisy Chain* dies immediately, her daughter years later) and unspecified accidents (a 30-year-old man in Meredith's *Diana*, a 15-year-old boy in *Eric*, a six-year-old girl in Sewell's *Amy Herbert* [1844]). More sensationally, in Kingsley's *Two Years Ago* a man drowns while in an opium-induced stupor, and surely Huck Finn's father dies in a drunken haze.

Most accidental deaths occur to children; functioning thematically, they often comment on the mother's role. *Eric* demonstrates the effect of inadequate care at a corrupt school: two characters die accidentally, and the hero dies from an unspecified illness after running away to become a sailor. Rotten conditions and inattentive school authorities lead to a girl's death in Brontë's *Jane Eyre* (1847), while society's rules may truly have murdered Hetty's child in Eliot's *Adam Bede*: although the death appears accidental, since the desperate unwed mother exposed her infant to conditions that made its survival unlikely, she is tried for murder. In Yonge's *Daisy Chain*, a child inadequately tended by her mother dies from the nurse's routine use of "Godfrey's cordial," or opium (568).

When Rose in *Amy Herbert* realizes her injuries spell death, her governess comforts her by talk of heaven, and Rose then speaks of angels coming for her. Sentimental depictions of a child's death appear also in Stowe's *Uncle Tom's Cabin* and Dickens's *The Old Curiosity Shop*. Little Eva and Little Nell die because of the harsh conditions they face and because they are almost too good to live.

But literature that realistically reflects high infant and maternal mortality rates is less sentimental. Miscarriages rarely occur (Hook's *Sayings and Do-*

45

ings [1836]), but infant deaths are common. Anne Brontë's *Agnes Grey* (1847) mentions a family of six in which four die as infants; Gaskell's *Ruth* has a family in which three of eight children die in infancy; and at the turn of the century, Carey's *Herb of Grace* speaks of a family of nine where only six survive infancy. These apparently casual references, just footnotes to family size, underscore why the harsh facts of infant mortality and child-bearing led to feminist reform efforts.

Deaths in childbirth occur with some frequency from Brontë's *Wuthering Heights* (1847) and Dickens's *Dombey and Son* (1848), through Thackeray's *Newcomes* (1855) and Eliot's *Scenes of Clerical Life*, to Moore's *Esther Waters* at the end of the era. Wood's *East Lynne* speaks of a nearly fatal labor and birth. When a woman has "taken ill" and given birth at home, her husband, recognizing she may die, is very grateful she survives (Eden, *House*, 160). Gilman's story *The Yellow Wallpaper* (1892) presents an extraordinary study of a severe postpartum depression. The more the heroine asserts her identity, the more insane she appears to outsiders. She confines herself to escape a society represented by an insensitive husband who adheres to current psychological theory about women and who enforces as "treatment" for his wife's depression a continued stultification of her identity. To be truly sane, she must appear mad, a moving feminist comment on prevalent attitudes toward women in their most female role: childbirth.

Under half the fictional deaths occur from realistic causes such as childbirth or physical illness, many of which comment indirectly on women's roles. The rest are either sensationalized or emotional and psychological deaths, the latter most commonly concerning women.

Stretching the capacity for credibility, Crowe's *Susan Hopley* contains drowning, murder, suicide, and random illnesses. Kingsley's *The Hillyars and the Burtons* includes a woman who drowns during a cyclone, and the title character of Linton's *Joshua Davidson* (1872) is killed in a riot of religious fanatics. Hardy's novels always border on sensationalism: Eustacia drowns (suicide or accident) and Wildeve drowns attempting to save her in *The Return of the Native* (1878); Tess's illegitimate baby dies and she murders her seducer in *Tess of the d'Urbervilles* (1891); Fanny and her illegitimate child die in *Far from the Madding Crowd* (1874); and there is a group murder-suicide of children in *Jude the Obscure* (1894). Hardy's deaths fit a pattern of sin and retribution usually revolving around women's sexuality.

Caught in the spell of men described as mesmerists, hypnotists, or spiritualists are Euphra in MacDonald's *David Elginbrod*, and the title character of *Trilby*, Du Maurier's famous tale of Svengali. Both women ultimately decline into death, Euphra by way of a painful madness. These stories work

46

in part because they simply exaggerate women's very real dependence on men. Trilby and Euphra die from emotional causes, but so do others who appear to suffer physically. An occasional straightforward suicide occurs (a minor character in Edwards's *Susan Fielding*, a major one in Lister's *Granby*), but characters—especially women—more often enter a "decline" with psychological origins. Fever, spine injury, and the all-purpose "decline" often mask death from unrequited love.

The sickly Linton in Brontë's *Wuthering Heights* simply lacks strength to live. In *Too Good for Him*, Marryat's tale of love, guilt, and repentance, an elderly character dies from an unspecified lingering illness and a boy from illness caused by a spinal injury. Perhaps because doctors truly couldn't help spinal injuries, or perhaps because such injuries permit a graceful decline with one's emotional and mental faculties intact, they are fairly common. As late as Gissing's *The Emancipated*, a 20-year-old woman dies that way. Margaret in Yonge's *Daisy Chain*, surviving the carriage accident that kills her mother and injures her spine, helps raise her motherless siblings. Although suffering severe physical injury, she finally succumbs only when she hears that her fiancé has died: she dies in part from that most rampant fictional disease, unfulfilled love.

To believe literature, the single greatest cause of death in the nineteenth century was love. Women suffer this ailment more than men, growing ill and dying from love—unrequited love, frustrated love, lost lovers—and they suffer it throughout the era: Lister's *Granby* (1826), Trollope's *The Three Clerks* (1858), Meredith's *Richard Feverel* (1859) and *Rhoda Fleming* (1865), Black's *A Daughter of Heth* (1871), Eliot's *Daniel Deronda* (1876), Broughton's *Dr. Cupid* (1887), Du Maurier's *Trilby* (1893), perhaps James's *Daisy Miller* (1879), and in a way, Chopin's *The Awakening* (1899). Despite an occasional male victim, like Rex Gascoigne in *Daniel Deronda* and Little Billie Bagot in *Trilby*, love was women's domain, and illness caused by love's failure fits the vision of women as sentimental and weak.

Betrayed by men they love and trust, perhaps first seduced by them, women die to make a moral and thematic point, as in *Rhoda Fleming* and *Adam Bede*. In *Richard Feverel*, an unfaithful husband and the trauma of an unacceptable marriage lead to brain fever and death for the charming, helpless Lucy Desborough. In Broughton's *Dr. Cupid*, saintly Prue declines and dies when the man she loves fails to return her affection. When love is unfulfilled through parental opposition, a woman's decline just might make a difference: Mrs. Woodward "almost brought herself to own that she would rather see her darling the wife of an idle, ruined spendthrift than watch her thus drifting away to an early grave" (Trollope, *Clerks*, 440).

Defying the norms can result in a decline, reinforcing the tremendous power of society against which feminists battled. The title character of Gaskell's *Cousin Phillis*, who contracts brain fever from the thought of revealing her love to a man and choosing the less acceptable suitor, regains her health and returns to "the peace of the old days" after acknowledging her error (157). Few women who break society's rules recover. Literature is rarely kind to women who defy accepted morality, whether they voluntarily engage in sexual activity or are coerced by an immoral man. Illness, madness, misery, and often death appear justifiable punishments.

Despite so many literary deaths, funerals tend to occur offstage, if at all. Real women played an important role after a death, but Mary Wodehouse tells her sister they need not attend their father's funeral: "it will be too much for you" and "ladies are not expected to have such command over their feelings" (Oliphant, *Curate*, 2:241). The rigid rules of mourning suggest how tightly society controlled behavior. Women plan the mourning attire— how dark the clothing, how long to wear it—and consider how the neighbors would react to the wrong degree of mourning (the right degree determined by issues such as how close the deceased was to the family). Couples might have to postpone marriage, leading to the kinds of plot complications that delight authors.

Most people accepted death, seeing it as a part of ordinary experience, and aided by religious faith. The inept title character of Oliphant's *The Rector*, who lies to a poor woman that she is not near death, contrasts with the young minister and his friend Lucy, who offer physical and spiritual comfort by acknowledging "their patient was dying" (37–38). Thoughts of heaven console far more sophisticated characters than Beth March or Little Eva. Although Frank Graham (Sinclair, *Holiday*) suffers miserably from fever and a painful battle wound, he refuses opium as he nears death, for he wants his senses clear when he goes to his God. Yonge's *The Heir of Redclyffe* asserts a profound faith in an afterlife, which comforts the dying man and his wife. The story also shows how women nurse the family member. Even when her husband can no longer swallow the medicine she offers, the young wife cannot grieve, for he appears peaceful. As dawn approaches, "he slept, but his breath grew short, and unequal; and as she wiped the moisture on his brow, she knew it was the death-damp. Morning light came on—the church bell rang out matins—the white hills were tipped with rosy light. His pulse was almost gone—his hand was cold." Once he calls her name "as if bewildered, or in pain"; she responds but "it was 'another dawn than ours' that he beheld, as his most beautiful of all smiles beamed over his face, and he said, 'Glory in the Highest!—peace—

good will.'" At his request she reads a prayer, and "even as she said 'Amen' she perceived it was over. The soul was with Him with whom dwell the spirits of just men made perfect; and there lay the earthly part with a smile on the face" (384–85). When she weeps, she mourns for herself, not him— for her loss, not his death, because religious faith prevails.

Characters die at home surrounded by their families. To aid plot or theme, authors grant them time for significant last words, even in an un-sentimental novel such as Moore's *Esther Waters*. Death is more natural than in our antiseptic modern world, where people usually die in hospitals, out of ordinary view. Yet death is dramatic, easily romanticized by literature.

Cholera caused many deaths, but unless pointing out the need for sani-tary reform or presenting an angelic character nursing the ill, literature doesn't say much about epidemics. Plot progresses better—and a point about women's roles is made—if a heroine falls ill when separated from her beloved. Literary deaths tend to uphold lingering female stereotypes. The good mother nursing her child or husband through illness to heaven, the saint declining gracefully to death, the martyr dying after sacrificing herself for another, or the sinner punished by death for sexual activity all reinforce traditional visions of woman.

The Changing Victorian Family

When Do People Marry?

Literature unrealistically depicts the age at which people married in the nineteenth century. Fiction most accurately pictures the youngest group: approximately one-third of characters wed between 15 and 19 until 1850, about one-fourth at midcentury, and one-eighth after 1900. The rise in literary marriages for the 20–24 age group mirrors reality at midcentury but disagrees sharply by peaking at century's end, when a marked decrease was evident in real life. Similarly, literary characters of the next age group (25–34) tend to marry later—as many as one in three in the final decades. Very few characters wed after the age of 35, however.

The figures underscore gender differences, routinely showing older men marrying younger women. This pattern is exploited in literature, as it mir-rors the real effects of war, emigration, economics, and social prejudice, and as it handily fits literary convention. For example, at least six times as many female characters as males marry before they are nineteen, while nearly all male characters delay marriage until they are twenty-five.

Literature blithely asserts that there are practical and philosophical reasons for a man to choose a younger woman, but that a woman should not marry a younger man. Age differences of 14 and 20 years are acceptable in Ward's *The Testing of Diana Mallory* and Brontë's *Jane Eyre*, respectively: in fact, Jane says, "More unequal matches are made every day" (152). While not treating them as "every day" events, fiction indeed depicts matches between an 18-year-old woman and a 45-year-old man (Hofland, *Daughter*), and even between a 25-year-old woman and a 70-year-old man (Trollope, *Orley*).

Widowers are often encouraged to remarry, widows almost never, exacerbating the age difference. Older men must beware of "the hundreds of unscrupulous hussies who take possession" of them (Collins, *Finch*, 132–33), while widows devote themselves to their children or to that ubiquitous category, "good works." Praise goes to widows who wear mourning for 20 years: "I think I may say on her behalf that she had never thought of marrying" (Trollope, *Orley*, 19). And blame attends those who remarry: "one husband is enough for any woman" (Carey, *Aunt Diana* [1892], 301); it would be "a desecration of his idol" if a widowed daughter remarried (Oliphant, *Agnes*, 208). Still, a woman who says "I have a—a horror . . . in general—of second marriages" later remarries (Oliphant, *Miss Marjoribanks* [1866], 2:88). Carey's *Lover or Friend?* merely warns widows not to be too forward in their search for new husbands, and one mother says that since her daughter and son-in-law "have been dead to each other for years," the younger woman is no "ordinary widow" who must "fill up a certain season of mourning" (Howells, *Landlord*, 287). Occasionally an older pair marries, perhaps for convenience (in Gaskell's *Wives and Daughters* the man gains someone to raise the children, the woman financial security) or perhaps for companionship in old age (Barr, *Jan Vedder's Wife* [1881]; Meredith, *Beauchamp*). As in reality, literary widowers find it easier to remarry than do widows. Varying over time, as many as half the widowers remarry, contrasted with less than one-third of the widows, thus mirroring accepted attitudes toward male and female roles.

In *Democracy* (1880), Henry Adams's satire on Washington society and government, Mrs. Lightfoot Lee properly devotes herself to good works until, still mourning her husband and child, she restlessly seeks excitement and power. At 30, she finds suitors in John Carrington and Simon Ratcliffe, 10 and 20 years her senior. Although she fears people saying she "came to Washington as a widow on purpose to set my cap for the first candidate for the Presidency" (58), she feels a "blind longing to escape from the torture of watching other women with full lives and satisfied instincts, while her own life was hungry and sad." Still, loving neither man and doubting Ratcliffe's honesty, she rejects both. She asks if "any life was worth living for a woman who had neither husband nor children," yet she also asks, "Was the family all that life had to offer? Could she find no interest outside the household?" (172–73). Neither she nor the author provides answers.

A few characters hesitate over a marriage between a younger woman and an older man, widowed or not, regardless of other factors of eligibility. In Meredith's *Beauchamp's Career,* one character is shocked to learn that a woman will marry an older man without love, but she merely obeys her duty to her father. An older man feels it "preposterous" that he loves a woman half his age; yet if he's "old enough to be her father," he is also "just the right age to combine the paternal with the conjugal affection" (Gaskell, *Ruth,* 188, 213–14).

That's the point, finally. Trollope's *Dr. Thorne* and Marryat's *Too Good for Him* are exceptional in saying that women mature faster and so should marry men their own age or older. The norm is that the man *must* be older; how else can he take care of his child-wife? This fits the image hovering over literature—the innocent ingenue exchanging her father's arm for her husband's before the altar. Women characters of 17 and 18 and even younger routinely marry, and the child-wife appears as a major element of plot in books before Dickens's 1850 work, *David Copperfield* and after Carey's 1894 novel, *Mrs. Romney.* Perhaps, as Carey's *Lover or Friend?* argues, a man should not be 15 years his bride's senior, just old enough to take care of her. "You will be my child as well as my wife," a man comforts his future bride (Carey, *Herb,* 75). Women should "acquire a wholesome sense of their helplessness, and a conviction that dependence on firmer minds and stronger frames than their own is their natural position" (Eden, *Couple,* 205). Women who reject this position risk ostracism or madness, as in Gilman's *The Yellow Wallpaper,* where the wife defies her husband's treating her as a child.

Stowe's feminist novel *My Wife and I* (1871) breaks the pattern in Harry Henderson's search for a wife. As a boy, he loves a "child-wife," five-year old "little Eve," who smiles "graciously" on "the lumpish, awkward Adam" (6); their Eden vanishes when she dies of scarlet fever. Describing the ideal woman he could someday merit, Harry's mother suggests "training men to be husbands" is as important as "training women to be wives" (40). His flirtatious "dream-wife" marries a rich man, leading Harry into brief misogyny. When he meets Eva, believing her engaged, Harry begins a friendship that prepares them for marriage based not only on love but also on respect, similar tastes, and a willingness to live simply and to work together. Women characters stress the need to modify relationships, education, and job opportunities to prepare them for solitary lives as well as marriage. Harry's cousin Charlotte observes that failure to marry will leave her "a cross-pious old maid, held up as a warning to contumacious young beauties how they neglect their first gracious offer" (107).

Charlotte is correct, for women soon drop from the category of potential brides. While Craik's *John Halifax* argues that a couple of 18 and 21 are too young to marry, and Yonge's *The Heir of Redclyffe* agrees about a pair of 20 and 21, Gore's *Mothers and Daughters* counters this by considering a 20-year-old woman past her prime. Jo fears she will be an "old maid" before she encounters the older, shabby, lovable Professor Bhaer (Alcott, *Women*). In 1901 an unmarried 29-year-old woman is unusual (Carey, *Herb*). To avoid this fate, women gradually redefine a good match: Clay's *Heiress of Hilldrop* says women of 20 expect to marry landed gentry, but at 27 or 28 they content themselves with curates and lawyers, even without money.

The fact that heroines marry older men supports the philosophical assumption of male superiority and the practical need for men to establish themselves before accepting responsibility for a family. Reflecting Victorian myths—and ignoring modern women's increasing financial independence—much popular literature pairs older, established men with younger women starting careers. Re-creating reality, most nineteenth-century heroines and heroes find marriage central, whatever their age or reason. But the reasons change as time passes.

Why People Marry: Duty versus Desire

"It is a truth universally acknowledged, that a single man in possession of a good fortune, must be in want of a wife": the first words of Austen's *Pride and Prejudice* (1813) say a lot about why people marry, at least in literature. Underneath the satire lie many assumptions: women must marry, all men are candidates, wealthy men are especially eligible; therefore, rich men must marry—and if they don't realize it, Austen implies, women will help them to their senses.

In reality, a married woman began the century with a status and position her unmarried sister lacked, but that did not mean she fared better. Once married, she could expect to be exhausted by the responsibilities of managing a large household, interrupted frequently by the dangers of childbirth. Her role had not changed since the eighteenth century, when *The Female*

Aegis; or, The Duties of Women described the important "influence of the female character" to improve the "manners, dispositions, and conduct of the other sex" as well as of children, and to lead both to "refinement."[14] Symbolically powerful, a woman actually depended on her husband's goodwill, for the law made him master of house and wife. She had no right to her own property, little control over her children's lives, and no practical solution for even the most disastrous marriage.

In *Women and Economics*, Charlotte Perkins Gilman deplored society's rigid differentiation of gender roles and the way women's "increasingly constricted" roles robbed their work of prestige as well as pay.[15] Her bold study envisions truly equal men and women coexisting in an economically differentiated society that accounts for and makes use of the talents and interests of individuals, regardless of gender. In her communal system, women who wish to cook or clean or raise children could do so for pay while others perform different tasks. Seeing no justification for society's assumption that housekeeping is a female job, her arrangement allows a woman to "stand beside man as the comrade of his soul, not the servant of his body" (237). To her, the "fear" that "fully independent" women "will not marry, is proof of how well it has been known that only dependence forced them into marriage": in a world where relationships are equal and democratic, "there will be needed neither bribe nor punishment to force women to true marriage with independence" (90–91).

Gilman's vision came to fruition only in occasional English and American experiments. Yet while the nuclear family remained a powerful myth and a continuing reality, feminists helped fulfill Gilman's prediction that women would no longer be economically dependent and that they would not have to find identity, social position, meaning, or job solely through marriage. From memoirs and from a changing literature, it seems they also helped create an atmosphere in which "true marriage with independence" between equal partners might more readily occur.

Literature defines romance as the prime reason to marry. Yet, realistically, many brides have other reasons: obedience to parents; an altruistic desire to help someone; a pragmatic search for security, position, or respectability. Heroines do, however, mirror social change, as they increasingly follow their hearts and minds in deciding whom to marry—or whether to marry.

Many women believe marriage will improve them or someone else. Charlotte Brontë's most overtly feminist work, *Villette* (1853), fits the first of these categories. Dorothea's marriage to Casaubon in Eliot's *Middle-*

march fits both: she wants to help him with his work, and, though perhaps unaware, to find significance for her life in a woman's only way—through a man.

Some later women reject the idea of marriage as social work designed to help the man, especially if that means to reform him. Confronted with a truly dissolute man, the heroine of Grand's *The Heavenly Twins* rejects marriage. In an unusual twist, Oliver earns no sympathy for considering marriage to Diana "a burden to be borne; an obligation to be met" because the taint on her family (*not* on her) might damage his political ambitions (Ward, *Diana*, 269).

For women, marriage realistically means security. In Trollope's *The Last Chronicle of Barset* (1867), the penniless Grace finds an excellent match in a widower with a young child. Similar situations occur in Mitford's *Atherton* (1854), Oliphant's *The Doctor's Family*, and Meredith's *Beauchamp's Career* and *Diana of the Crossways*; even the unmercenary March family rejoices at Amy's good fortune in marrying the wealthy Laurie in *Little Women*. New alternatives to marriage made this less significant, yet literature suggests that marriage provides not just material comfort or financial stability but purpose and meaning. As young women in Broughton's *Nancy*, Grand's *Babs the Impossible* (1901), and many other works put it: what else is there?

Marriage can confer position and respectability on both men and women. In the most obvious case, Fanny's pregnancy in Ward's *Diana Mallory* shocks Diana, but she knows the solution is marriage. Society requires marriage for a potential politician in Meredith's *Beauchamp's Career*. Marriage as a mutual bargain appears with unusual directness in Marryat's *Too Good for Him*, where the woman knows she gets a husband and the man knows he gets a mistress for his house. The impact of marriage on status measures men's and women's relative social power: "A man raises a woman to his own standard, but a woman must take that of the man she marries" (Trollope, *Dr. Thorne*, 80).

This is an advantage for a woman who marries up (a common event in literature). The far less common instance of the woman who marries beneath her is shown with poignant realism in Jackson's *Ramona* when the half-Indian heroine disgraces her adopted Spanish family by choosing an Indian husband. The pair become wanderers trapped by racial prejudice, the greed of white settlers, and the government's betraying agreements with Native Americans.

On the other hand, the belief that social and moral progress accompany economic progress has such power that Howells's *The Rise of Silas Lapham* is based on the very theory it denies. Silas assumes financial success will confer status, but what the nouveau riche Laphams do not know constitutes a lesson in nineteenth-century society. At first unaware that living in "an unfashionable neighborhood" is a "personal disadvantage" (22), they later plan a showy house in a good neighborhood. But they don't know how to spend money: European travel is beyond their imagination, their clothes are "rich and rather ugly," and their house is decorated "with the costliest and most abominable frescoes" (23). Daughters Irene and Penelope take dancing lessons, but fail to attend private classes or even to realize that such classes exist. Tom Corey, from old money and high society, becomes interested in Penelope, while Irene cares for him; but for a Corey to marry either girl is a step down, and a man who marries out of his class is disadvantaged. Silas's home reveals the disparity: "There was everything in the house that money could buy. But money has its limitations." Tom's mother adds that "taste" marks the difference between financial and social progress (91). Visiting the Coreys, Lapham learns he is "not a gentleman," for he speaks incorrectly, doesn't know what to discuss, and drinks too much wine. Yet he proves himself a gentleman when he refuses to repeat the kind of shady deal that made him rich, thus beginning his economic fall and moral rise. Poor again, he earns one character's acknowledgment that he "behaved very well—like a gentleman" (273). These studies of limited social mobility are more striking because American; English literature demonstrates even more strongly that breeding and education determine status. Nearly all literature assumes that social position matters in making a match.

Since marriage can offer improved financial or social status for the bride's family, the heroine's mother and others frequently discuss the groom's situation. These ideas become somewhat more overt as the years pass, especially when realism replaces sentimentality, as in Broughton's *Miss Litton's Lovers*, James's *Washington Square* (1880), Grand's *Babs the Impossible*, and Ward's *Marriage a la Mode* (1908). Young women want to help their families: Gaskell's title character in *Sylvia's Lovers* realizes marriage will enhance her family's financial position and provide comfort for herself. Less generously motivated is Peter in Reynold's *The Soldier's Wife* (1852), whose daughter's marriage will give him "a sort of borrowed relation of the lustre of rank" and the right to "dub himself 'a gentleman'" (5).

In *Little Women*, when Meg overhears people say that her mother plans for her daughters to marry successful men, she is stunned and hurt. Asking "Marmee" for the truth, she receives typically pure advice: "I want my daughters to be beautiful, accomplished, and good; to be admired, loved, and respected; to have a happy youth, to be well and wisely married, and to lead useful, pleasant lives. . . . To be loved and chosen by a good man is the best and sweetest thing which can happen to a woman and I sincerely hope my girls may know this beautiful experience" (118). When Meg marries a good, poor man, Marmee asks only that John "keep free from debt and make Meg comfortable" (232). Social position mattered more in England, but financial security mattered everywhere. Given women's dependence on their husbands for financial and social well-being, the emphasis on a "good match" makes sense. But underlying Marmee's words is the truth that a woman's *emotional* well-being also depends on making a good match, something neither status nor money guarantees.

Love and happiness matter more to heroines than to parents, and children—especially girls—must obey their parents. But gradually women insist on their rights in marriage as in other areas of life. A Frenchman asserts that "it is of more consequence that a girl pleases her parents than herself," but her British listener naively responds, "In this country, girls arrange their own marriages" (Black, *Daughter,* 124). In Grand's *The Heavenly Twins,* a girl rejects the man her father chooses, although in traditional terms he is an excellent match: when the man turns out a dissolute rake, the father recognizes his daughter's wisdom.

Authors continually warn against marrying only for money. Bulwer's *Cheveley* (1839) demonstrates the emotional distress such a marriage can cause. From the earliest novels, love can conquer, even when the alternative is a wealthy, titled man, as in Gore's *Mothers and Daughters.* Austen's characters amuse us by directly acknowledging the power of social position to influence a match, but they are right. In *Pride and Prejudice, Sense and Sensibility* (1811), *Persuasion* (1818), *Mansfield Park* (1814), and *Emma* (1816), young women explore the relative importance of status or security and a sound relationship based on respect and solid affection, if not passionate love. Reactions to Emma's continuous meddling reveal Austen's views. Trying to raise Harriet's social position, Emma fails to consider the extent to which Harriet and her potential suitors internalize society's views of rank; Harriet would be uncomfortable with a man above her station. Significantly, Emma fails to acknowledge the power of emotion: people fall in love with whom they wish, not with whom she wants them to, and that's as true for herself as for Knightley or Harriet.

Love accompanied by money is best of all. Still, as in Gore's *Progress and Prejudice,* the choice and power lie with the man. Eden's *The Semi-Attached Couple* argues that happiness requires both love and material security. A few novels even overtly dispute worldly reasons to marry or delay marriage. In Trollope's *Orley Farm* (1862), Felix has a lower social rank, no money or job; but since he is a good, honest person, Madeline's parents accept him. Even more strongly, the heroine in Craik's *John Halifax* refuses to wait until the hero can support them comfortably: because she trusts, respects, and loves him, they will marry now.

As time passed, more heroes and heroines prevented misery by heeding warnings such as this: "The secret of much, though not of all, the unhappiness of the marriage state lies in the glaring unsuitability of mind and temperament betwixt those whose separate lives are about to blend and commingle into one current. Men marry for wealth, for connection, for that dazzling but evanescent gift, a beautiful face and form: women marry for position, by sheer force of circumstances, or for a home. Marrying *alone* for these reasons involves not a blessing, but a curse" (Guyton, *Married*, vi–vii).

Increasingly, characters marry simply for love. Even shared interests are inadequate without love, decides the heroine in Gaskell's *North and South*. Rejecting Laurie's proposal in *Little Women*, Jo explains she cannot love him: "I'm happy as I am, and love my liberty too well to be in any hurry to give it up for any mortal man." Laurie rightly predicts "a time when you *will* care for somebody, and you'll love him tremendously, and live and die for him" (403). Accepting her capacity for so great a love, Jo insists that only then could she marry.

Literature reflects society's ambivalence and confusion about sex, an area especially fraught with myths. The relatively recent debunking of Victorianism led to two popular theories: Victorians were either sexually repressed or rank hypocrites who spoke one game while enthusiastically engaging in another. Neither extreme is correct. Although some contemporary books describe women as asexual creatures or dangerous sirens, others consider female sexuality more reasonably. Arguments against abstinence more than balance arguments against sexual excess, within or outside of marriage. Prostitutes flourished in big cities, but their lives were not wholly degraded, nor were they doomed to misery.[16] People tried to suppress adolescent sex and supported a blatant double standard, condemning sex before or outside of marriage for women but often condoning it for men. Yet this was neither a new attitude (Puritans differentiated the punishments for intercourse with a married woman or man), nor was it totally old-fashioned. Without countenancing unchanneled or uncontrolled sexual expression, Victorians acknowledged the reality and power of sex and its implications.

In his pioneering study of Victorian sexuality, Steven Marcus quotes extensively from William Acton, considering his *Functions and Disorders of the Reproductive Organs* (1857) typically contradictory and conservative.

For instance, Acton states that childhood is asexual, then devotes pages to preventing premature sexual activity. He decries the evils of childhood sexuality (masturbation leads to insanity), premarital sex, and sexual excess within marriage (besides inducing heart failure and memory loss, sexual indulgence can distract a man from his work and lead to ruin). He insists that women neither need nor enjoy sex.[17].

Despite Acton's popularity, many defied his premises. Elizabeth Cady Stanton argued that "a healthy woman has as much passion as a man" and "needs nothing stronger than the law of attraction to draw her to the male."[18] Physicians like Drysdale also regarded sex as pleasurable, not merely functional, and certainly not morally, physically, or emotionally evil. Even before Drysdale, Richard Carlile's *Every Woman's Book: or, What is Love* (1825), selling some 10,000 copies in two years, considered women's sexual needs and discussed birth control (Branca, 132).

Morality remained a vital force in popular attitudes. Some felt middle-class sexual restraint justified a man's having a mistress or seeking a prostitute, but virtually everyone expected women to deny or repress their sexuality. Intercourse during pregnancy was considered dangerous, and women were to help men curb their sexual desires then and at all other times. Encouraging sublimation, writers recommended active sports for boys, delicate flirtation for girls, and carefully selected books for both. But, as Marcus observes, literature devoted to sex may have been intended for the same people who read Eliot and Dickens, since references to those "family" novelists occur in pornographic fiction (225–26). And in marriage, sex was accepted—if not understood—at least in the world outside literature.

Avoiding a discussion of sexuality, literature merely hints, veiling the sensual in sentimental and romantic terms. A heady romance during a typically rapid courtship in Eden's *The Semi-Attached Couple* is about as far as an author dares go, and significantly, this relationship almost results in a failed marriage. Early in the era, characters discuss love but avoid its physical side. Though later characters may not discuss or consciously consider sexual attraction and gratification, they do act on these human needs.

Some authors explicitly confront the topic in terms like these: should young men and women remain innocent or learn enough about their feelings and desires to avoid trouble? "Fallen women," whose lives demonstrate the evil outcome of passion, appear throughout the period, making it obvious that authors deal implicitly with sex. One sensationalistic novel, Helme's *The Farmer of Inglewood Forest* (1825), aptly subtitled *An Affecting Portrait of Virtue and Vice*, examines the lives of a decadent man and the pure girl he seduces. Cajoled into a secret marriage, she ends up utterly miserable, finally a prostitute. Far less melodramatic, Gaskell's tellingly subtitled novel *Wives and Daughters: An Everyday Story* shows how a woman can be drawn into a secret marriage and a man be trapped by sexual indiscretion. The forest scene in Hawthorne's *The Scarlet Letter* displays an unusual recognition of sexual power. After months of repression, briefly freed from a Puritan society mimicking Victorian times, Hester literally lets down her hair. Suddenly she is handsome and sensual again: a smile was "gushing from the very heart of womanhood," "a crimson flush was glowing on her cheek"; "her sex, her youth, and the whole richness of her beauty, came back" (213). The traditional temptress, she has power to lead Dimmesdale to fulfillment or damnation. Books that thus present either Eve the temptress or Eve the fallen woman veil their discussion of sexuality in strong language and symbolic hints. The truly direct discussion of sex, whether positive or negative, is pretty much reserved for later literature.

Grand's turn-of-the-century novels argue vehemently that innocence creates problems. In *Babs the Impossible*, the heroine is so innocent and so "starving for a caress," she does not realize the sexual impact of a kiss for herself or the man (353). Grand is not alone in acknowledging sensual needs with unusual directness. In Ward's *Marriage a la Mode* a woman admits she married her husband from "a sudden gust of physical inclination" (189). In the 1870s and 1880s, authors acknowledge the power of sex more cautiously. A character in Collins's *Poor Miss Finch* realizes her beloved has changed, for she no longer feels a "delicious tingle" when they touch (424). Broughton's *Second Thoughts* (1880) concludes with what was, for the time, a fairly racy love scene: the man "is madly kissing the hem of her gown" as the woman "cries, below her breath, panting and almost inarticulate," to ask what he is doing. He proposes, she accepts, and "he enfolds her slender body with the passionate vigor of his fond arms; and she, yielding to that loved and desired embrace, falls forward weeping on his neck." At the extreme, Egerton's *Keynotes* (1893) shocked readers with its explicit discussions of women's frustrations and lack of knowledge about male or female sexuality.

In contrast, Hungerford's *Molly Bawn* (1895) presents the typical ingenue: "Kiss you! . . . No, I think not. . . . I don't believe I should like it," she says to her fiancé, adding in total seriousness, "Do all women kiss the man they promise to marry?" (55–56). Less absurd but equally strong in asserting women's inherent innocence is Ward's *Diana Mallory*. Learning of her unmarried cousin's pregnancy, Diana experiences the "agonized shock and recoil with which the young and pure . . . receive the first with-

drawal of the veil which hides from them the more brutal facts of life."
Overcoming her "maiden panic," her "cloistered innocence," Diana helps
her cousin (458–59). Such attitudes sometimes linger, a result of women's
upbringing and a cause of marital problems. As a woman in Moore's *A
Mummer's Wife* says, at best she "always complied with the ordinances of
the marriage state without passion or revolt" (89). Only in the new century
do authors deal more directly with issues such as frigidity (Wells's *Tono-
Bungay* [1909], for instance).

By the end of the period, sex is very much an issue, even a focal point
of the story. We do not have to wait for Lawrence's *Sons and Lovers* (1913)
or *Women in Love* to see the power of sex acknowledged for good or ill,
although no mainstream nineteenth-century author proposes that sex outside of marriage is innately good. Hester tells Dimmesdale, "What we did
had a consecration of its own" (*Letter*, 205), but Hawthorne's sympathy does
not mean total exoneration. In *Far from the Madding Crowd, Tess of the
D'Urbervilles*, and *Jude The Obscure*, sexual desire traps Hardy's characters
into inappropriate marriages or illicit relationships, all ending miserably.
Philip's sexual ties to Mildred in Maugham's *Of Human Bondage* (1915)
nearly ruin him. He is rescued by Sally, a good woman who is not too pure
to have sex with him before marriage. When Sally thinks she is pregnant,
Philip reluctantly concludes he must marry her. Learning "it was a false
alarm," he realizes he's not "glad," so he proposes. (606) They seem to share
a healthy relationship, marrying because of love and compatibility and with
full knowledge of each other's sexual and human natures. The differences
in attitude and openness between a book like this and those a century earlier
are stunning.

Attitudes toward love change, too. No longer accepting love simply as
an overpowering emotion, some characters ask what love means, just as
they ask what marriage should be and whether it is necessary. Philip in *Of
Human Bondage* examines the impact and significance of the loves he
experiences, as do James's characters in *The American* (1877), *Daisy Miller,
The Golden Bowl* (1904), and *The Portrait of a Lady*. Later authors like
Woolf and Lawrence allow their characters to explore the many facets of
love, homosexual as well as heterosexual, and to see it as immense, frightening, and transforming. In Woolf's *The Voyage Out* (1915) and *Night and
Day* (1919), and Lawrence's *Women in Love*, couples ask overtly what characters in less open and less psychological novels explore covertly: Do we
really love each other? What is platonic or romantic or sexual love? Should
love lead to marriage? How does love transform both lover and beloved?

Obviously by this time, people's attitudes toward getting married had changed a great deal. Their reasons for *not* marrying changed as well, altering with society.

Why Not Marry?

Under normal circumstances, men determined who would marry—however much women might, according to the stereotypes, maneuver prospective husbands or sons-in-law. Until late in the period and for good practical reasons alone, most women preferred to marry. The single woman had to find shelter in a relative's house: normally she lived with her parents until they died, then became a companion or unofficial nurse for another relative, gaining an anomalous and tenuous status. Still, as women achieved greater independence and divorce became more feasible, women often worked before marriage and prepared themselves for the possibility of remaining single. Even choosing not to marry became a viable option, as it had always been for men.

Rarely reflecting this change realistically, literature tends to regard single men as eligible bachelors, single women as "old maids" or "fallen women," not as "new women" or "bachelorettes." Unmarried people become symbols: the saintly woman whose fiancé drowned while serving his country inspires others through self-sacrifice and virtue; the curmudgeonly old maid who found no proposal matching her proud expectations lives alone and unhappy; the bachelor uncle whose beloved rejected him for lack of money or position inspires his niece or nephew to disdain materialism. The reasons for not marrying change throughout the period, but attitudes toward the importance of marriage alter even more. Still, heroines rarely remain single. They may believe they want to be free, as Jo March put it, or may feel they must care for their orphaned siblings or widowed fathers; but sooner or later the situation alters or they simply change their minds.

Until midcentury, a misalliance based on social or financial position is the most common reason to postpone or reject marriage. This is true in several Austen novels as well as works like Lister's *Granby*, Thackeray's *The Newcomes*, Edwards's *Susan Fielding*, and Alcott's *Rose in Bloom* (1876).

Women's dependent position makes finances matter, leading to complications in the plot: a younger son is a poor match because he has no money (Broughton, *Good-bye*); a man hesitates to marry a wealthy woman, fearing people may accuse him of marrying for money and being unable to fulfill a man's responsibilities (Broughton, *Thoughts*; Yonge, *Daisy*); a lost will motivates plot (Clay, *Heiress*). Less melodramatic stories might raise the issue of prudence (wait until you can afford to marry) versus love (marry now). In Oliphant's *The Perpetual Curate*, the unhappy Dora, who lost her love 30 years before, warns the hero not to follow her path or even that of a married couple who prudently waited 10 years. Dora's story convinces Frank that happiness outweighs financial risk. Feelings tend to win in both realistic tales and romanticized ones like Mitford's *Atherton*, where missing heirs and sudden revocations of love solve the problem; or Jackson's *Ramona*, where obeying the call of love gives the heroine a few intensely happy years followed by great sorrow.

Believing their child can find a wealthier suitor or otherwise disapproving the choice, parents threaten to cut off income. Parents insist their child (usually a daughter) marry for money or position or even, in Egan's sensationalistic *The Flower of the Flock* (1859), to help her family out of trouble. If the girl agrees, like a good daughter, she tends to find a troubled marriage, especially in later works like Grand's *Babs the Impossible*. But sons or daughters who reject their parents' demands risk being punished financially and socially. To avoid that risk in Bury's *Separation*, a man makes a false marriage, with much pain to his wife, his child, and himself. Far less dramatic but equally painful effects occur in Austen's *Pride and Prejudice* when Lydia elopes with Wickham in a marriage justly seen as "so imprudent a match on both sides" (202). Disobeying parental desires results in misery in Meredith's *Richard Feverel*, Oliphant's *Agnes*, and other works.

In contrast, virtue reaps rewards. In Stowe's *The Minister's Wooing* (1859), Mary rejects James in obedience to her family's edict that she wed within their faith. Mary is his "living gospel" (29), the "image" which protects him from temptation as a sailor. Hearing of his death, Mary devotes herself to good works in a "state of self-abnegation . . . not purely healthy" (273). Agreeing to marry the minister, she goes to him as a nun to a convent; but when James reappears, saved in body and soul, the minister releases Mary from her vows. She and James wed, as the narrator insists women find no calling higher than marriage: "The fair poetic maiden, the seeress, the saint, has passed into that appointed shrine for woman, more holy than cloister, more saintly and pure than church or altar, a Christian home" (410).

Duty to one's family, unlike money or social differences, remains a good reason for not marrying throughout the era. In Alcott's *Rose in Bloom*, the talented orphan Phoebe feels she owes it to the Campbells, her adopted family, not to marry their beloved Archie. She tries to earn their approval through work and self-denial, but only after she performs the womanly task of risking her life to nurse Rose's uncle do the Campbells fully accept her as Archie's fiancée.

More typically—and true to social expectations—a young woman sacrifices her happiness to care for her family, often because of her mother's death. In Carey's *Aunt Diana*, Alison's sense of duty teaches her how to serve her widowed father and younger siblings; responsible for the household, she even encourages cheery conversation at breakfast. Alison marries only when the next sister can take her place. The two oldest daughters in Yonge's *The Daisy Chain* never marry. The sickly Margaret runs the household and provides emotional care for the family until she weakens, and Ethel takes over. Ethel consciously decides to stay with her family: "the misty brilliant future of mutual joy dazzled her! But there was another side: her father oppressed and lonely, Margaret ill and pining . . . the children running wild; and she, who had mentally vowed never to forsake her father, far away, enjoying her own happiness" (433–34). That vow, easy to make in the abstract, is harder to keep. But marriage would be "wrong" considering the "state of things . . . at home" (436). Later she confirms her choice: "she had her vocation, in her father, Margaret, the children, home and Cocksmoor [a school she founds]; her mind and her affections were occupied, and she never thought of wishing herself elsewhere" (637).

Ethel's remaining a spinster is a hard decision, for at midcentury only two kinds of women failed to marry: pure "old maids" and sexually active "fallen women." Though society approved the former and disapproved the latter, it didn't like either very much. Instigating and modeling change, the New Woman frightened, distressed, and disgusted most of her sisters, but she inspired a few.

Old Maids and New Women

Magazines such as *Godey's Lady Book*, edited by Sara Josepha Hale, celebrated woman as a domestic being dedicated to serving her family. In the 1870s and 1880s, Hurricane Nell and Calamity Jane romped through the pages of the dime novels, acting with all the vigor and energy of female Western heroes. Although Calamity Jane hardly represented the norm, mainstream magazines around the same time acknowledged a new dimension: while continuing to reinforce woman's domestic role and to exalt her as the source of civilization and culture within her proper sphere, even the first issues of the *Ladies Home Journal* included articles about work and wages. Elizabeth Cady Stanton and Susan B. Anthony edited a magazine called *Women's Journal* (later renamed *Revolution*), carrying articles on work, dress reform, and other items of interest to the New Woman. Charlotte Perkins Gilman spoke for a small band of increasingly vocal and influential women when she expressed skepticism about the cult of pure womanhood in works like *Women and Economics* and *The Home*. Since Stanton's, Anthony's, and Gilman's readers did not need converting, shifts in traditional domestic magazines more significantly reveal society's new ways.

Yet ideas evolved slowly. Literature frequently describes spinsters in the most unflattering terms: "old cats" (Ward, *Diana*, 119); a woman with the heart of an "angel" but "a little dumpy body, with a yellow face, and a red nose" (Kingsley, *Two Years*, 472). They must follow "the rigid punctilio" of maidenly behavior (Mitford, *Village*, 85). Gossips and complainers, they are faultfinders, rarely satisfied. Jo and Amy both suffer the trials of working for their querulous maiden aunt in *Little Women*, and Austen's Emma is not alone in mocking such creatures. But just as Emma learns she should not make fun of Miss Bates at the Box Hill picnic, so others display sympathy. In *Shirley*, Charlotte Brontë pleads, "Reader! when you behold an aspect for whose constant gloom and frown you can not account, whose unvarying cloud exasperates you by its apparent causelessness, be sure that there is a canker somewhere, and a canker not the less deeply corroding because concealed." The woman who unconsciously motivates this plea is "solitary and afflicted," "corpse-like" and unsmiling. But the heroine learns "the old maid had been a most devoted daughter and sister, an unwearied watcher by lingering death-beds" whose labors earned her the wasting illness which "now poisoned her own life." This impoverished woman who still keeps a "wretched relative" from utter ruin "was rather to be admired for fortitude than blamed for moroseness" (163–64).

But even when presented sympathetically, as in Gaskell's *Cranford*, spinsters are seen as incomplete. Realistically, they tend to be poor, lonely, dependent on relatives. One kind aunt says she will have no child "to cheer my old age" (Carey, *Aunt*, 31). Ethel knows that although she "was truly a mother to the younger ones," they will "find others to whom she would have the second place" (667). To love "heartily" and selflessly, knowing she will never stand first in anyone's heart, takes great fortitude and, for Ethel, great religious faith. She is one of many single women who give unstintingly of themselves, like the woman Ward describes as a "tired saint" (*Diana*, 359).

Late in the century, Gissing's *The Odd Women* portrays several spinsters—"odd" because they have not married and work outside the home. Some never have the choice to marry; others reject marriage altogether. Most successful among them is Rhoda Nunn, who founds a business school to help single women achieve more comfortable and useful lives. Yet she is not a sympathetic character, in some ways fitting the negative stereotype of the old maid.

Ethel of *The Daisy Chain* remains single out of love and duty to her family, reasons her contemporaries understand and praise. Throughout the period, having more options, men can focus on a career or simply choose to remain free, usually without losing face. But in some later novels, women make those same choices, for reasons Ethel's contemporaries would have found incomprehensible.

As early as 1866, Oliphant presents a 29-year-old who thinks it more fun not to marry. Agreeing with her, one woman says, "it would be very foolish of Miss Marjoribanks to marry, and forfeit all her advantages, and take somebody else's anxieties upon her shoulders, and never have any money except what she asked from her husband" (*Marjoribanks*, 3:67); however, the freedom-loving Miss Marjoribanks ultimately succumbs. Her contemporary, Lily in Trollope's *The Last Chronicle of Barset*, rejects marriage: having once loved, she feels she no longer has a whole heart to give; and having been betrayed, she no longer fully trusts men. Lily would have married had her lover not betrayed her, and Miss Marjoribanks ultimately does marry. After exploring some new reasons for remaining single, literature favors marriage.

Carey's *The Mistress of Brae Farm* (1896) reveals a newer attitude, though the novel is ultimately conservative. For the title character, "marriage was not . . . the aim and object of her life; she gloried too much in her freedom to yield her liberty lightly." Wealthy, attractive, and kind, she "had her chances," but "she was not a submissive woman; it would be difficult for her to yield to another person's judgment" (46–47). Strong as these statements sound, she worries if she is normal. Although there is "nothing missing in her life," she is "dimly conscious of unknown capacities in her nature" (203). Unfortunately, she realizes these capacities too late, losing her former lover to her cousin. Planning "to take up her changed and marred life as best she could," she thinks, "if I live to be an old woman, I shall never suffer such pain again" (416, 422). Unusual in focusing on a woman who does not marry, the novel portrays her with rare sympathy, though her contemporaries would call her "unwomanly" and anyone would see her as somewhat self-centered. But the main point, the moral, remains clear: it is a mistake not to marry.

Stowe, in *My Wife and I*, sympathizes with the desires of the New Women, Caroline and Ida, for education and a "life-work." But she heaps scorn on the radical woman, Audacia Dangyereyes, who smokes, visits men in their rooms, and announces she will live as any male can in New York. Stowe endorsed domesticity in much of her work, coediting the best-selling *American Woman's Home*, and editing the magazine *Hearth and Home*. This split also appears in Alcott's writings. In *Little Women*, Jo and Meg work at 15 and 16; with their father a Union Army chaplain, the family needs their small earnings as companion to an elderly aunt and as governess. Yet both marry. Jo tries the independent life: serving in the home of a family acquaintance provides shelter and income while she experiments as an author. Yet love motivates her as much as a desire for independence. Believing that Beth loves Laurie, she hopes her absence will teach him to reciprocate. This does not occur, but Jo falls in love; ultimately she marries *and* writes, but as revealed by *Little Men* (1871) and *Jo's Boys* (1886), writing always comes second to her extended family. For feisty, independent Jo, marriage matters just as much as for the domestic Meg.

Olive Schreiner's life reveals even more of the pressures on the New Woman than does her striking representative of the type, Lyndall in *The Story of an African Farm* (1883). An ardent feminist, Schreiner worked in South Africa and in England for women's issues, including suffrage and trade unions. When she finally married, her husband took her last name and supported her efforts. But they often lived apart, and she was a sickly woman, unable to bear healthy children or to fulfill her goals as a writer.

Celia Madden rejects marriage in Frederic's *The Damnation of Theron Ware*. Celia's bright red hair should warn the innocent, egocentric Theron: she is unmarriageable because of "the bold, luxuriant quality of her beauty, the original and piquant freedom of her manners, the stories told in gossip about her lawlessness at home, her intellectual attainments, and artistic vagaries" (83). A talented musician, she arouses Theron with intellectual talk, impassioned renditions of Chopin, and self-described "pagan" or "Greek" attitudes that imply an intense but untouchable sexuality; and she stuns him with her views on marriage. When he says men would fight for her, she counters that he is "old fashioned" to think "women must belong to somebody, as if they were curios, or statues, or race-horses." She insists,

"I am myself, and I belong to myself, exactly as much as any man. The notion that any other human being could conceivably obtain the slightest property rights in me is as preposterous, as ridiculous, as—what shall I say?—as the notion of your being taken out with a chain on your neck and sold by auction as a slave." Theron correctly stammers, "that is not the generally accepted view," but Celia's words reflect changing attitudes (213).

The staunch feminists Zenobia of Hawthorne's *The Blithedale Romance* (1852) and Olive Chancellor of James's *The Bostonians* (1886) are seen very negatively by their authors and most characters. Priscilla, the "snow-maiden" foil to Zenobia's dark beauty, is not the traditional blond heroine, although Miles Coverdale so regards her. Zenobia's hothouse flowers aptly represent her voluptuous nature and the existence of some false note about her. She tantalizes Coverdale and the reader, hinting at her sensuality and hiding the truth about Priscilla, whom she symbolically dresses in white and literally controls through the mesmerist Westervelt. Zenobia's uncertain role as a feminist spokeswoman frustrates modern readers: although she argues that women can achieve full lives without marriage, she ultimately commits suicide for a man unworthy of her love. Far less attractive, Olive Chancellor is grasping, impassioned, frustrated, and an unacknowledged lesbian who cannot see that her attempts to control Verena and submerge her personality in the "cause" destroy Verena's freedom just as do Basil Ransom's attempts to force the girl into the feminine mold. Women's roles changed, but not enough to allow most authors—or readers—to hold positive views of ardent feminists.

Fallen Women

Sexually active women may escape the stigma of being unwomanly, unfeminine, or lesbian, but they are still anathema. If seen as pure, innocent victims of evil men, they earn more pity than blame, yet society rarely exonerates them. But seen as the daughters of Eve, seductresses whose sensuality can destroy themselves and their men, they receive no mercy.

With rare exceptions, literature says sex belongs within marriage. In *Lady Rose's Daughter* (1903), Ward's heroine is the "illegitimate child of a mother who had defied the law for love." She tries to be "free—like my parents—from all these petty strivings and conventions." But if "the depth of passion in her . . . stirred, and intoxicated" her potential lover, it also leads to "a curious diminution of respect" (302–6). She agrees to meet him in Paris, but they fail to consummate their relationship and are grateful to be saved from "an abyss" (365).

Not all women are spared the "abyss," and whoever instigates the relationship, the woman suffers when an unmarried couple engages in sex. The story of Eden hovers behind the image of the fallen woman, especially in American fiction. The ambiguity of Eve's both succumbing to Satan and tempting Adam lingers as well, adding to society's complex and ambivalent attitudes toward woman as mother, temptress, and saint.

Elsie Venner (1861) so obviously connects its heroine to the original Fall that Holmes refers to Elsie as "Eve" in his 1891 preface. Temptress and seductress, Elsie is identified with snake imagery, much as is the satanic Chillingworth in *The Scarlet Letter*. Yet while accepting the destructive nature of her sexuality, Holmes also explores the culpability of society and the men she encounters. Unable to fit into the normal life of her community, she is both stultified and alienated.

Literature often establishes a symbolic contrast between the dark lady, the temptress Eve, and the innocent blond ingenue, the Virgin Mary. In Melville's *Pierre* (1852), blond Lucy Tartan, a ministering angel to be worshiped but not touched, is foil to the dark and vibrantly sensual Isabel Banford. Isabel's role fits the book's subtitle, *The Ambiguities*: like Eve, she is a powerful force, neither pure good nor pure evil. If she tempts Pierre, she also brings him to life. Pierre should marry Lucy but treats her like a sister; his true sister, Isabel, he loves as a wife. Destruction is assured, and it is complete.

Though leading men astray, temptresses like Isabel offer a vitality missing in the blond angels. Hester Prynne conveys such ambiguity. When she emerges from prison, the Puritans see a tall, dark, strong woman who has emblazoned a brilliant scarlet letter on her breast; no Puritan and few Victorians would acknowledge Hawthorne's vision of her as a Madonna. To Dimmesdale, Hester offers hope and freedom, a new life away from their stultifying society; but there is deception in their passion and in her failing to tell him about Chillingworth until it is too late. And, while Hester feels their sexual relationship had its own "consecration," she may misread Dimmesdale in believing he shares that view.

Occasionally a more sensational novel like Bulwer's *Cheveley* argues that a woman who falls must have begun with questionable virtue. But Hardy in *Tess* does not expect us to sympathize with Alec when, reformed from seducer to preacher, he brands Tess a "temptress" and "a dear, damned witch of Babylon" (369). Not Eve the seductress but the innocent virgin prevails, especially in popular domestic writing. Blame goes to the man and the situation. Whether in a romance like Reynolds's *The Soldier's Wife*, a more realistic work like Gaskell's *Ruth*, or a late novel like Moore's *Esther Waters*, the story is the same. Women fall because they are friendless, lonely, and scared—innocent children unprepared to face a man's or their own sexual drives. "Passion and shame had set their marks upon the child's forehead": such words convey the standard attitude. An older man responds, "Of course she has done wrong. I don't mean to defend her—but, after all, she is but a child. Poor little thing! Her mother died, you know, when she was a baby. She had nobody to tell her how to behave." In contrast, "every gentleman" must believe the man displayed "vileness" (Oliphant, *Curate*, 83–85, 92–93).

A fallen woman may redeem herself through good works (Collins, *New Magdalen* [1878], Hawthorne, *Letter*), a virtuous life (Gaskell, *Ruth*), or even becoming a nun (Moore, *Sister Teresa* [1901]). Occasionally a seducer repents, as in Meredith's *Rhoda Fleming*. Eliot, in *The Mill on the Floss*, satirizes contemporary morals when she says "public opinion" would have accepted Maggie's elopement if she married Stephen and returned with a large trousseau (428). Meredith satirically presents Bella's insisting on her right to live as she will, to maintain a house where men visit her, keeping her in the "luxuries" she "can't do without"; the author comments that she "was best in her character of lovely rebel accusing foul injustice. 'You tell me to be different. How can I? What am I to do? Will virtuous people let me earn my bread? . . . Do you expect me to bury myself alive? Why, man, I have blood; I can't become a stone'" (*Feverel*, 375).

But Bella is exceptional. Normally, a woman who falls is doomed forever, called an "outcast prostitute" (Gaskell, *Barton*, 151) or considered dead by her father (Meredith, *Fleming*, 136–37). No effort wipes out the stain of sin: her neighbors may eventually reinterpret Hester Prynne's letter as signifying "Able," but they still ask her to sew shrouds, not bridal veils or christening gowns. Crane's naturalistic novella *Maggie: A Girl of the Streets* (1896) poignantly describes a woman's total degradation. Maggie "blossomed in a mud-puddle" (17), innocent in spite of her slum upbringing. But once fallen, she rapidly slides downhill, depicted by parallel scenes in a high-quality beer hall, a seedy one, and finally the streets. In the last pages, Crane shows her propositioning ever more disreputable men, until she commits suicide in the blackness of the river.

In Hardy's bleak novels, sin inevitably leads to intense suffering and often death. *Tess* certainly presents a double standard about sex, but men also suffer: Tess loses her child, her position, her lover, and ultimately her life;

her seducer dies as well. In *Far from the Madding Crowd*, Fanny and her illegitimate daughter die, and in *Jude*, sexual desire leads to uncountable miseries: Arabella commits bigamy, Sue marries unhappily, Jude dies, and the children of Sue and Jude's marriage die through suicide and murder.

Only in the new century does literature suggest that sex outside of marriage need not doom the participants. From Wells's *Ann Veronica* (1909), aptly subtitled *A Modern Love Story*, to the heroes and heroines of Lawrence's work, characters may hesitate for personal reasons, but neither they nor their authors automatically condemn sexual relationships. In Galsworthy's Forsyte Saga, including *The Man of Property* (1906) and *In Chancery* (1920), we sympathize with the unhappily married Irene, who has two affairs, and we despise her husband, Soames, who tries to maintain the old view of his wife as property. By the time of World War I, literature could echo society in damning men like Soames and Theron Ware, and Irene could echo Celia Madden's scornfully reversing the old position: "That is not the generally accepted view."

Some authors even argue that the sexual double standard should die with the nineteenth century. In Forster's *Howards End* (1910), having accepted Henry's admission of an affair during his first marriage, Margaret is furious when he insists she abandon her pregnant sister. He stammers, "the two cases are very different," and, incredulous, she cries, "You shall see the connection if it kills you, Henry! You had a mistress—I forgave you. My sister has a lover—you drive her from the house." She notes that he betrayed his first wife, her sister "only herself": "You remain in society, Helen can't. You have had only pleasure, she may die." Speaking for Margaret, the narrator concludes, "Oh, the uselessness of it" (308). But the feminists' mission, the effort and struggle were not useless if they created characters like Margaret and the conclusion Forster draws—and readers who would accept such scenes. Ironic circumstances force Henry to accept Helen into his home, and the novel ends with a picture of a very new family: Henry; Margaret, his second wife; Helen, her unmarried sister; and Helen's illegitimate son, the inheritor of the new world.

In much early twentieth-century literature, such as Wharton's *The House of Mirth* (1905) and *The Age of Innocence* (1920), and Sinclair's *The Three Sisters* (1914), women remain sexually and socially confined in stultifying roles, no matter how they struggle. But characters such as Gudrun and Ursula in Lawrence's *Women in Love*, and Katharine in Woolf's *Night and Day* reveal new values through the questions they ask and the answers they give about marriage. Earlier characters ask: If I don't marry, what else is there? Modern characters ask: Why marry? That is a change indeed.

When Marriage Fails

Rarely dealing with unhappy marriages, even as laws and attitudes changed, literature almost never considers divorce. A man's infidelity, a misalliance, or a woman's discontent causes sorrow but not legal action. Reflecting society's assumptions and readers' wishes, wedded couples live happily ever after—or at least live together ever after.

Most literature about troubled marriages understandably focuses on women. Law and attitude favored the husband; even if denied legal freedom, he had far greater freedom of action. Most literature reinforces the moral that a woman (or less often a man) must stick with a marriage. Less conservative writers suggest that women's real legal and financial position offers no option: marriage is still indissoluble, but for very different reasons. Yet slowly, hesitantly, as society changed, literature began to consider when divorce might be justified.

The battle in society over marriage and divorce laws raged for decades. While feminists argued that women deserved equal rights in marriage and divorce, for they should not be economic, social, or sexual slaves, altering these laws struck at the very heart of the womanly ideal.

Opponents of divorce raised both religious and social objections. Although Scotland had long experience with laws granting relatively inexpensive divorces and permitting divorce to husbands and wives for similar causes, conservatives claimed that rewriting the laws about marriage would undermine family life, destroying society's most sacred institution. The women's movement helped establish conditions that made divorce more acceptable. Typical among reformers, Elizabeth Cady Stanton focused on divorce not as a social problem but as an individual right, one of the many new options available to women.

At first, only the wealthy and highly determined could divorce, and men always found it far easier to divorce than women did. If husband and wife separated, society blamed and denigrated the woman, considering her immoral, an unfit mother. Until the Infant Custody Act of 1839 English mothers had no legal right to appeal for access to their young children or even to care for those under seven.

The Matrimonial Causes Act of 1857 gave middle-class Englishwomen access to divorce, creating a new court and significantly reducing costs. Yet under its provisions a husband could win a divorce if his wife committed adultery, whereas a wife needed to prove not only her husband's infidelity but also his desertion, cruelty, incest, rape, sodomy, or bestiality.[19]

In time, social conservatives joined feminists and radical reformers in protesting costly, difficult, and unfair laws. Although Alexander Walker argued that intellectual and physiological differences made women's "sphere" the right one, he decried the "absurdity" of laws that meant that "a mere error in choice . . . doomed" a couple "to perpetual suffering," whereas "if they will only add a crime to this," they can be "rewarded by being set free." Suggesting ground rules such as postponing divorce if there are young children, Walker asserted that wives and husbands should have equal "right or power" in divorce.[20]

Even if a woman could obtain a divorce, she usually could not support herself and her children. Changing that situation required laws such as the Married Woman's Property Act (1870) in England and a series of such acts in individual American states (14 by 1860). Giving women rights over their property and earnings, these laws made it profitable for married women to work for pay. Additional laws were enacted later in the century, but the slow nature of reform, economic realities, the idealization of womanhood, and the almost mythic reverence for the family explain why the number of divorces, though growing, remained low, and why at first men filed more petitions. In England, even as the number of divorces quintupled between the 1860s and 1890s, men still filed the majority (McGregor, 36–41). More generous American laws led to some 7,000 divorces in 1860, 60 times the number in England; and by the end of the century, two-thirds of all divorces were granted to women.[21] On the frontier, divorce wasn't always necessary, since a man could simply leave home, assume a new identity in a new community, and marry again. That may explain the frequency of bigamy and desertion as cited causes for divorce in the United States. Although divorce remained the exception in both nations, laws and attitudes toward marriage and divorce most decidedly changed.

Eliot's *Middlemarch*, aptly subtitled A *Study of Provincial Life*, presents the literary norm: realizing his mistake soon after marrying Rosamund, Lydgate knows he must make the best of it. Usually literature featuring separation or divorce is sensationalistic or proselytizing for reform. In representative fiction up to midcentury, fewer than one in 100 male characters divorce, a figure that doubles in literature published between 1876 and 1901 and reaches more than one in 20 in works published between 1901 and 1920. The mark of the women's movement is seen in changes for female characters. Only one in 100 risk divorce as late as the final quarter-century. But works published from 1901 to 1920, generally taking place in the last decades of the century, feature more divorced women than men. While the percentage remains low (about one in 13), the change is significant, perhaps suggesting new attitudes toward divorce and women's roles, and also new freedom for writers to confront sensitive issues.

Sensationalism and Middle-Class Morality

In early literature, separation or divorce tends to fit a pattern of exaggerated problems. Redolent of sensation, exaggeration, and the gothic, rather than moral condemnation, Helme's *The Farmer of Inglewood Forest* contains a bad marriage, a duel, seduction, and elopement. Hook's slightly more realistic *Merton* (from *Sayings and Doings*) rivals Helme with a secret marriage, some questionable marriages, lawsuits, jail sentences, death, divorce, and an unusual remarriage. In Kingsley's *The Hillyars and the Burtons*, remarriage and separation fit a pattern of disaster: four widows, false arrest, a lost will, emigration to Australia, and drowning in a storm at sea.

Hardy nearly always features marital failure. In *Tess*, which includes murder and hanging, Angel invokes the double standard (Tess should forgive his premarital affair, but he cannot forgive hers) and causes the separation of husband and wife. *The Mayor of Casterbridge* (1886) has a widow, a fake widow, bigamy, and remarriage. For sheer sensationalism, *Jude* wins with what Sue calls a "natural marriage" but others call an affair, bigamy, separation, murder, and suicide.

Problem marriages normally evoke direct or implied moralizing. Secret engagements and elopements create bad marriages, say Bury's significantly titled *Separation* and Meredith's more realistic *Richard Feverel*. Relationships fail if people don't know each other before marriage (Eden, *Couple*), or marry for the wrong reasons (Estella in *Great Expectations* [1861], Louisa in *Hard Times* [1854]), or both (David and Dora in *David Copperfield*). Parents forcing children to marry causes problems, as with Catherine Linton and Linton Heathcliff, the second generation of unhappy pairs in Brontë's *Wuthering Heights*. Carey's *Herb of Grace* offers an extreme situation with a reminder of social attitudes about divorce: Leah's father twice coerces her to marry against her will, and divorce is out of the question.

As reformers arguing for new laws insisted, failed marriages injure the participants, a point Meredith frequently makes. Like the better-known *Richard Feverel*, *Diana of the Crossways* shows how a couple with different values bickers, reconciles "for the sake of decency," then "breaches . . . the truce." Both are "deformed by marriage": she sees "the man behind the mask" but loathes "glimpses of herself, too, the half-known, half-suspected, developing creature claiming to be Diana" (104).

In *Janet's Repentance* (from Eliot's *Clerical Life*), Janet's alcoholic husband beats her until she desperately defies him. Barred from the house in a storm, she turns to alcohol. Though she nurses him when he dies, reform comes too late, and her life ends in miserable repentance for sins modern readers understand and forgive. Among her contemporaries, only feminists battling for new laws would prefer her behavior to that in Hofland's *Patience* (1825): one character suggests Dora divorce her debauched, unfaithful husband, but after she helps him, his reform and love repay her virtue. In case anyone could possibly miss the thesis, the narrator intones, "Christian patience alone had sustained her" (306).

In Barr's *Jan Vedder's Wife*, middle-class morality and religion again defeat the evils that attend a bad marriage. The restless Jan prefers tavern to job, but his wife's rejection harms them both. At last he reforms, she grows kinder, and they reunite in an atmosphere of Christian forgiveness and a promise for the future. Not Christian virtue but a good Jewish man guides Gwendolyn in Eliot's *Daniel Deronda*. Gwendolyn pays for marrying for money and position. Without a marriage settlement, she cannot escape her predicament, so Daniel guides her to make the best of her situation. She finds a reward in a peaceful life, secure in her own virtue.

Gissing's *The Emancipated* demonstrates that elopement, always bad but worse with an unsuited pair, may lead to distress, illness, separation, an affair, and an infant's death. Rather than supporting conventional morality, the novel scores points against social and legal double standards. It defies the myth that women can reform immoral men. One woman angrily insists her husband has no "right" to "demand more of me than I of you" (420). But he correctly notes that even the law distinguishes between men's and women's infidelity.

When Julia in Bulwer's *Cheveley* becomes an abused wife in a horrid marriage, she knows that "the frightful power that is vested in men" means "there is no redress for a woman, publicly or privately." In a neat bit of propaganda that plays up to middle-class nervousness about reform, Julia insists she is "no advocate for the ridiculous and immoral chimera, called the 'Rights of Women.'" She dismisses the "right" of women "to kill their fellow-creatures as soldiers, cajole them as statesmen, or cheat them as lawyers"; rather, "a woman's proper and only empire is her home": "it never can or ought to be any other; but still there should be some cruelty-to-animal act that would extend its protection to her in that sphere" (225–26).

Separation and Divorce

Given contemporary laws and attitudes, literature's serious treatment of separation and divorce makes sense. In Ward's *Lady Rose's Daughter*, a couple who consider marriage "a mere legality" that must not prevent "happiness," still assert that "divorce was in itself impious" (21). An acquaintance, peeved to be "kept in the dark" about their affair, is "insulted" out of "Vanity!—not morals" (89). But the attractive pair "cared much and ardently for 'man'; and very little, comparatively, for men" (99). Most characters, shocked by the affair, invoke their responsibility as models, arguing that no one of their stature has the "right to do anything which may lead others to think lightly of God's law" (151). Since society's law reinforced "God's law," feminist authors sometimes focus on bad marriages to assert the need for reform in attitudes or laws or both.

The rare separation often creates other problems. Even when separation comes from family or financial pressure, difficulties occur (Eden, *Couple*; Broughton, *Nancy*). Isabel, of Wood's *East Lynne*, jealous of her husband's apparent interest in another woman, goes to the sea for her health; her lonely isolation leads to increased jealousy and distrust. Ruin follows inexorably, as she becomes pregnant by another man. Changed beyond recognition and believed dead, she becomes governess to her own children. The initial act of separation seals her fate, with no sympathy: "How fares it with Lady Isabel? Just as it must be expected to fare, and does fare, when a high-principled gentlewoman falls from her pedestal. Never had she experienced a moment's calm, or peace or happiness" (278).

A stigma attaches itself to a woman separated from her husband, almost regardless of justification. Whatever the initial cause, if the separation ultimately involves sexual infidelity, as in *The Awakening* or *The Scarlet Letter*, this may seem reasonable. But the stigma is equally strong and surely unfair when a woman whose husband has been jailed for 14 years adopts the approved role of widow, for "a woman is bound to defend herself and her children" (Carey, *Lover*, 274). Even in the new century, Sophia of Bennett's *The Old Wives' Tale* passes as a widow when separated from her husband; she also lives abroad, supporting herself by running a pension in Paris. In contrast, Howells presents a "rather anomalous lady," Mrs. Vostrand, who lives apart from her husband but on "apparently perfectly good terms with him" and functions "so discreetly and self-respectfully that no breath of reproach had touched her" (*Landlord*, 88). Though a sophisticated Boston woman accepts the Vostrands' relationship as "one of the most obvious phases of the American marriage" (91), it is far from usual. By leaving her disreputable husband in Gissing's *The Emancipated*, Mrs. Travis damages her own reputation. One man admits her act distresses him because "he was in the position of a husband who fears that his authority over his wife is weakening. Mrs. Travis, as he knew, was a rebel against her own husband— no matter the cause. She would fill Cecily's [his wife's] mind with sympathetic indignation; the effect would be to make Cecily more resolute in independence" (298).

Separation is bad, divorce far worse. A widower may make a fine match, but not a divorced man, let alone a divorced woman. A character in Wood's *East Lynne* piously intones, "Whosoever putteth away his wife, and marrieth another, committeth adultery" (317). Clive in Thackeray's *The Newcomes* and Isabel in James's *The Portrait of a Lady* gain release from troubled marriages only when their spouses die. Death may punish one who breaks society's rules, but, given both law and mores, a fortuitous death may be the only escape from a bad marriage.

When some members of high society accept a divorced man in Gore's *Mothers and Daughters*, the virtuous middle class quickly finds fault: contrasting two definitions of morality, the novel staunchly reaffirms traditional values. Fifty years later, in Ouida's sensationalistic *Moths* (1880), a mother can still force her former lover and daughter to marry. The unfaithful, abusive man imprisons his wife, who obeys him utterly, bound by her belief in convention: "The woman who can wish for a divorce and drag her wrongs into public—such wrongs!—is already a wanton herself" (398). Miserable years of virtue finally reap the reward of a quiet life with a loving man.

The idea that virtuous self-denial produces rewards recurs in Anne Brontë's *Tenant of Wildfell Hall* (1848), a diatribe against women's helplessness, society's willful blindness, and contemporary laws. Loving the profligate Arthur Huntington, Helen Graham accepts the notion that a woman can reform a bad man: "If I hate the sins I love the sinner, and would do much for his salvation" (147). Together only one month after their engagement, she realizes that he drinks, gambles, and keeps bad company. She admits, "I cannot shut my eyes to Arthur's faults, and the more I love him the more they trouble me" (179). Marrying him anyway, she learns she cannot influence him, for he believes a wife is something "to love one devotedly and to stay at home—to wait upon her husband, and amuse him and minister to his comfort" (233). Helen stays with Arthur even when he brings his mistress to live with them, but later says, "We are husband and wife only in name. . . . I am your child's mother, and your housekeeper, nothing more" (304). Only when he encourages their toddler to drink does Helen finally leave. Her child's needs, not her own, guide her quiet life as a "widow" at Wildfell Hall, where she can wean her son from alcohol. Society and her family side with her husband. Finally his death releases her and she can marry her confidant, Gilbert.

An occasional male character suffers as do women from society's views. Rochester in Charlotte Brontë's *Jane Eyre* cannot divorce his wife, though her family failed to warn him of her hereditary madness. Knowing his pain, Jane forgives his considering bigamy but won't accept him while his wife lives—however she lives. The fire that blinds him kills his wife, releasing him from a dreadful marriage. Craik's *John Halifax* also argues that a bad marriage cannot excuse adultery, and Halifax cites the Ten Commandments to reinforce the immorality of both adultery and divorce.

Beyond the issue of attitude, the law erected practical barriers to divorce, as outlined by Dickens in *Hard Times*. Seeking help from the rich Mr. Bounderby, the laborer Stephen Blackpool notes, "I ha' read i' th' papers that great fok . . . are not bonded together for better for worst so fast, but that they can be set free fro' *their* misfortnet marriages, an marry ower again." Mr. Bounderby piously mumbles, "There's a sanctity in this relation of life . . . and—and—it must be kept up." Pressed to acknowledge "there *is* such a law," Bounderby quickly adds, "It's not for you at all": "It costs a mint of money . . . You'd have to go to Doctors' Commons with a suit, and you'd have to go to a court of Common Law with a suit, and you'd have to go to the House of Lords with a suit, and you'd have to get an Act of Parliament to enable you to marry again" (68–69). But if Stephen's poverty leaves him no choice, at midcentury members of the middle class had little choice, either.

Two generations later, Linton's *Christopher Kirkland* reveals a changing society when a character comments that it is no longer "subversive" to obtain "divorce by mutual consent and without the necessity of committing a crime." This new "facility of divorce," replacing "falsehood" and "crime" with "the honest confession of incompatibility," seems "a just relief" and "an accumulation of virtue for the community" (207). This view would not be liberal for reformers like Mary Wollstonecraft, Lucy Stone, or Caroline Norton. But it was for literature, with its hesitant, troubled approaches to divorce.

Stressing the misery of life rather than the wages of sin reveals a new attitude in *A Mummer's Wife*, but Moore still shows that divorce leads to evil. Deserting her sickly, cantankerous husband to elope with an actor, the heroine enjoys brief success on stage and with her new man. But a neatly constructed plot leaves her ill and ornery, until she finally loses both her second husband and her life.

Confronting the evils of contemporary marriage laws, Howells's A *Modern Instance* (1881) argues that divorce, while not good, is necessary. The relationship of Bartley Hubbard and Marcia Gaylord seems doomed from the start. Rightly jealous (Bartley kisses Hannah, his redheaded coworker), angry, and hurt, Marcia breaks the engagement, but then begs him to return—a pattern repeated in marriage. They fight, she locks him out, then welcomes him back. He wastes money, drinks, and is bored with family life; Marcia wrongly accuses him of renewing his relationship with Hannah and he disappears. Months later, friends learn Bartley sued for divorce: Marcia's failure to appear in an Indiana court in three days will prove that *she* abandoned *him*, thereby justifying the divorce. Love, hatred, and vengeance lead her to fight. Yet when she wins and her father countersues for divorce in her name, she cannot hurt Bartley. He again flees, telling a friend "we ought to be free," for "if our marriage had become a chain . . . we ought to break it" (507).

Bartley's friend agrees that when marriages are "hells" where slavery replaces self-respect, they should "be broken up!" (325). One woman cries, "To suppose that such a notice as this is sufficient! Women couldn't have made such a law" (462). Her listener notes the unfairness that the laws differ between states. A friend tells Marcia that the issue is social, not personal, for one divorce leads to another, spelling the end of civilization. Since no one believes Bartley and Marcia's marriage improves them or civilization, Howells rejects another argument against divorce.

Blaming law and custom for the wasted lives that result from failed marriages, Grand's novels reveal the evolution of feminist thought by 1900. *The Heavenly Twins* shows how women's upbringing and treatment cause unhappy marriages. Since Colquhoun has the requisite job, background, and money, Evadne's father does not mention he is a reprobate. Learning the truth minutes before marriage, Evadne rejects the role of woman as savior, saying such forgiveness condones misbehavior and women should not be sacrificed to men. She accuses her parents of a double standard, arguing they wouldn't allow—let alone force—a son to marry a woman with Colquhoun's reputation. Bound by propriety and fearing scandal, they refuse to stop the wedding. Later she tries to save her friend Edith from the same mistake, but Edith will not listen. So both women face endless misery. Like Howells, Grand observes the importance of the suffrage movement: "There is no law . . . either to protect us or to avenge us. That is because men made the law for themselves, and that is why women are fighting for the right to make laws too" (307). Learning of her husband's illegitimate child, Edith returns home, near mental collapse. Without her family's support, Evadne can be free only upon Colquhoun's death. Remarried, she struggles with morbidity and fears a breakdown; later, in *The Beth Book* (1897), she reveals how a bad marriage blights her entire life.

Destroying the written proof of her husband's evil ways in the spirit of goodwill, the title character of Grand's *Ideala* has no grounds for legal separation or divorce, even when he bars her from the house. This strong feminist novel condemns women's upbringing and current divorce laws. Feeling she has no real life, Ideala poignantly says, "I am one of the weary women of the nineteenth century. No other age could have produced me" (15).

Early in the new century, when literature more openly explores the reasons for and effects of separation and divorce, it still treats the issue gravely. Most characters in Wharton's *The House of Mirth* accept divorce, but not all welcome divorced women into their homes: "Some one said the other day that there was a divorce and a case of appendicitis in every family one knows," but people wonder "what society is coming to" (41). Clara Dawes in Lawrence's *Sons and Lovers* faces unhappiness after returning to her husband; Marion's frigidity in Wells's *Tono-Bungay* leads to a weakening of her relationship with her husband, then to his infidelity, finally to their divorce. Ellen Olenska in Wharton's *The Age of Innocence* marries a foreigner, then compounds her error by leaving him and seeking a divorce— unacceptable behavior in the New York society of the 1870s. Her family and friends insist she would be better off *with* her husband, who is despicable in some vague but terrible way. Treated as an outcast woman of questionable repute, Ellen learns she must "sacrifice" her chance at freedom and a new life "to preserve the dignity of marriage" and "spare" her family "the publicity, the scandal" (140). In Galsworthy's *The Man of Property* and *In Chancery* we sympathize with Irene and wish her well in her marriage to the divorced Jo, yet her divorce from the insensitive traditionalist Soames is fraught with pain and much concern about society's reaction. Couples like the gambler Dartie and his unhappy wife, Winifred, remain married, regardless of the quality of their lives.

Ward contends in *Marriage a la Mode* that separation without scandal can be justified far more easily than divorce. Compared to England, Daphne accurately notes, in America "if the marriage doesn't work out, divorce is the answer" (36). Suggesting girls are so sheltered they often err in choosing a spouse, she wants to "retrieve" her own "mistake" and "free herself" (191). Though admitting children must be "considered," she adds in a modern note, "how can it do children any good to live in an unhappy home?" (36). Initially euphoric that life is no longer "closed, as in a sense it is, for every married woman," in an "intoxication of recovered youth and freedom" she decides "my first duty is to myself" (196). But the novel insists that hers is a fool's happiness and that she should not regard divorce so lightly. The divorce granted in America is not recognized in England, leaving Daphne, Roger, and their child in anomalous positions; Ward observes that America's legal system means people divorced in one state may be "bound" in another. (266) Gradual debasement leads Roger to drop out of "decent society" (259), while Daphne, impassioned by feminism, stops caring for her friends or her responsibilities. Ultimately Roger dies, unhappy and ill, and Daphne isn't much better off.

Accepting divorce, Ward says it must be seen very seriously. She has no sympathy with the "ever-spreading restlessness and levity, a readiness to tamper with the very foundations of society, for a whim, a nothing!" (267) People should not believe marriage can end without penalty, for "there are divine avenging forces in the law they tamper with" (267), and marriage is "the supreme test of men and women. If we wrong it, and despise it, we mutilate the divine in us" (290).

New Laws, New Attitudes

Edward Bellamy's *Looking Backwards* (1888) carries the subtitle, *2000–1887*. Today, looking back over even more years, we see how much society has changed. From 1800 to 1900 and beyond, as Ward says, marriage has something "divine" about it. A citizen of the nineteenth century who "tampered" with that "holy estate"—by any attempt to redefine men's and women's roles—risked a great deal. Yet the act of tampering, performed by brave and sometimes desperate people, freed women from the bondage of unjust laws and stultifying lives. It also freed men from assuming total financial responsibility for a family and being forced into certain molds of behavior.

The laws and attitudes of today developed during the nineteenth century, in part as a result of the women's movement. However different from the utopia feminists dreamed about, society has been transformed. Freeing women to be themselves, feminists opened new options for relationships within marriage and outside traditional boundaries. Those options go beyond relationships as well, for the women's movement argued that important as love and marriage may be, women can have more options in their lives. The right to vote or to work, new educational opportunities and jobs—these also come from the reformers of the nineteenth century.

The Brontë Sisters

Courtesy of the National Portrait Gallery, London

Education: "The Bars Go Down"

The heroines of romance and drama to-day are of a different sort from the Evelinas and Arabellas of the last century. . . . Women are growing honester, braver, stronger, more healthful and skilful and able and free, more human in all ways.

The change in education is in large part a cause of this, and progressively a consequence. Day by day the bars go down.

—Charlotte Perkins Gilman,
Women and Economics (148–49)

In Eliot's *The Mill on the Floss*, Maggie's father worries that she is "too 'cute [acute] for a woman . . . an over-'cute woman's no better nor a long-tailed sheep—she'll fetch none the bigger price for that" (10). Many voices in literature and society argued that a woman who sought an education was an aberration—a "blue stocking," "Girton Guy," or "long-tailed sheep." But reflecting and causing changes in social conditions and attitudes, reformers labored to take down the barriers to full educational opportunities for women, essentially to allow them to catch up with men. Educational reform forced people to examine deeply held beliefs about women's nature and roles, touching on cherished values and raw nerves. As a result, education became a major battleground for the women's movement.

Literature sometimes presents realistic educational options for boys and girls, men and women, but more often reflects an ideal. Not questioning the value of education for middle- and upper-class men, characters fear that educating laborers might be good for the individual but bad for society—or even bad for the individual, leading him away from accepting what his "betters" taught. Most literature sees education as irrelevant for working-class women; for middle- and upper-class women, some degree of polish and accomplishment might be valuable but real education seems useless or dangerous. Feminist attitudes toward education rarely appear, though authors sometimes prod gently. As the "bars" went down in society, both feminists and traditional writers explored the controversy over whether women could or should be educated, and if so, how.

"A University may be considered with reference either to its Students or to its Studies," wrote the eminent Victorian John Henry Newman.[1] When considering how women's education changed, both matter, as do the actual schools. Technological, utilitarian, and "modern," Victorians delighted in statistics: the numbers and types of schools and students, years of schooling, even literacy figures, newspaper circulation, and library borrowings attest to the great impetus for educational reform and the real gains in mass education.[2] Such facts also help explain why women sought educational reform.

While some modern historians claim that contemporary writers exaggerated in their routine laments about education, they did not need to exaggerate much. Primary education might mean haphazard instruction at home or in a private school run by an elderly woman who felt no need to provide space, heat, or instruction. Relying on beatings and rote learning, government and better private schools were noisy, overcrowded, and under-ventilated. Several hundred students often had one barely qualified teacher who was helped by assistants, slightly advanced students who passed on the rudiments of information (or misinformation) learned from past assistants. Religious groups feared government intervention; parents impeded progress when they worried more about a school's social reputation than its academic quality, or when they withdrew children to work on the farm, in factories, or in the family business. From the poorest dame school for workers to the finest preparatory school or university for the upper class, boys' educational opportunities outstripped girls'.

During this century of change, there was an explosion in the number of students attending at least some kind of school.[3] Educational reform intertwined with other major social issues and directly affected women's changing roles, arousing joy in some people and fear in others. Elementary school enrollment tripled in England between 1830 and 1880, then nearly doubled again in the next 30 years; by late century, education until age 12 was both compulsory and free. In both nations, higher education grew more slowly, primarily through private efforts. A few new secondary schools and universities accepted women. Hundreds of new centers for training teachers underscored the improved status of education.

Change also occurred in the nature and structure of education, thanks to the expansion of the middle class, a growing awareness of the working class, the Industrial Revolution, foreign competition, new professions and a new professionalism, and an atmosphere of social and intellectual reform. Two principal theories about education identified different problems and offered different solutions. One was evangelical in origin and humanistic in philosophy, emphasizing the personal value of a liberal education; the other, utilitarian in origin and resultingly pragmatic in philosophy, focused on political, social, and economic goals.

Some questioned government's role in private schools, even in regulating safety standards. But in America, states and localities became involved, and by late century the federal government took stands on child labor, education, and racial segregation in schools. In England, two decades before Victoria's rule, Lord Brougham introduced into the House of Lords a bill acknowledging education to be government's responsibility and an object worthy of tax revenue. New laws limited the hours children could work and required periods of education during work breaks, established school inspection, and took some of the responsibility for children's well-being out of parents' hands. One innovation with doubtful benefits involved paying for "results," measured by attendance and performance in such areas as reading, dictation, and sums. Although this encouraged falsified attendance records and rote learning, government intervention also helped introduce subjects like science, provide merit grants for good teaching or a clean and orderly building, and establish the value of a library or visual aids.

The major barrier to progress for women came from the fear that for them, as for workers, education might be detrimental. Learning might distract laborers from their duty or lead them to rebel; women were physically, mentally, and perhaps morally unfit for serious intellectual effort; and both groups might be led astray by their reading, if they understood it. The workers' case was more easily argued: education made economic sense and might guide them to a virtuous life free of alcohol, atheism, and criminal behavior. Attitudes toward women's education changed more slowly. The cult of femininity and the idea of women's proper sphere raised difficulties:

education contradicted the notion that women were inferior, gentle, emotional, and not very bright. Reformers had to explain how education enhanced women's performance of their "proper" roles—or be prepared to defend altering those roles.

Literature reflects all the concerns about education: should it be practical or liberal? how does it affect social status and job preparation? who should pay for it? what should be taught? who should teach? Each of these questions affected women, as did even more basic questions: are women educable? and is it right to educate them?

Educational Theories

In spite of its title, Alcott's *Jo's Boys* depicts a college that offers women as well as men a practical and liberal education. Coeducation was as unusual in Alcott's day as the attempt to combine utilitarian and evangelical values. Personal effort makes Jo's vision real, a truth seen in virtually all the educational advances.

In reality, idealistic and practical interests motivated the government and middle class. Education offered social and professional advancement as well as leisure occupation. Traveling lecturers, cultural societies, and groups such as the British Mechanics' Institutes offered informal education in the arts, travel, science, and technology, as well as classes in mathematics, mechanical drawing, language, writing, grammar, and elocution. The popular self-help schemes, mutual improvement societies, and reading—especially books like *Self-Help* by Samuel Smiles (1859)—suited contemporary values and the American ideal of the self-made individual.

Dickens's *Great Expectations* demonstrates how women like Estella can rise through education. A more common formula is for education to help make a man a gentleman; his wife then becomes a lady through him. "I was but a poor uneducated artisan, and he [the Vicar] was a gentleman and a scholar," says the title character of Linton's *Joshua Davidson* (46). The effect of education on status appears in Joshua's concern that he is "not refined in the same way perhaps as a gentleman, so far as manner and little observances went; a man speaking with a provincial accent, and dressed in fustian and coarse clothes" (181). Such refinements can be learned. To rise above the working class, the hero of Craik's *John Halifax, Gentleman* educates himself: illiterate at age 14, by 18 he learns Latin, the mark of an educated man. In America, the self-made man might become a gentleman:

Holgrave, with only "a few winter months' attendance at a district school," has, by 22, successfully worked as journalist, writer, salesman, mesmerist, and photographer (Hawthorne, *The House of Seven Gables*, [1851], 152). Women can learn the accomplishments and graces needed for gentility, as the title character in Oliphant's *Agnes* does, thanks to her father's wealth. Wharton's heroines display the educated lady's behavior and accomplishments: May Archer in *The House of Mirth* reflects her husband's ideas about literature, having none of her own, but she can negotiate her way in New York society, give a party, and gracefully win an archery tournament.

Sometimes literature reflects middle-class resentment of the worker's rising through education to challenge the status quo. A self-educated character in Reynolds's *The Soldier's Wife* explains that "people in high life don't like humble persons, such as I am, to have much learning: they think it opens our eyes to the injustice of the system which keeps the millions poor that the few may be rich": having actually said so, he is guilty of "disseminating seditious ideas amongst the villagers" (6). Yet, as Linton reminds the middle class, its members likewise rise through effort—including education—and often against the desires of their social superiors, defying "a caste-Providence": "the same spirit of determination" helped force a "reception on anything like terms of equality" from nobles, "men who had at heart the great truth of human equality and human rights" (*Joshua*, 146).

Besides recognizing the value of education—at least some education, for at least some people—reformers in society and literature considered the nature and quality of the system. Thomas Huxley, grateful that by the 1860s almost no one "dares to say that education is a bad thing," still observed "a buzz of more or less confused and contradictory talk about education."[4] Utilitarians believed educating the masses was both politically and socially necessary in order to prevent unrest and enhance the nation's competitive position; a practical education trained aspiring middle-class businessmen, engineers, and doctors. Evangelicals contended that education was ethically and socially necessary: by enhancing personal moral and spiritual growth, it enhanced society; liberal education helped the middle class emulate those above them.

Huxley among others insisted that "the masses should be educated because they are men and women with unlimited capacities of being, doing, and suffering," and that "people perish for lack of knowledge." Newman, discussing primarily the middle and upper classes, believed that a liberal education helps form a lifelong "habit of mind" with "attributes" of "freedom, equitableness, calmness, moderation, and wisdom . . . a philosophi-

cal habit." To him, knowledge was "not merely a means to something beyond it . . . but an end sufficient to rest in and pursue for its own sake," a
"philosophical" not "mechanical" end ("Knowledge Its Own End," parts
1 and 2). Defying the prevailing utilitarianism, these reformers include
women in their concerns, acknowledging that a lack of education limits all
human life.

Utilitarians valued "useful" knowledge and feared lagging behind in technological development and industrial achievements. John Stuart Mill
claimed a utilitarian education gave him excellent analytic powers at the
expense of the powers to feel or imagine.[5] But reformers like Herbert
Spencer argued for a scientific education, not an "ornamental" one of reading and the arts.[6] Such an argument underscored contrasting attitudes about
the purpose and propriety of educating men and women.

As schools were established for different reasons, by religious groups,
individuals with a personal theory, or groups of parents banding together,
virtually all reformers, in literature and society, said that gender and rank
determine the right education. Eliot's title character in *Adam Bede* attends
a night school for workers; Linton's Joshua Davidson attends a day school
for the lower-middle class; Kingsley's characters in *The Hillyars and the
Burtons* train as apprentices. From different classes, Lucius and Perry in
Trollope's *Orley Farm* attend different private boarding schools. In Howells's *The Landlord at Lion's Head*, farm boy Jeff Durgin's attending Harvard seems shocking and ludicrous, and he fails to fit in educationally or
socially.

The middle class could choose between private and public schools for
boys, boarding schools or the right governess for girls. Captain Warkworth
in Ward's *Lady Rose's Daughter* believes his Charterhouse education raises
him above his parents; Jacob Delafield, in the same novel, feels that Eton
and Oxford helped him become a barrister and a gentleman. Trollope
mocks the established pattern in *Dr. Thorne*, suggesting that mere attendance at Eton and Cambridge no longer guarantees becoming a gentleman,
though it certainly helps.

Ultimately, new job opportunities and demands led many middle-class
characters to acknowledge (and bemoan) the inadequacy of a traditional
genteel education. Harold Romer of Broughton's *Miss Litton's Lovers*
(1880) realizes his "gentleman's education" from Harrow and Cambridge
will not help him find work. In *North and South*, Gaskell asks, "What in
the world do manufacturers want with the classics, or literature, or the
accomplishments of a gentleman?" One manufacturer, "a pretty fair classic"
scholar, elaborates, "what preparation" did Latin and Greek offer "for such

a life as I had to lead? None at all. Utterly none at all." Although his questioner pursues the humanistic belief in liberal education—"Did not the recollection of the heroic simplicity of the Homeric life nerve you up?"— the utilitarian answers, "Not one bit! . . . I was too busy to think about any dead people, with the living pressing alongside of me, neck to neck, in the struggle for bread" (82). The hero of Disraeli's *Coningsby* (1844) learns the lesson of the age: while a classical education was "very admirable" and something "all gentlemen should enjoy," he really needs "two educations," "one which his position required, and another which was demanded by the world" (167).

For women, just dreaming of school and university education, the issue arises differently. And since education affects women's roles as wives and mothers, defining appropriate learning is especially hard. Knowing Latin and a little Italian makes Phillis superior and an inappropriate wife to the engineer Paul in Gaskell's *Cousin Phillis*. For the sake of her son, Gaskell's title character in *Ruth* educates herself above her status as a dressmaker, even learning Latin so that she can foster his advance. At a higher social level, the neglect of Grace Rosenberry's education means that she can only become a lady's companion, not a governess (Collins, *Magdalen*); so, too, Alcott's heroine in *Work* is limited by her lack of education. Responding to such problems, Mrs. Lassingham in Gissing's significantly titled novel *The Emancipated* wants to guarantee her niece Cecily an education that will prevent her from "stumbling": her education should do more than shelter her or prepare her for marriage; it should ensure that "she respects herself" and is fit for any society and any kind of life (129–30). This idealistic vision, like Alcott's in *Jo's Boys*, moves far beyond simply reevaluating men's traditional classical education or introducing the first reasonable opportunities for women. Reformers, authors, and thus characters began to see the limitations of a traditional genteel education and the need to create something new, for men and for women.

Teacher Training

To the extent that the quality of education depends on the quality of the teacher, education could only improve. Initially, "pupil-teachers" provided an apprenticeship that permitted more than 100 students in primary classes. Later, teachers trained in "normal" schools and universities gradually replaced or at least supplemented "dame-schools" and semieducated "monitors." James Kay-Shuttleworth, who promoted school inspections, sought better teacher training: he received little support for avoiding what he called "mechanical drudgery," but encouraged recruiting and helped found a teachers' college (22–29). Large increases in pupil-teachers and certified teachers led to some lowered standards, yet by 1900 teachers needed more than a minimal primary education. The gradual abandonment of one-room schools made the system of using assistants fade in importance. By the last decades of the century, teachers had professional organizations and colleges had departments of education. Such changes helped enhance curriculum and the quality and status of teachers. This had a special impact on women, as teaching, always an option for unmarried women, became a profession.

The training of teachers, governesses, and tutors appears when literature focuses on a future teacher, tracing his or her education and experience, or when a book discusses the effects of a teacher—usually an inadequate one—on the hero or heroine. The lives and jobs of teachers form an important part of the changing role of women on both sides of the desk.

Typically and realistically, fiction's teachers are poorly trained, especially in the proliferating private schools. Two years as an articled pupil followed by some time as a junior teacher forms the unusually long training of the governess Edith Scott Proctor in Guyton's *Married Life*. Although Sophia Barnes of Bennett's *The Old Wives' Tale* never teaches, she studies as a pupil-teacher from age 15 to age 17. Sue Bridehead in Hardy's *Jude the Obscure* attends a boarding school for teachers, a sort of "normal school," and Frances Henri in Brontë's *The Professor* pays to learn grammar, history, geography, arithmetic, and French by serving as needlewoman and pupil-teacher in a Belgian school.

The quality of teachers varies tremendously by time and location, especially in private schools. England's "public" schools and America's upper-class private schools sought teachers (usually men) of good social and educational background; the new private schools fussed far less about training and background. A character in Carey's *Lover or Friend?* wonders if any good private school dared hire a man of so questionable a background that he applied under an assumed name. But the local grammar schools, where girls might receive some education, simply took what they could get: a man with an Oxford degree (Carey, *Men*), a woman with a high school diploma (Lawrence, *Rainbow*). In Eliot's *The Mill on the Floss*, when Tom's father seeks advice about teachers, Mr. Riley parrots the traditional view that "all the best schoolmasters are of the clergy. The schoolmasters who are not clergymen, are a very low set of men generally . . . men who have failed in other trades, most likely. Now a clergyman is a gentleman by profession and education, and besides that, he has the knowledge that will ground the boy, and prepare him for entering on any career with credit" (21). Though usually motivated by money, at least clergymen had completed a university education, which was more than could be said for most teachers, including all women.

In economic straits, Gaskell's Miss Matty considers teaching. But she barely plays the piano, cannot draw, and lacks knowledge of "the branches of a solid English education—fancy work and the use of globes—such as the Mistress of the Ladies' Seminary, to which all the tradespeople in Cranford sent their daughters, professed to teach" (*Cranford* [1853], 199–200). These very minimal criteria are impossibly difficult for Miss Matty. At least she knows her limits, unlike many gentlewomen seeking work as teachers.

A distressingly typical man heads a miserable school in Farrar's *Eric*: "a scholar and a gentleman, early misfortunes and an imprudent marriage had driven him to the mastership of the little country grammar school; and here the perpetual annoyance caused to his refined mind by the coarseness of clumsy or spiteful boys, had gradually unhinged his intellect." He believes "it was an easier life by far to break stones by the roadside than to teach" (8). Even people with far better intentions than this sadistic schoolmaster lacked real qualifications, especially since teaching often attracted those desperate for work. A refreshing exception, Mr. March in Alcott's *Jo's Boys* loves to teach and inculcates a love of learning in his students—male and female.

The differences between boys' and girls' education meant that governesses needed far less preparation than tutors. When Brontë's title character in *Agnes Grey* needs work, her mother stresses her unusual talents: "music, singing, drawing, French, Latin, and German . . . no mean assemblage" (54). Agnes is qualified to teach her male pupil Latin and prepare him for boarding school while she contributes to the superficial education and polish required for her female pupils. More typical is Miss Osborne, weak in French, music, and drawing, and less knowledgeable in German, but still an adequate governess for the daughter of the house (Carey, *Men*). Lucy Snowe, in Brontë's *Villette*, serves as a cross between lady's maid and governess for the headmistress's children in a French school simply because she speaks English. To tutor boys requires greater qualifications but holds little more appeal: Hugh Sutherland is a university graduate who finds "the state of his funds rendered immediate employment absolutely necessary"; knowing the "one way in which he could earn money without yet further preparation"; is through tutoring, he plans "to look about" while in the job, for he hopes not to follow those who "once going in this groove, can never get out of it again" (MacDonald, *David*, 210).

Aiming directly at utilitarianism in *Hard Times*, Dickens makes his satire obvious even in the schoolmaster's name:

Mr. McChoakumchild . . . and some one hundred and forty other schoolmasters had been lately turned at the same time, in the same factory, on the same principles, like so many pianoforte legs. He had been put through an immense variety of paces, and had answered volumes of head-breaking questions. Orthography, etymology, syntax, and prosody, biography, astronomy, geography, and general cosmography, the sciences of compound proportion, algebra, land-surveying and levelling, vocal music, and drawing from models, were all at the ends of his ten chilled fingers. He had worked his stony way into Her Majesty's most Honourable Privy Council's Schedule B [the 1846 syllabus for teacher training], and had taken the bloom off the higher branches of mathematics and physical science, French, German, Latin and Greek. He knew all about all the water-sheds of all the world (whatever they are), and all the histories of all the peoples, and all the names of all the rivers and mountains, and all the productions, manners, and customs of all the countries, and all their boundaries and bearings on the two-and-thirty points of the compass. Ah, rather overdone, McChoakumchild. If he had only learnt a little less, how infinitely better he might have taught much more! (9)

Thus Dickens demonstrates the link between teacher training and educational philosophies, and suggests the importance of educational reform to men and women, in literature as in life.

Preschools: Out of the Mother's Hands?

Although most middle- and upper-middle-class children received their earliest education at home from their mothers, some joined the children of workers, artisans, and the lower-middle class at infant schools or preschools, private institutions. The best of these, designed like good modern day-care centers, still faced the same objection of separating children from their mothers at a formative age. Yet as one writer argues, not all mothers make good teachers and most are overburdened; besides, children benefit from a school's stimulation and discipline.[7] In a still familiar plea, this reformer notes parents' responsibility includes giving attention to the schools and supporting teachers through adequate pay and assistance. A contemporary shows the balance of physical and mental activities, stimulation and rest, discipline and learning in the program of a well-run school: during the eight hours from opening hymns to closing prayer, students read or are read to (often from Scripture); study numbers, geography, writing, objects and forms, morality, and religion; and get four or five periods of exercise.[8] A school like this was exceptional. Most remained more like the dame schools: a little singing, maybe a little reading or sewing, and in general very little care from an untrained woman teaching out of financial desperation.

Focusing on and idealizing the middle class, literature tends to ignore even the finest infant schools. Until about age five, boys and girls receive nearly identical care, often sharing a nanny or a governess who functions more as a nurse than a teacher. They may learn some rudimentary lessons in the schoolroom, but formal education comes later and differs greatly in demands and opportunities for girls and boys.

The Differences Between Boys and Girls

Literature realistically differentiates between boys' and girls' schooling, saying a well-educated boy attends a university after fine preparation, while a well-educated girl attains the polish of genteel accomplishments. After sharing a governess, boys go away to school or graduate to tutors, while their sisters stay with the same nursery governess, study casually with their parents, or spend a year or two at a finishing school. In Thackeray's *Pendennis* the boys study classics and mathematics at the university; the girls learn music, a few French and English poems, drawing, and scraps of German from a governess. The Grantley boys in Trollope's *The Warden* attend boarding school while the girls have a governess. In Sinclair's *Holiday House*, Laura Graham, an unusually well educated upper-middle-class girl, studies French, Italian, geography, and history as well as arithmetic, reading, writing, and spelling; her brothers add Greek, Latin, and higher mathematics.

English and sometimes American boys may round off their education with a Grand tour, ranging from a season in Paris to a jaunt through Italy and Switzerland to a year or more in countries as exotic as Egypt, Israel, and Turkey. Girls travel so rarely that those who do seem unusually wealthy, like Milly Theale in James's *The Wings of the Dove*, or exceptionally modern, like Ward's heroine in *Diana Mallory*. Limited family money always goes to boys. Mary Hargood gets what education she can by listening to her father read out loud while she works, and she works "to provide . . . her young brothers a solid classical education" (Gore, *Progress*, 139–40). This attitude is typical, and it angered reformers in literature as in society. As

93

Grand says, "it is customary to sacrifice the girls of a family to the boys; to give them no educational advantages, and then to jeer at them for their ignorance and silliness" (*Beth*, 114). Understanding the catch-up game for girls requires a brief look at boys' education.

Lower-middle-class boys—sometimes with their sisters—usually had one teacher with many assistants, a cheap system perhaps fitting the practical model of mass production, but producing poorly educated children with no love of learning. Though occasionally educated at home, sons of military, clergy, business, and professional men generally attended either superior day schools or boarding schools. Utilitarian or classical, the curriculum might stop at basic skills like reading, writing, and arithmetic, or add practical business skills such as bookkeeping, some advanced arithmetic, and a smattering of French or German. Schools designed to appeal to parents' upward mobility featured the accomplishments of upper-class education.

At least early in the century, lower-middle-class boys left school by 13 or 14, to serve apprenticeships or go to work. Beyond a social assertion, education was a practical necessity for middle-class boys, especially as more professions became available (engineering, architecture, civil service), more jobs became professions requiring advanced education (medicine, law), and more entrance exams developed (civil service, universities, and military academies). New schools, unlike the traditional ones, tried to prepare students for careers in commerce or industry, or for the professional exams. The prestigious private schools did not welcome middle-class boys, and of course accepted no girls. The situation in England was especially striking, for the seven boarding schools (Charterhouse, Eton, Harrow, Rugby, Shrewsbury, Westminster, and Winchester) and two day schools (Merchant Taylors' and St. Paul's), founded centuries earlier, drew their students from the aristocracy and gentry and had close links to the two great universities. Their education was traditional, their ambience unique. Not until late in the century did their graduates enter medicine or business rather than exclusively joining the government or the military or returning to their landed estates. Such schools had become an *idea* by the nineteenth century: a society of boys trained to be leaders and gentlemen through a rote classical education, Christian guidance, self-governance, and games. The exclusion of girls reinforced the idea that women stood outside the real world of potential leadership and social action.

So long as universities maintained the classical tradition and so long as upwardly mobile middle-class boys aspired to college, schools that prepared future university students remained unchanged. But, science and modern languages gradually appeared in the curricula, and, as more middle-class children aimed for college, schools had to include the kinds of literary culture that every university-bound child would once have imbibed at home. By 1900, as university departments began training secondary-school teachers, the modern secondary system had begun.

Typically idealizing the situation, representative fiction has one and a half times as many British youth attending ancient public schools as new private schools; depending on the time period, as many as one in three go on to Cambridge or Oxford, no more than one in 30 to the new universities. Exceptions exist, especially in America: Christopher Newman, the archetypal self-made man in James's *The American*, leaves school by 14, and by 36 earns enough through business to travel to Europe seeking culture and a wife. But even in America, such stories are rare: most literature implies a norm that truly was not a norm.

A few authors toy with unusual educational plans. Sir Austin Feverel, believing "schools were corrupt," devises a doomed "system" that tries to protect his son from pernicious influences such as women (Meredith, *Feverel*, 16). Characters engage in experimental study for specific goals, such as the title character of Eliot's *Daniel Deronda*, who adds Hebrew, Jewish history, and law to his traditional Eton and Cambridge education. Fitting popular utilitarianism, in Grand's *Babs the Impossible* Montacute's tutor provides practical training to run an estate along with an appropriately highbrow classical education. Still, most fictional boys follow the path of tutor, private school, and university, underscoring the contrast with their sisters' impoverished educations.

Fictional schools, like real ones, vary greatly. Huck Finn's adoption by the Widow Douglas means new clothes, no smoking, and a chance to attend a very basic school. In Dickens's *Great Expectations*, Pip's adoption by the mysterious individual who wants to make him a gentleman saves him from apprenticeship and a bad evening school. Walter Gay in Dickens's *Dombey and Son* leaves a weekly boarding school when apprenticed at 14, while the wealthier Paul Dombey attends an absurdly pretentious boarding school that feeds six-year-olds Greek, Latin, ancient and modern history, orthography, and weights and measures—a diet that may help explain Paul's early death. David Copperfield experiences the worst and best of private schools, tormented rather than educated at Mr. Creakle's, then sent to Dr. Strong's school, a "gravely and decorously ordered" institution that appeals "to the honour and good faith of the boys," giving them "a part in the management of the place, and in sustaining its character and dignity" (227–128).

In a satire about the way real schools defined themselves according to their potential clientele, Dickens describes Dotheboys' Hall in *Nicholas Nickleby* (1839) as a brutal school that exists to earn money for Squeers, who blatantly lies about everything, including teacher qualifications, curriculum, and buildings. Appealing to every educational faction, Squeers advertises that Nicholas, his unknown apprentice, is "a gentleman's son, and a good scholar, mathematical, classical, and commercial" (111). Similarly, Farrar's *Eric: or, Little by Little: a Tale of Roslyn School* displays a school where students cheat, lazy teachers cane pupils, and everyone indulges in bullying, hazing, and alcohol. This popular sentimental and propagandistic novel contrasts the playing field's ideal of morality and courage and the reality of cheats and bullies. Closer to the ideal is Rugby under Dr. Arnold, presented in Hughes's "true picture" of "everyday school life," *Tom Brown's Schooldays—By an Old Boy* (269). Dr. Arnold, wisely appreciating tradition without fearing change, guides Rugby from "monstrous licence and misrule" to order established "with a strong hand" (114). Since "by far the most important part" of education occurs "out of school hours" (56), much education occurs in formal games, informal competitions, and opportunities for older boys to serve as dorm masters. Though bullying and cheating remain, learning to be a good sport matters as much as learning to be good at sports. Tom wants to survive academically, equal "any fellow, lout or gentleman" in sports, "please the Doctor," and leave a good reputation. Asked why he attends Rugby, Tom echoes literature's norm: "I don't know exactly. . . . I suppose because all boys are sent to a public school in England" (278–79).

Still, literature sometimes sees the limits of a classical education. In Dickens's *Bleak House*, such an education and the law case of Jarndyce versus Jarndyce share blame for Richard's unsettled attitude. Maugham, in *Of Human Bondage*, reflects real fears about a new headmaster's proposals for modernization (56–71). Students and teachers "hoped fervently" that the school "would remain true to its old traditions," teaching "the dead languages," revering the classics as more "noble" than mathematics, avoiding modern languages and science. The headmaster, a brilliant former student but a linen draper's son who attended school on scholarship, introduces new instructors (none ordained), new courses, and an influx of city boys. Common sense and current events replace cramming, to Maugham's obvious approval.

Given the real difficulty of admission at prestigious private schools and the increasing discontent with traditional education, the fact that so few characters attend other kinds of schools confirms literature's conservatism. Acknowledging the unlikelihood of attending a traditional private school, in *Tono-Bungay* Wells considers the schools designed by and for the middle class. A dingy school has students who enjoy "spiritual neglect," fight, smoke, imbibe alcohol and "the uncensored reading matter" of the local store, play cricket "without style" on a "bald" field, and are led by a "lout of nineteen, who wore ready-made clothes and taught despicably," although the headmaster offers some mathematics (34–35). Not especially good, not especially bad, this was truly the kind of school most *real* middle-class boys could expect to attend either for their final education or as a step toward the university, while their sisters watched and protested outside the door.

After preparatory education, real upper-class youth initially chose from among Oxford and Cambridge in England, or from Princeton, Yale, and Harvard in America—all teaching the liberal arts and offering an academic challenge to the serious student, a continuation of prep-school life to the playboy. Gambling, drinking, and high bills were common even at Oxford and Cambridge, where most students entered the clergy. But admission required appropriate preparation and often a personal connection, mostly excluding the middle class, and the elite schools conferred social status and a passport to advancement.

Responding more quickly to change, the less expensive alternatives designed for youth whose educational, social, or religious background barred them from the great universities provided choices among secular, scientific, and professional subjects. They taught economics, engineering, law, botany, Sanskrit, Hebrew, and the social sciences; students especially sought laboratory sciences and medical programs. Sometimes supported by local industries or governments, universities might emphasize areas such as mining, textiles, or agriculture. West Point and Sandhurst added algebra, astronomy, navigation, and surveying to their curriculum, though they did not abandon French or fencing, drawing or dancing. The traditional universities gradually changed, so that by late century Oxford and Cambridge abolished religious tests, and in both nations, schools added science and preprofessional training. Most startling of all, women began to study at colleges near men's schools or to attend coeducational classes.

But, unlike their real counterparts, most male characters follow the upper-class route from tutor or prep school to Oxford or Cambridge if English, Harvard or Yale ("Cambridge" and "New Haven") if American. Roger Barnes attends Eton and Oxford (Ward, *Marriage a la Mode*), as do Mark and Hugh Davenport (Gore, *Progress and Prejudice*). Usually, if one character in a novel attends a particular school, so do others: in Gore's *Mothers and Daughters*, three of four Etonians go on to Oxford (the fourth drowns while still at Eton), while in Disraeli's *Coningsby*, the title character and at

97

least three other men take a second popular route, from Eton to Cambridge. Although the hero of Thackeray's *Pendennis* attends the generic "Oxbridge," more than one character notes that "it was the Cambridge men who were always good mathematicians" (Eliot, *Mill*, 23). Disraeli's emphasis on the links between attending Oxford or Cambridge and obtaining political power informs novels such as *Tancred* (1847) and *Vivian Grey* (1826), again indicating how educational barriers created other barriers for women.

Other options suit specific careers: Sandhurst makes professional sense in Lever's *Our Mess: Jack Hinton, the Guardsman*, as does medical training for doctors John Bold (Trollope, *Warden*) and Philip Carey (Maugham, *Bondage*). Social and financial concerns send Will Ladislaw abroad after Rugby (Eliot, *Middlemarch*) and force Alaric Tudor to work his way through a German university (Trollope, *Clerks*). George Ponderevo, in Wells's *Tono-Bungay*, follows a surprisingly real path from a bachelor of science at London University to a scholarship for advanced scientific work at another London school. If the rigors of education on either side of the Atlantic seemed unappealing, students could enjoy conversation and the pursuit of genteel academic failure, or follow Jeff's example, rarely attending class at Harvard and getting into mischief (Howells, *Landlord*). The danger of being "sent down" for misbehavior lurks over many students (worrying their homebound sisters), and others leave school when family circumstances change—two devices that serve plot well.

While students usually ignore practical considerations, Trollope, probably for personal reasons, condemns the new professionalism that altered real education. "Competitive examinations" might "give an interesting stimulus to young men at college," but they are "a fearful thing for a married man with a family" who assumed promotion comes from hard work and seniority. The rising "standard of education" means "the prodigy of 1857, who is now destroying all the hopes of the man who was well enough in 1855, will be a dunce to the tyro of 1860." Workers wonder what will be required tomorrow. "It may one day be conic sections, another Greek iambics, and a third German philosophy" (*Clerks*, 62). If men felt insecure as changing job definitions altered education and the workplace, women longed to have the opportunity to learn conic sections or Greek iambics. But education for women always came second to men's in value and thus in pace.

Grand's *The Beth Book* presents the feminist anger that helped cause reform in its depiction of educational differences in the Caldwell family (114–21). The girls briefly attend day school; then, while their brothers study at a national school, they pick up scraps of education from the school-master after hours. When Captain Caldwell dies, his widow decides she must "give her boys a good start in life," though that would leave no money for the girls. Choosing to educate the girls herself, she provides a Bible, an arithmetic text, a French grammar, and "Pinnock (an old-fashioned com-pilation of questions and answers)." After "two or three dreadful hours" each morning, mother and daughters remain "free for the rest of the day" and the daughters remain essentially uneducated. Even inheriting money from a maiden aunt doesn't get Beth an education. Mrs. Caldwell convinces her it "would really be a fine, unselfish thing" to give her brother the funds, and Beth wears hand-me-downs so Jim can afford "to swing a cane, smoke, drink beer, play billiards, and do all else that makes boys men in their own estimation at an early age" (224). This is an accurate portrayal of pervasive favoritism.

Reflecting real values, literature suggests that, finances aside, educating women is inappropriate, unnecessary, and potentially damaging. In Yonge's *The Daisy Chain*, Ethel struggles to keep up with her brother Norman's education, but household tasks make this increasingly difficult (181–83). Her sister's suggesting she quit horrifies Ethel, for she and Norman "have hardly missed doing the same every day since the first Latin grammar was put into his hands." Margaret observes that since "Men have more power than women," Norman must be able to "do more than a girl at home." Yet Ethel rightly counters that "he has so much more time," devoting all day to learning while she must cram her studies into rare free moments. Margaret's response stresses not injustice but reality: to match his achievement and go to the university, Ethel would have to give her "whole time and thoughts to it," and "what would it come to?" A degree? A job? Ethel explains she only wants education, but Margaret insists that being "a useful, steady daughter and sister at home" is more important. Dissatisfied, frustrated, and beaten, Ethel concedes, "I suppose it is a wrong sort of ambition to want to learn more, in one's own way, when one is told it is not good for one." To her brother she hints at a feminist position but retreats: "I was just going to say I hated being a woman, and having these tiresome little trifles—my duty—instead of learning, which is yours, Norman." Norman also presses her to conform, since objecting to her role "would have been very silly of you; and I assure you, Ethel, it is really time for you to stop, or you would get into a regular learned lady, and be good for nothing." This is routine for Yonge's novels, which display women's superiority while declaring the divine appro-priateness of their inferior positions.

Equally poignant, in Eliot's *The Mill on the Floss*, Maggie Tulliver has the love and ability to learn, while Tom lacks both. But relative ability and interest don't matter. Maggie's father reflects current attitudes if not language in saying an educated woman is "no better nor a long-tailed sheep" (10). His reasoning is simple, his motivation practical: Tom needs "an eddication as'll be a bread to him" (9); Maggie needs one that will produce a husband.

When Maggie visits Tom at his classical "academy," she again enjoys reading his books. But his continued education lets him outstrip her, and he quickly leaps to the popular explanation: asserting "girls can't do Euclid," he asks his master for confirmation, "Can they, sir?" Mr. Stelling sententiously responds, "They can pick up a little of everything, I daresay. . . . They've a great deal of superficial cleverness; but they couldn't go far into anything. They're quick and shallow" (134).

This devastates Maggie but pleases Tom. His pleasure pales when he realizes a smattering of Latin, Euclid, and Greek and Roman history has no practical use and cannot get him a job to support his mother and sister. But neither he nor any other character realizes that Maggie, a mere girl, might merit an education—practical or classical. Girls, after all, are "shallow" and "superficial"; education cannot help them and it might well harm them. This literary norm against which Eliot, like other writers, gently inveighed, reflects with fair accuracy the attitudes against which *real* women fought.

A Genteel Education for Girls

The same questions haunted women's education as men's: what is the future student's role in life? what should it be? how should education foster that role? Asked about women, these questions offered a painful challenge to fundamental assumptions. Reformers like Sarah Grimké in *Letters on the Equality of the Sexes* argued that women needed education to perform their part of the world's work, but Grimké spoke for the minority in defining that work as existing outside the usual "sphere." In *Women and Economics*, Gilman explained that traditional education reinforces society's ideal of women gaining identity through relationships with men. But by the century's end, as indicated in the quotation heading this chapter, literature reveals a change: the new heroines "look" and "behave" differently, laying aside "the false sentimentality, the false delicacy, the false modesty, the utter falseness of elaborate complement and servile gallantry which went with the other falsehoods." Gilman praised education as both "cause" and "consequence" of this change (148–49).

The process of transforming society and literature took time and great effort from dedicated reformers, mostly women. Gilman joked that people who speak of women and men having different brains or emotional makeup might as well speak of their having different livers (149). But many critics of education for women seemed willing to believe that women's livers differed, too: they felt women were truly inferior, and that their education was therefore necessarily different, if not irrelevant. Opponents of women's education cited moral, physical, and religious arguments attractive to listeners who preferred women to stay in their sphere, limited to "women's work." But industrialization provided pragmatic reasons to educate female laborers, and in time the middle class either accepted the argument that education could enhance women's traditional roles or eased the commitment to a traditional view of women, making progress possible.

At first middle-class girls attended a private day or boarding school (a "ladies' academy") or were educated at home. A family with three or four daughters found one governess cheaper than school fees, and in rural areas or the American frontier, mothers necessarily became teachers. Girls in the lower-middle class, attending a dame school or a government school with laborers' children, learned the rudiments of the "three Rs" plus a little needlework. Their slightly better-off middle-class sisters added singing, cooking, geography, history, and French to that curriculum, and rarely a little mathematics or science. Haphazard curricula depended on teachers' abilities, and school costs were high. In many schools, the Bible served as a text for reading, history, and geography. Newly popular "readers" offered extracts in difficult styles and on subjects with little appeal for children. Education meant memorization and testing, drilling with books or flash cards to review grammar, Biblical geography, or arithmetic tables. For girls as for boys, the goal fit the times: not to encourage intellectual curiosity or imagination, but to give boys useful and improving information and to prepare girls for marriage. Since a woman's education was not supposed to make her self-supporting, just enhance her value on the marriage market, many parents were reluctant to spend money educating their daughters.

Different reasons for educating girls and boys implied different education. Girls' schooling was designed to relieve their boredom and enhance their ornamental qualities; even on the frontier they learned the "feminine" accomplishments of singing and drawing, playing an instrument or sketching, doing needlework or reading aloud. Boys read books for their utilitarian value, with a goal of factual knowledge, or they studied the classical curriculum, with a goal of attending a fine university. Girls read to achieve a vague touch of literary culture, some acquaintance with great and popular authors. A lecturer for "a School of Female Tuition," explaining that "a certain degree of knowledge is both ornamental and useful" but need not and should not be the same as that gleaned by men, taught morality, domestic duties, dress, and "the influence of the Female Sex in Society, as Daughters, Wives, or Mothers."[9]

Until midcentury, representative fiction depicts about the same number of girls being educated in schools as by governesses at home; of those who attend school, nearly three-fourths go to boarding schools. By 1900, the situation changes: 10 times as many girls attend school—private or public, day or boarding—compared to those studying with governesses. Accurately reflecting social change, literature also describes what girls study, attitudes toward educating girls, and girls' schools. Perhaps because women rarely considered attending college, literature less frequently exaggerates their education, presenting a conservative but fairly realistic picture. In fact, following society's lead, authors downplay the education of girls. Unlike a hero, a heroine isn't defined by her school; her education is unimportant.

At home or school, the goal of a girl's education is gentility. In Howells's *The Rise of Silas Lapham*, the nouveau riche parents realize they "didn't go to work just the right way" for their daughters' schooling. After public school, the girls tried being "finished" at a private school but did not fit in: "We ought to have got them into some school where they'd have got acquainted with city girls—girls who could help them along" (23–24). Social position matters even more in England. When Estella is sent abroad "educating for a lady" (Dickens, *Expectations*, 137), the language may not be genteel, but the idea is. And the idea dominates literature, enhancing its conservatism. Yet, direct comments in feminist novels and more delicate exploration in some popular literature offer questions about women's education as they do about women's roles. Feminist literature especially explores the connection between the two topics.

Home Education

With the notable exception of the heroine of Grand's *The Beth Book*, incompetently taught by her uninterested mother, girls educated at home usually have a governess. Ada Clare's governess in Dickens's *Bleak House* offers French, geography, music, singing, and needlework, while Brontë's

Jane Eyre teaches her pupil to play the piano, use globes, read poetry, and write little essays. At the least, governesses teach reading, writing, sums, and needlework; better governesses add such refinements as a foreign language (a little French), some history and geography, dance, and music (usually the piano and often just enough to accompany oneself or another vocalist). Even girls needing to work and thus seeking a practical education often receive only a useless veneer of genteel accomplishments.

Mocking the norm, Eliot describes Mrs. Transome's "superior governess" in *Felix Holt*. This teacher "held that a woman should be able to write a good letter, and to express herself with propriety on general subjects. And it is astonishing how effective this education appeared in a handsome girl, who sat supremely well on horseback, sang and played a little, painted small figures in water-colour, had a naughty sparkle in her eyes when she made a daring quotation, and an air of serious dignity when she recited something from her store of correct opinions." Eliot warns that "such a stock of ideas may be made to tell in elegant society, and during a few seasons in town," but provides no "perennial source of interest" and no "safe theoretic basis in circumstances of temptation and difficulty." Even Mrs. Transome learns that "what she had once regarded as her knowledge and accomplishments had become as valueless as old-fashioned stucco ornaments, of which the substance was never worth anything, while the form is no longer to the taste of any living mortal" (26).

Girls from wealthier families might have special masters for French or German, music or dance, but they learned little of practical use and nothing in depth. Gillian's stopping lessons at 14 to care for her widowed uncle and his children characterizes women's position; but, given what was available in education, she doesn't miss much (Broughton, *Thoughts*). By 16 or so, a girl would be out of the schoolroom, her governess dismissed, her education finished.

Educational distinctions may result from studying with a governess or at school, or from the teacher's background and educational theories. In *Bleak House* Dickens observes how differently Ada Clare and Esther Summerson are educated: Ada has a genteel governess while Esther studies at a local day school to become a governess. Gaskell's heroine in *Sylvia's Lovers* can barely read, write, or add, but her expectations—marriage in a lower-middle-class home—make refined accomplishments superfluous. Agnes, in Dickens's *David Copperfield*, is educated at home while dainty, accomplished, delicate Dora studies in Paris; the practical Agnes not only cares for her father but also teaches little girls.

Schools for Girls

Reflecting reality, literature normally says that while governesses and schools could be good or bad, utilitarian or genteel, women's education always merits a distant second place. Few heroines spend much time in school, and their education is seldom stressed. A heroine who says she is "out of the schoolroom" could be referring to an education that occurred in her home, a neighbor's home, or a more formal school, and may have lasted years or just months. Eleanor Milroy in Collins's *Armadale* (1866) studies with a governess until 16, then spends six months at boarding school. Ordinarily, such "finishing schools" provide little if any substantial education. A girl who briefly attends school in France, Germany, or Switzerland, as does Genevieve Vostrand in Howells's *The Landlord at Lion's Head*, receives the special polish of a little sheltered travel, since women did not mimic their brothers' grand tour as the final phase in their education.

In literature as in life, girls' schools vary by type, size, and quality. The few convent schools receive praise for social and academic reasons: the title character of Disraeli's *Sybil* receives a good convent education; Julie's education at the hands of Ursuline nuns helps overcome her illegitimacy, making her an acceptable lady's companion (Ward, *Daughter*). Although education in small groups is common (Miss Wade is educated with nine other girls in Dickens's *Little Dorritt* [1857]; Mary Snowe has three classmates in Trollope's *Orley Farm*), Madame Beck's unorthodox French school in Brontë's *Villette* has 100 day students and 20 boarders, with an unusually large staff of 12 teachers.

Hofland's *The Daughter of a Genius*, tellingly subtitled "A Tale for Youth," conveys much about middle-class attitudes toward education. The widowed Maria Albany, through errors bred of materialism and pride, must support herself, her daughter, and her huge house; she chooses to start a small school in the house. Soon bored, she turns over the teaching to her assistant and the housekeeping to thirteen-year-old Little Maria. No parents withdraw their daughters until Maria marries an adventurer six years later. Then Little Maria runs the school, and, since her high moral standards override her haphazard academic background, enrollment again rises. This institution's growth, failure, and rebirth show the relative weight of social propriety and education. The school breaks its promises to teach French, drawing, dancing, and music; the original headmistress never taught and could not even prevent the servants from stealing; but none of this matters like one whiff of scandal.

In *A Modern Instance*, Howells suggests that Marcia's two years at boarding school give her an advantage over the other girls in town. But the advantage is social—the broadening experience of meeting girls from Augusta, Bangor, and Bath—not educational or practical. She obtains "a great proficiency in the things that pleased her, and ignorance of the other things," justifying her father's attitude: he "had no great respect for boarding-schools, but if Marcia wanted to try it, he was willing to humor the joke" (102). Unfortunately, girls honestly seeking education found that many schools were jokes—or worse.

The coeducational school in *Hard Times* emphasizes facts, facts, and more facts; its pragmatic, even inhumane approach, exemplified by the aptly named Mr. McChoakumchild, allows Dickens to satirize school reform. Yet, in *The Old Curiosity Shop* he displays the need for reform: Mrs. Wackles's day school offers English grammar, composition, geography, dumbbells, writing, arithmetic, dancing, marking, needlework, and samplering, along with "general fascination" (3), taught by the semieducated Wackles sisters using such methods as "corporal punishment, fasting, and other tortures and terrors" (68).

Still, even this school of incompetents or the one Beth and Amy dislike in *Little Women* can't match the Lowood School in Brontë's *Jane Eyre*, the equal of Dotheboy's Hall in *Nicholas Nickleby*, but presented without Dickens's satirical leavening. Jane is sent to Lowood to learn enough to be a governess—and to be out of her guardians' way. A charity school, Lowood has many pupils who have lost one or both parents. Besides fees, the school solicits subscriptions to educate and care for 80 students aged 9 to 20, but very little money actually goes to the girls or their education.

The school emphasizes virtue and duty with a curriculum designed to prepare girls for a hard, independent life. Prayers precede and follow silent meals; plain clothes and food attempt "to mortify . . . pride" (33). Rather than learning fancy needlework, girls make their own clothes. Subjects such as the globes, history, grammar, writing, arithmetic, drawing, French, and a little music train future governesses and teachers. Older girls carry supper trays, shelve books, and check the younger girls' neatness. The schoolroom is cold and dimly lit, the girls share mugs and beds, and no one pays much attention to their physical or mental well-being. A typhoid epidemic forces officials to realize the effects of semistarvation and neglect. New inspectors "combine reason with strictness, comfort with economy, compassion with uprightness" to create a "truly useful and noble institution" (81). The story highlights the lack of standards and the power of a school's leaders.

Brontë makes an effective contrast by placing Jane as an assistant in a fine country school. Initially attended by 20 rough, illiterate girls, the school eventually serves three times that number, teaching appropriate behavior, neatness, and manners as well as reading, writing, sewing, history, and geography. This school derives its excellence from three unusual people—university graduate St. John Rivers and his sisters, Diana and Mary, who surprisingly also hold advanced degrees. Jane learns much from her experiences with these three, while Brontë demonstrates the value of a good education not just for the wealthy and not just for men.

Stowe likewise reflects the important work of a few dedicated reformers determined to make a sound and valid education available for women. In *My Wife and I*, two of Harry Henderson's sisters mimic real women's situations when they found a seminary to help fill the educational gap girls face in their community. Women like Brontë and Stowe used their literature to make a point, and both were heard.

Beyond Gentility

Early in the century, Jane Austen describes the value of a simple, traditional education. Praising a good village school in *Emma*, she says that it is not "a seminary, or an establishment, or any thing which professed, in long sentences of refined nonsense, to combine liberal acquirements with elegant morality upon new principles and new systems . . . but a real, honest, old-fashioned Boarding-school, where a reasonable quantity of accomplishments were sold at a reasonable price" (14). The "little women" of Alcott's novels, educated at home and at school, learn practical skills and womanly refinements, avoiding merely "feminine" accomplishments. Meg works as a governess out of necessity, not love of teaching. Many Alcott characters, including Marmee in *Little Women*, Jo in *Little Men* and *Jo's Boys*, and Dr. Alex Campbell in *Eight Cousins* (1874) and *Rose in Bloom*, espouse a philosophy of good health and a balanced education; some proclaim the advantages of coeducation and higher education for women. After Rose withdraws from a fashionable boarding school that had crammed useless snippets of knowledge into her head, leaving her uneducated, nervous, and unwell, her uncle Alex establishes a healthy home regimen. While Rose lovingly mocks it ("We will set up a school where nothing but the three Rs shall be taught, and all the children live on oatmeal, and the girls have waists a yard round"), her physical and emotional health improve (*Cousins*, 89). Other writers suggest the inadequacy of even a solid basic education, especially given women's changing roles. Not surprisingly, women writers present the strongest cases for reform and the most examples of new kinds of education.

Just about the time Dr. Campbell established Rose's new schooling, the real physician Edward H. Clarke, although acknowledging that men and women might have equal intellectual potential, still insisted that their education, like their lives, should differ. His book *Sex in Education* surveys the physical and emotional debility resulting from a woman receiving a man's rigorous schooling: "neuralgia, uterine disease, hysteria, and other derangements of the nervous system," and even sterility. Blaming the problem partly on timing (the most strenuous educational years coincide with the onset of menstruation), Clarke cites case after case of women whose education leaves them sickly (if also scholarly); his descriptions would certainly discourage aspiring students.[10] He might have learned from the fictitious Dr. Campbell's experiments.

Even more conservative theorists than Clarke argued that women lacked men's intellectual capacity and thus, unable to evaluate what they read, would be led astray by education; if educated like men, they would become like men. Women's roles differed, their spheres of activity differed, and so should their education. But a "different" education really meant no education: separate proved inherently unequal for genders as for races. The early reformer Hannah More suggested that "the natural and direct tendency of the prevailing and popular system" of educating women serves disastrously "to excite and promote those very defects which it ought . . . to remove."[11] She sought "female virtue" and a Christian education, acceptable to early reformers but wholly inadequate for later ones.

Emily Davies, prominent midcentury advocate of women's education, argued that women, like men, benefit from a liberal education. Knowing the issue of girls' schooling hinged on "the larger question of women's place in the social order," she accepts "so far as it goes, and with explanations" the common idea that women's education should "make good wives and mothers." She observes that transferring the definition to men makes its limits obvious: "an education which produces the best husbands and fathers is likely to be in all regards the best," simply because "the best man in any capacity must be the man who can measure most accurately the proportion of all his duties and claims, giving to each its due share of his time and energy." But she defies traditional male and female spheres as well as utilitarian educational theory when she adds that men and women are not better parents for neglecting other obligations: the best education makes a student the best person possible, regardless of future roles or gender.[12]

Women increasingly faced long years of single life, even if they eventually married. Wars, emigration, and other factors reduced the number of eligible men, and men also postponed marriage for economic or career purposes. Single women needed something to fill their lives, and many needed an income. Dinah Mulock Craik, relatively conservative and vehemently opposed to sexual equality, linked the problem to education. In her view, the "chief canker" in the lives of middle-class women is "the want of something to do." The problem is that "young ladies" are not "brought up to do anything," unlike their brothers who know "from school days" that they are "to do something, to be somebody." Men train for "counting-house, shop, or college," while women, lacking a "clear future," receive education with "so little that is substantial, real, and of practical utility," half the girls' schools in existence could be shut without loss. But Craik pleads for the schools' "reformation," not "annihilation": "there are none too many of them, if they can be made what they need to be."[13]

Activists tried both reforming old schools and founding new ones. Several schools were opened by women unable to get the kind of education they wanted. When Middlebury College barred the self-educated Emma Willard from attending classes to improve as a teacher, she developed her own curriculum and training programs. Her petitions to the New York State Legislature to fund girls' education also failed, but, with the support of the town council, she founded the Troy Female Seminary in 1821, a model for the education of young women. As early as the 1830s, some women spoke on behalf of secondary education for women, either liberal or practical. Lady Mildred Ellis argued that women should be able to work in jobs as various as "practical chemistry," "mechanical arts" like engraving, gilding, and watchmaking, or "the useful trades, such as bookselling"; she proposed schools to teach girls reading, writing, and arithmetic before they chose a trade.[14]

For a liberal higher education, Mary Lyons founded Mount Holyoke College for women, and Oberlin became the first coeducational college. Education became more professional, as organizations like the Governess's Benevolent Institution offered shelter and employment help for English-women after 1844, and evening lectures began at King's College in 1847, a first step to formal education for women at the college.[15] In the audience at the packed introductory lectures sat several women who became leading spirits in English educational reform: Dorothea Beale, Frances Mary Buss, Sophia Jex-Blake, and Elizabeth Day. Within a year, Queen's College opened; as was often true, this college had to function as a preparatory school, offering English, theology, history, mathematics, Latin, modern languages, natural philosophy, the fine arts, and teacher training. Women educated there or inspired by this example soon founded Bedford College and two important secondary schools: the North London Collegiate School (opened by Frances Mary Buss in 1850) and the Cheltenham Ladies' College (1854, under the guidance of Dorothea Beale). Without eliminating "female accomplishments," such schools emphasized solid subjects like literature, history, ethics, religion, and philosophy.

In response to the women's campaign led by Emily Davies, the Taunton Commission on English boys' education agreed to investigate the condition of girls' secondary education. Acknowledging the girls' deplorable situation, the commission forced the government to act. Although the government established more than 80 endowed schools for girls in the last quarter century, at the same time some 900 new or revised plans for boys' schools were approved (Dent, 29). Thus, private efforts remained essential.

By the 1890s a handful of high schools offered both classical and pragmatic subjects from Greek to bookkeeping, from physical education to physical sciences. The new availability of higher education for women gave these schools a goal as well as curricular guidance. Girls' schools offered less science and math; girls also took less science and math at coeducational schools, and fewer girls than boys attended secondary schools. When schools became coeducational, hostility often ran deep. Yet by midcentury, supporters could point to positive experience, arguing that coeducation produced better manners in boys, less sentimentality in girls, and more orderly classrooms, without requiring that girls be educated like boys.

As late as 1907 theorists spoke of the need to distinguish boys' and girls' education: "bodily strength and needs are different," "boys are probably more original; girls more imitative," and, in any case, the "normal work of woman is to be maker of a home, to be a wife, and above all a mother."[16] Nearly a century of reform had not eliminated such ideas.

Part of the effort for reform occurred in literature, especially in the proselytizing novels of feminists like Grand. In *The Heavenly Twins*, Evadne studies anything she can—Italian, German, and French; bandaging and first aid; anatomy and physiology. Her parents disapprove, saying her reading makes her disobedient. They are right, for when she teaches herself advanced math after her father says no woman can learn arithmetic, she understandably questions his other decrees. The twins of the title also try to sabotage their parents' educational plans: though Angelica has a governess and Theodore a tutor, they arrange matters so both learn math, history,

Latin, the Bible, literature, the arts, physical education, and natural history. Still, Theodore attends Sandhurst and then joins nearly all the novel's other men at Oxford, while Angelica stays home.

An education that keeps her a perpetual "amateur" bores the title character in *Babs the Impossible*. Yet, better off than most, she studies with a governess until 15, spends two years at a good Parisian boarding school, then continues lessons at home with a "tutoress," a university-educated woman who encourages her wide-ranging interests. The heroine of *Ideala* pleads for an education almost as shocking to her contemporaries as it would have been to her grandmothers: from personal suffering, she believes "an ideal of marriage should be fixed by law," with college courses and exams to be passed and a "standard of excellence" to be met before people can marry (150).

Though few writers speak out as plainly as Grand, many recognize the need for change. Carey, in *Aunt Diana*, sees a value in Alison's continuing lessons for two years after finishing with her governess. She learns music, Latin, and history from a male neighbor, painting from her aunt. Her 17-year-old sister's studying only French and singing is seen as unfortunate. Still, Carey decries too much education: Alison's friend Anna enjoys history, Latin, literature, and geometry, but must quit studying because her doctor fears for her health, and her mother and sister fear for her femininity. At 17, Muriel Hillyard wants more education, but her family and friends consider this ridiculous. Although she has a "solid, useful education," including Latin, geometry, and English literature, she feels she "lacks accomplishments" (Carey, *Men*, 242). Of course, men in the same social and financial position as Anna, Muriel, or Alison attend the university.

In *Jo's Boys* and *Little Men*, Alcott's sequels to *Little Women*, Jo acts on advanced educational ideas. With money from the philanthropic Mr. Lawrence, guidance from her father and husband, and support from her family, she organizes first a boarding school for boys and later a college where men and women receive the same education and encouragement to become the best people working at the best career possible. No one ridicules Nan for wanting to become a physician; no one ridicules Daisy for wanting to raise a family. Female students gratefully learn needlework and listen to good conversation with Amy and Meg, for Jo hopes to keep these bright, educated women out of the unpleasant category of bluestockings. But with the prime goal a sound education, all rejoice when a woman speaks at graduation. It is significant that Jo, a successful author, rarely seems to write and leaves the teaching to her father and husband, but it is more significant that Alcott, in her very popular novels, gently insists on the need for new kinds of education for women.

A more strident yet uncertain reformer, Dorothea Brooke, despising "domestic music and feminine fine art," seeks greater education (Eliot, *Middlemarch*, 47–48). She hopes to learn Latin and Greek not "entirely out of devotion to her future husband," but because "those provinces of masculine knowledge seemed to her a standing-ground from which all truth could be seen more truly." Eliot observes, "she had not reached that point of renunciation at which she would have been satisfied with having a wise husband: she wished, poor child, to be wise herself." So Casaubon helps her study Greek, but she is "a little shocked and discouraged at her own stupidity, and the answers she got to some timid questions about the value of the Greek accents gave her a painful suspicion that here indeed there might be secrets not capable of explanation to a woman's reason." If she doubts women's ability, her father knows that "such deep studies, classics, mathematics, that kind of thing, are too taxing for a woman—too taxing, you know." Casaubon, "evading the question," explains, "Dorothea is learning to read the characters simply," to save his eyes. Her father acknowledges, "Ah, well, without understanding, you know—that may not be so bad. But there is a lightness about the feminine mind—a touch and go—music, the fine arts, that kind of thing—they should study those up to a certain point, women should; but in a light way, you know" (47–48). In a Grand novel, Dorothea would grow to represent women who need and deserve education, but Eliot mixes sympathy with mockery.

To the end of the era many men agree with Dorothea's father and many women share Dorothea's doubts along with her interests. But a few authors, insisting women are educable and should be educated, demand that their education equal men's in depth, length, and quality. Some, like Gissing in *The Odd Women*, suggest the need also to teach secretarial and business skills to let women enter new fields. Others take a stronger and more difficult step, arguing that women deserve exactly the same options as men, including university degrees.

Higher Education: The Final Bars

In Gore's *Women as They Are*, comments at a Mechanics' Institution reveal literature's prevalent attitude toward the "bluestocking," or educated woman. Saying "the ladies" would not enjoy the lectures, the speaker condescendingly adds that women may be capable "of appreciating scientific knowledge, and matters requiring deep thought" but warns "a learned lady was not always a very popular person, and a 'blue' was looked upon as something in the light of a learned pig." His comments meet with "loud laughter" (259).

In the real world, women did not laugh at such comments. Frustrated and angry, they instead took action. Bedford College, the first woman's college in the University of London, was a step toward higher education, yet it necessarily admitted girls at 12 and taught preuniversity courses. The same pattern occurred in America, where women's colleges, starting in the 1830s, often had to provide a preparatory education before or in addition to higher education. Critics liked to ask why no women geniuses existed, no great women scientists or philosophers or artists; their question implied that women lack the talent, drive, or intellect needed for such success and, by extension, for advanced education. That women lacked opportunity, not ability, became apparent thanks to the untiring efforts of the reformers.

After midcentury, Cambridge and Oxford allowed women to sit for entrance exams, while a series of women's colleges were founded in America: Vassar, Mount Holyoke, Smith, Wellesley, Bryn Mawr, and "Harvard Annex" (Radcliffe). Like many reformers, Mary Lyons, founder of Mount Holyoke College, and Sophia Smith, who endowed Smith College, believed that educating women enhanced their ability to influence society through contributing as workers, teachers, and mothers. To help foster womanly traits, Smith College established small "houses" led by "house mothers" who modeled conservative upper-middle-class values, a system lasting until new attitudes introduced student "head residents" a century later. Following Oberlin's lead, other male schools opened their doors, including Boston University, Cornell, and the University of Michigan by the 1870s. Spearheading the battle for reform were women who recognized the terrible waste of their lives in a society that denied them the right to develop their interests and talents. In *Twenty Years at Hull House*, Jane Addams describes her frustrations as a woman bright enough to read and write Greek and enjoy mental and moral philosophy, history, art, and literature, but forbidden by her father to attend Smith. Faced with such situations, feminists acted.

When Cambridge and Oxford started examining schoolboys in the 1850s, in an effort to admit candidates from outside the ancient public-school system, Emily Davies fought to persuade the universities to examine women as well. Both sexes objected: Dorothea Beale questioned women's openly competing with men, and others argued that boys might discount the exams if girls took them, too. But to Davies, separate exams reinforced the idea that women's and men's education should differ. In time, some women took the standard Cambridge locals, while others took a special exam established in 1869, emphasizing teaching qualifications. That same year, five women persuaded Cambridge professors to lecture for them. In 1870 the women passed bachelor's level examinations, and in 1873 three of them earned honors on the higher examination, the tripos. Although the women took the exams unofficially and earned no degrees, this spelled the beginning of Girton College. The earliest students primarily sought teacher training, but by 1887, 127 women had passed the bachelors' examinations in fields as diverse as classical philology, mathematics, and natural science (the most popular areas), philosophy, history, modern languages, and theology, and another 29 passed the tripos (Stock, 180–81).

Meanwhile, Newnham College was founded near Cambridge, started by Anna Clough in 1871 and incorporated in 1880. Determined to avoid obvious competition with men, Newnham focused on secondary teachers, expecting its graduates to enhance girls' education, not receive degrees. Yet in just a few years, 80 percent of the students were preparing for the tripos as well as the first college examinations (Kamm, 260).

Initially, visitors from Cambridge or graduates of Girton and Newnham served as tutors and lecturers for both schools. But when male professors felt it more convenient for women to attend regular classes (strictly by the professor's choice), properly chaperoned women listened to selected lectures. By the 1880s men and women could potentially receive identical educations and pass identical exams at Cambridge. Still, the women had no official recognition and could not earn degrees. One objection to granting women degrees was the fear they would compete with men for jobs, yet women were barred from most of the jobs graduates sought. Not until 1921 did women receive limited Cambridge degrees (stripped of voting rights): the men's degree provided the right to vote on issues affecting the future of the university, and fear of women's influence was one reason authorities fought against giving them traditional degrees. Not until 1948 were women granted degrees equal to those of men.

Oxford administered some exams for women in 1884, opened all classes and exams by 1894, and granted degrees in 1920. Lady Margaret Hall and Somerville College founded in 1879, St. Hugh's in 1886, and St. Hilda's in 1893 rapidly progressed from training teachers to offering university preparation. Yet the women constantly depended on men's goodwill: until World War I, men could refuse to let women sit in on their lectures.

Considering the barriers to acceptance, let alone a degree at Cambridge or Oxford, it must have been primarily the symbolic value of the ancient universities that kept some women from choosing the new schools that welcomed them. Others took advantage of the fact that the University of London granted women degrees in 1878 and that Victoria University in Manchester, though refusing to admit women to certain classes, gave them degrees from its inception in 1880. Women's long history as governesses and teachers led to much progress in this area; women could choose between normal schools and new institutions like the Maria Grey Training College (1877) and the Cambridge Training College for Women (1885). Very few women obtained broad university educations during the period; support for edcation or research in women's colleges barely existed; students had no prizes or scholarships, faculty often had no offices. Still, the bars were coming down.

When Virgina Woolf wrote A Room of One's Own in the 1920s, the way she distinguished the physical conditions, educational opportunities, and atmosphere at English men's and women's colleges applied even more to earlier times in both nations. Faculty and schools for women lacked the great universities' prestige and academic traditions. For instance, the first president of the all-woman faculty at Wellesley, Alice Freeman Palmer, took charge at 26.[17] While higher education opened new careers, even the very select women who attended college primarily chose traditional fields (classics, English, languages, ancient and modern history) and traditional jobs (writing and teaching). A survey of Vassar graduates in 1895 revealed that many attended graduate school to prepare for careers in law and medicine, but many chose to teach (often at Smith, Wellesley, Vassar, and a few coeducational schools like the Massachusetts Institute of Technology); about two-thirds eventually married (Firor, 69–73).

The drive for new professions for women fostered new educational opportunities. For example, in the 1860s in England, women could not attend medical schools or present themselves for examination; by 1900, women could study medicine at more than a dozen schools, either with men or alone, and could earn degrees.

Elizabeth Blackwell's story typifies the prejudices the pioneers faced and the energy and courage these women needed. A story that crosses the Atlantic, it suggests that America, while slightly ahead of England, erected most of the same barriers. Deciding to become a doctor, Blackwell faced a situation in which the traditional role of women in medicine (practicing midwifery or charity medicine, founding hospitals, serving as nurses) had lessened. Men had taken over many of women's earlier medical tasks, women were barred from training, women and men could not study anatomy or physical processes or diseases together, and men could not teach women such subjects. Persisting, Blackwell applied to 29 schools in the United States before the Geneva College of Medicine in New York accepted her. That school allowed the students to vote on her admission after establishing that one negative vote could debar her. Ironically, her application was considered only because no American medical school, unlike their British counterparts, had officially excluded women, so foreign was the notion that one might apply. Although graduating at the top of her class in 1849, Blackwell, a social pariah, chose not to march in the commencement parade for fear it was not ladylike. After additional training, she tried to practice medicine but was denied access to hospital wards. Support from Quakers interested in her lectures to girls on hygiene and physical education enabled her to open a dispensary. In time, she raised money to found the New York Infirmary, a 40-bed hospital staffed by women including her sister Emily. Partly because Blackwell prepared army nurses for the Civil War, she earned the support of male doctors and in 1868 was able to open the Woman's Infirmary Medical School.

Meanwhile, other women battled for the right to obtain a medical education in England (Stock, 205–6). Elizabeth Garrett-Anderson sat in medical classes at Apothecaries Hall in London and paid tutors to cover classes that banned her. Though passing the medical examination in 1860, she was refused a degree; eventually the University of Paris granted her one. When Sophia Jex-Blake and six other women gained access to Edinburgh University's Medical School after a long fight, male students' opposition prevented their getting degrees. In the face of such treatment, Jex-Blake and Garrett-Anderson founded a medical school for women. Hospital wards finally opened for the students in the 1870s, and in 1877 the University of London admitted women to medical examinations and granted them degrees.

The story of Florence Nightingale's revolutionizing nursing also exemplifies how one person's efforts enhanced educational and professional opportunities. Nursing sisterhoods in England first received formal training in 1848, when St. John's House was established as a school: two years of classes preceded five years of additional training while living in the hospital. This isolated life helped foster demand for reforms. During the Crimean War, Nightingale saw the impact of poor sanitation and poorly qualified nurses, and acted on what she saw. Like Dorothea Dix during the American Civil War, she became a hero for reforming army medicine. That helped gain support for her plans, leading to the creation of a nursing school at St. Thomas' Hospital in London in 1860. Denying the tradition of women's instinctive knowledge, Nightingale believed nurses required professional education and sought to remove their training and disciplining from the hands of male doctors and hospital administrators. She established nursing as a true profession.

Additional educational progress occurred outside the classroom. University extension courses responded to workers' and women's desire for higher education. For example, in 1867 the North of England Council for Promoting the Higher Education of Women began a lecture series that, though controlled by professional men, was organized and patronized by women. As more than 100 such courses of demanding lectures with readings and examinations appeared around the country, women flocked to them, comprising up to two-thirds of the students in the Oxford Extension courses in 1888–89.[18] Still, even some early modern authors experienced the continuing limits in women's education: May Sinclair's first formal schooling occurred at 18, when she entered Cheltenham under Beale's tutelage; Virginia Woolf studied in her father's library while her brothers attended Cambridge. Given the realities of higher education, women sought education where they could find it, and given their desire to advance in this area, they created opportunities where there were none.

Unlike such reformers, most characters in literature see no need to educate women and, like the speaker quoted earlier, regard an educated woman as "a learned pig." As one woman says to another: "Mathematics! Science! Why, what can you want to make yourself hateful for, like a Girton College guy?" (Ouida, *Moths*, 23).

Would-be students might well find such attitudes disheartening, yet even a more sympathetic voice can convey discouragement. Well's free-thinking heroine in *Ann Veronica* decides to go to London University without her father's approval. But her brother cautions, "the world isn't ready for girls to start out on their own yet. . . . Babies and females have got to keep hold of somebody or go under—anyhow, for the next few generations. You go home and wait a century, Vee, and then try again. Then you *may* have a bit of a chance" (131).

Such views make clear why parents routinely discourage their daughters' thoughts about higher education. Muriel Trevor in Carey's *The Mistress of Brae Farm* reads until midnight, studying Greek, Hebrew, and Latin. As usual, no one takes seriously the desire of this bright, dedicated, motivated woman to attend university.

In fact, very few women characters consider higher education, or if they do, it is a brief and halfhearted thought. The plot of Edwards's *Girton Girl* (1885) endorses the norm that women do not truly desire education, and that marriage is the right and best goal. Marjorie long and loudly proclaims her determination to attend college. In spite of the difficulties and her friends' insistence that higher education is just a fad, she finds a tutor to prepare her in mathematics and classics. But predictably, Marjoie finds her tutor more appealing than his subjects: having fallen in love, she struggles only briefly before reaching the expected conclusion, gladly giving up her education, career goals, and ambition for her beloved and a traditional marriage.

This pattern has very few exceptions, usually occurring in the works of feminists like Grand or avant-garde writers like Lawrence. While Lawrence's women may attend art school or even university, as do Gudrun and Ursula in *The Rainbow* and *Women in Love*, since they also engage in sexual relationships outside of marriage and one experiments with lesbianism, they are hardly representative.

A rare female university graduate, Barbara Land, notes the irony that men, displaying ambivalence toward educated women, talk one way but behave another. While "extolling the virtures" of the excellent but boring "gentle ladies of a by-gone day," men "built [clubs] everywhere to escape from their society." But now "those palatial buildings are being gradually deserted for the smaller mixed clubs" where men and women "associate . . . on equal terms." Grateful that the former "sentimentality" about women has been replaced by "respect," Land insists "a well-behaved woman may go almost anywhere unmolested" (Grand, *Babs*, 343–44). Grand's heroine in *Ideala* says women can truly fulfill the old ideal of leading people to social and moral reform, if they first receive a good education. She declares, "A woman may do anything which she can do in a womanly way" and the old idea of a woman's "sphere" is "nonsense" (188).

Less unrealistically optimistic about the impact and acceptance of the New Woman and the value of educating women, Stowe still presents some remarkable characters. She makes a strong case for higher education, tying it to women's need to find something worth doing. In *My Wife and I*, when the Henderson men go off to college, the women found their own seminary, but they note that at least some New England colleges admit both sexes, with good results: the quiet, refined women receive no less education than the men. Harry's cousin Caroline and another woman, Ida, express their frustration that men's education serves a purpose but women too often waste their talents and the years between a minimal schooling and marriage. These women seek independent lives, hoping to be doctors. Foreshadowing Woolf's vision, Caroline insists, "I want what any live woman wants; I want something of my own; I want a life-work worth doing." But "the world seems all arranged so as to hinder my getting it. If a man wants to get an education there are colleges with rich foundations, where endowments have been heaped up, and scholarships founded, to enable him to prepare for life at reasonable expense. There are no such for women, and their schools, such as they are, infinitely poorer than those given to men, involve double the expense" (111–13). Her simple ideal is to receive the same education as her brother, but she cannot act until her father dies. Then she works on a newspaper in New York while Ida serves as a clerk in her father's business; both save their money, and, as the novel ends, they sail to France for medical school.

In her gently liberal way, Alcott presents not only an idealized coeducational college but several characters who seek higher education. In *Rose in Bloom*, Phoebe uses her years of specialized musical training to support herself by singing in churches and private gatherings; in *Jo's Boys*, Nan studies medicine. Though Plumfield School and Lawrence College may be dreamworlds, Alcott encourages her characters—and by extension, her readers—to reach for their dreams. Her women realistically struggle for education and appropriate jobs (as she proves in *Work* [1873]), but she won't let them quit. She generally gives them a choice of marriage or education and career, and she suggests the advantages of the first option: after proving herself as a singer, Phoebe happily accepts a traditional married life. Through direct moralizing and plot, Alcott warns educated women to remain feminine, not to behave as bluestockings. Though limited, her reform is real and her influence probably more pervasive than that of the feminist writers, for her message has a sugar coating and her works were widely read.

Characters like Caroline and Ida, who brave a trip to France for medical school, or Nan, or even Phoebe, are exceptions, as were their counterparts in life. Even more conservative than society, representative literature presents no female characters at any university or in any formal higher education until the final decades of the century. Then, only one in 100 women attend universities; in novels published just after 1900, about one in fifteen receive some kind of university education. Only a few dedicated and determined authors directly address the issue of women's education—especially higher education—with a goal of reform. But, just as in reality, those few finally did make a difference.

While often unrealistic, literature offers intriguing insight into a few schools, especially a few bad private schools. It describes some basic features of girls' education, and it shows some of the impact of educational reform. Tending to inflate men's education and downplay women's, it emphasizes the ideal and mimics society's goal of gentility. Female characters and real women who sought to change their roles by increased education and new opportunities found barriers erected by the stereotypes of genteel femininity. Yet a few women made a difference, exploring new ideas in literature and enacting them in life. Gradually the "Angel of the House" gained real educational opportunities, and the New Woman opened the door a few inches. As Elizabeth Blackwell sailed from England to America to attend medical school, so characters like Caroline sailed from America to France; both reached their goals, and both provided role models for other women.

Florence Nightingale

Courtesy of the National Portrait Gallery, London

CHAPTER
4

Employment: The Angel
Takes Flight

In the fiction of today, women are continually taking
larger place in the action of the story. . . . They are
no longer content simply *to be*: they *do*.
— Charlotte Perkins Gilman,
Women and Economics (150)

Victorians worked hard and took their jobs seriously, motivated as much by
a cult of work as by potential social and financial rewards. Society castigated
slackers and the unemployed as frivolous and immoral or patronized them
as creatures in need of higher guidance (which members of the middle class
happily supplied). The hardworking were rewarded with equal fervor. The
conflict between this ideal and that of the Gentle Lady living as the "Angel
of the House" helped to convince many real women and literary heroines
that they could not simply "be"; they had to "do."

Job advances led to improved standards of living, wages, and real earnings, as well as an enhanced sense of personal worth, the right to feel
virtuous. Many believed social progress more or less automatically attended
an earnest attitude toward work. Compared to today, people devoted more
time to their jobs and did not welcome distractions. They rarely sought
pleasure in work, and many of their amusements, such as attending lec-

tures, reading serious books, or running charitable bazaars, contained elements of work. A virtuous necessity, work established social and spiritual worth and guarded against financial and moral ruin. This was the guiding principle of society, yet it truly applied only to men.

Work conferred respectability upon men but not women. The middle-class woman who *needed* to work usually experienced frustration if not despair; *choosing* to work could precipitate a family crisis. The hobgoblin of respectability planted a huge obstacle in women's path to better jobs. Reformers had to combat the beliefs that working for pay decreased a woman's femininity, detracted from her mission as wife and mother, and proved her father or husband had failed to provide adequately. Slowly and with great difficulty, reformers forced society to accept the fact that women could work and even be considered professionals. But questions about equal pay and opportunities, the suitability of certain jobs for women, or combining a career with marriage or child rearing, linger into the twentieth century.

Attitudes toward Work in a Changing Society

From stable agricultural and commercial economies in the eighteenth century, England and America rapidly industrialized.[1] Farmers traded their plows for industrial tools, individual craftsmen making part of a complete product joined a chain of manufacture, small workshops disappeared or became large factories. Towns grew up around a factory or mine. Railroads wound through the English countryside, bringing workers to jobs, materials to factories, and manufactured goods to seaports, where steamships carried international trade. Concentrated populations needed shops and services, enticing more people to cities. Workers thronged into urban tenements, while the newly prosperous middle class sought suburban retreats.

Increased respectability and status often meant more than money. A master at a fine private school stood above one at a lesser private school, and both outranked schoolmistresses. The big city hospital nurse rated above her country sister. Professions, requiring advanced training and relying on mental rather than physical skills, earned more status than commerce or industry. Manufacturers and their families could achieve gentility through work, whereas artisans and laborers could hope only for respectability. Most people knew not to flaunt financial success; money helped, but wealth acquired through personal effort aroused a snobbish unease in more established families.

A rapidly changing society increased economic strain and social tension, leading to labor strikes, calls for government intervention on behalf of child laborers, and demands for minimum safety regulations. Newspaper articles focused on the plight of seamstresses, the morals and health of factory girls, and the use of small children and pregnant women to haul coal. Less visible but equally profound reactions affected family life and relationships, especially as women's roles altered.

The changes for women were stunning. Women entered the work force in new numbers and new fields. Documents about women's jobs can be misleading, since they usually define women working part- or even full-time in their husbands' shops or fields as "dependent" or "unoccupied"; even at century's end, this remains the largest class of women. Yet by 1900, the number of women engaged in manufacture had quadrupled, those in commerce and trade had quintupled, and women professionals had increased even beyond that.

Onetime farmers, skilled craftsmen, and small shopkeepers, who previously worked at home with their sons as apprentices and their wives and daughters as assistants, found life transformed. In factories and large stores, wives and children might not obtain work, might not choose or be allowed to train with their husbands and fathers. The family no longer functioned as a unit. At every level of society, families and individuals experienced dislocation and a restructuring of old patterns. Focusing on family life, literature reflects its authors' and readers' profound, often traumatic reevaluation of men's and women's roles. As Eliot writes in *Felix Holt*, "These social changes . . . are chiefly public matters, and this history is chiefly concerned with the private lot of a few men and women; but there is no private life which has not been determined by a wider public life" (45).

Like their real counterparts, men in literature expect to work hard and reap the benefits, and they expect women to remain inside the home. But literature does not truly reflect the impact of the Industrial Revolution on jobs and working conditions, or on women's lives. Women in literature struggle to craft new roles, but only a few—financially desperate or reform-minded—seek paid employment. Barely aware of social change, Cedric's friend and sister offer the routine options, asking "what are we to do with him" if he fails the civil service exam? "He has utterly refused to enter the church or to study for the law. He has no taste for engineering or architecture, and we should not care for him to be a businessman." The friend, suggesting Cedric could become a teacher in a good private school, agrees, "There is a limited number of professions, certainly" (Carey, *Herb*, 3).

Nearly half the men in representative novels enter the church, military, or government at midcentury; most of the remainder divide fairly evenly between law and medicine on the one hand, and the life of a country squire on the other. Even at the end of the century, the same jobs employ almost half the male characters, with just one-fifth in business, manufacturing, or new fields like engineering, the jobs that truly absorbed most men. The great majority of women—nine out of ten in the early decades, eight out of ten in the last—stay at home. Only in novels occurring right around 1900 do significant numbers of women labor for pay: then about one-fourth work as writers, nurses, companions, and teachers. Conservative and idealistic about employment, literature nonetheless realistically portrays the importance of work in defining personal and social value and the agonies women faced because of the dichotomy between that view and society's attitude toward *their* working. Work might be good for everyone else, but not for the Angel of the House.

For men, the value of work is clear. Richard Carstone in Dickens's *Bleak House*, lacking the motivation his society considers a virtue, fails in medicine, the military, and law, then descends into debt and a secret marriage. It takes his wife's guidance to make Oliver in Oliphant's *Oliver's Bride* treat being a barrister seriously, and his failure to work symbolizes his moral weakness: Grace helps him accept responsibility for his job *and* for ruining an innocent girl. Helen recognizes that any "useful trade, or profession, or employment" would help reform her husband from his alcoholic debauchery (Brontë, *Tenant*, 220). While providing such guidance is ordinarily women's work, a male friend of the bored, debt-ridden, sickly, immoral Henry Fitzharris takes on the task, saying a combination of divine and human effort can cure his "disease": "The human agency required in your case, is an active and laudable pursuit, fitted to your age, your capacity, and your situation in life" (Bury, *Separation* 1:30).

While work is often seen as man's salvation, that attitude rarely touches women. Remarkable in many ways, the bored and wealthy Mrs. Lightfoot Lee of Adams's *Democracy* seeks employment, but the work is rooted in tradition. Having inspected hospitals and prisons, examined poverty, and performed philanthropy, she decides to study government by visiting Congress and dining with prominent officials. Peggy Lambton keeps busy with household duties and volunteering at the local workhouse, and she worries that her younger sister, Prue, has no "serious occupation" (Broughton, *Cupid*, 90). Like real women, these characters stay occupied as volunteers, as dilettantes. Few men would apply to women Madame Pratolungo's belief that work enriches everyone's life and "nobody has a right to be idle" (Collins, *Finch*, 68).

Upper-class characters work as lawyers, ministers, government officials, and bishops; they also socialize together, illustrating one way a husband's occupation affects his wife. Demonstrating the nicety of social distinctions, Howells's A *Modern Instance* explains that "Mr. Phillips's father had been in business on that obscure line which divides the wholesale merchant's social acceptability from the lost condition of the retail dealer." When he dies, his son "emerged forever from the social twilight" to become a man of leisure and a gentleman (35). David Copperfield is properly placed not in a countinghouse with lower-class workers, but as an articled clerk or secretary, or reading for the law. Finances force a hero who expected to be a genteel clerk or officer to assume his father's job as a tailor. Yet, since he possesses the "bearing and character . . . of a gentleman," society accepts him (Meredith, *Evan Harrington* [1860], 301).

For a man, status comes less from money than from the right school, neighborhood, and job; for a woman, it comes from her father's or husband's job. One character notes, "I don't think our being poor ought to signify a bit. . . . Papa is a gentleman, and a clergyman, and mamma is a lady" (Trollope, *Chronicle*, 537); another is introduced as "Mr. Amos Ford, attorney-at-law, and (consequently) gentleman" (Hook, *Sayings*, 104). When a day-school graduate and apprentice teacher becomes private secretary to an upper-class man, the position alters his status, so he "dressed like a gentleman" (Kingsley, *Hillyars*, 158–59).

For a woman, work means an almost automatic loss of status. When Hepzibah Pyncheon opens a shop, she reflects the norm, saying, "I am a woman! . . . I was going to say, a lady—but I consider that as past" (Hawthorne, *Seven Gables*, 42). The democratic Holgrave considers Hepzibah more "heroic" than any other lady in her family, for she has joined in the "united struggle of mankind" (43). Describing Phoebe, the narrator envisions a utopia where "ladies did not exist. There, it should be woman's office to move in the midst of practical affairs, and to gild them all—the very homeliest, were it even the scouring of pots and kettles—with an atmosphere of loveliness and joy" (73). But he speaks for the minority. Far more usual is a suburb where "the men went daily to their offices or countinghouses, and the women depended for society on long morning visits from London friends and relations" (Eden, *House*, 12). For much of the century, whomever they depend on for "society," women clearly depend on men's work for rank as well as economic survival.

In *Sybil*, Disraeli's novel of social reform, poverty and disease hide beneath the town of Marney's pastoral veneer, for no significant manufacturing means no jobs. As conditions worsen, laborers burn hayricks, loot, and riot, shocking the upper classes. A few good people try to bridge the gulf between the "two nations" of rich and poor, and some workers obtain better jobs. When the unsympathetic Lord Marney complains that increased pay just lets the workmen "spend their money in the beer-shops," Mr. St. Lys blames women's changing roles. He excuses "a poor man" who seeks "solace" or "refuge" in a tavern when he returns from work to find "no home," no fire or meal, because his wife, "the partner of his life, wearied with labour in the field or the factory, [is] still absent, or perhaps in bed from exhaustion." He notes, "We have removed woman from her sphere; we may have reduced wages by her introduction into the market of labour; but under these circumstances what we call domestic life is a condition impossible to be realised for the people of this country" (120).

Children quickly imbibe society's rules, as Grand's *The Beth Book* reveals. When Sammy asks what her father "was," meaning what did he do, Beth answers, "He was a gentleman." Pressed further, she adds, "an officer and a gentleman." Surprised that Beth doesn't understand what he means when he calls his father a "retired gentleman," Sammy explains, "When you make a fortune you retire from business. Then you're a retired gentleman." Beth objects that "gentlemen don't go into business. . . . They have professions or property." Though Sammy says "It's all the same," Beth insists "It isn't," and Sammy laughs, "Yah! *you* don't know" (166).

As the traditional social markers of various jobs changed, the Sammys of reality and literature found it increasingly hard to "know" whether a man was a gentleman and his wife, a lady. For a woman who worked or wanted to work outside the home, the situation was even more complex and difficult.

"Comfortable" and "Uncomfortable" Workers

When the title character of Eliot's *Felix Holt* becomes a journeyman watchmaker, he knowingly takes a step down from the options his education offers. Even in a book about radical politics, Felix must justify his decision. Preferring crafts to bank or office work, he asks, "Why should I want to get into the middle-class because I have some learning?" He feels laborers and artisans who "forsake their born comrades and go in for a house with a high door-step and a brass knocker" are not rising, at least not morally (59). Though Sewell accurately notes that "not all the rank in the world will make persons ladies and gentlemen without manners" (*Amy*, 246), manners alone cannot confer gentility. *Felix Holt* patronizes "one of your middle-class upstarts who want to rank with gentlemen, and think they'll do it with kid gloves and new furniture" (29). But through effort—and especially through the man's having the right job—families can achieve some gentility, learning manners and earning kid gloves.

For men, new jobs often brought exciting options, from furniture to housing to political and social power; for women, that same rise in family status might actually limit job options, since middle- and upper-class wives were to enjoy genteel leisure. Recognizing the tensions created by being plunged into a confusing world of new roles for women and changing roles for men, Wakefield titled the middle class the "uneasy" class (60–84); but most called them "comfortable," in contrast to the "uncomfortable" workers. Thomas Wright offered a contemporary guideline relating class to job: those above the "working man" are "the employing, or genteely-employed."[2]

Occupation and income traditionally define class, as every character in literature knows. In the 1860s, Dudley Baxter attempted to divide the whole English population into stratified classes based solely on men's income and ranging from the upper class (earning £1,000 to £5,000 a year, sometimes more), through three divisions within the middle class, to unskilled laborers and agricultural workers, earning under £100 per year.[3] Women who performed the same work as men earned so much less that Baxter observes, "in the great majority of occupations the average wages of a boy, a woman, and a girl, added together amount to those of a man" (*National Income*, in Best, 97).

As the middle class expanded, so did their income, but more income often meant disproportionate expenses: servants, travel, books, and furnishings maintained the genteel life defined by magazines and literature. Novels and neighbors taught the wife of a new doctor or merchant that she needed a seven-room house staffed by two or more servants, while the wife of a professional or tradesman wanted at least one female servant to cook and clean. For a son to enter law, medicine, or the church required fees for college, suitable clothing and furnishings, and the ability to purchase a legal or medical apprenticeship or practice or to obtain a parish. A daughter preparing for marriage needed an appropriate "finishing" school and clothing, while an unmarried daughter had to be maintained for life.

The "comfortable" class, fearing a slip in status, felt uneasy because the lower-middle class often shared laborers' jobs and working conditions. Moving from country to city didn't guarantee work, especially for the unskilled, since applicants often outnumbered jobs. Employers controlled wages, hours, and conditions, keeping the first low, the second long, and the third pretty miserable. In industry and manufacture, workers faced 12-hour days in noisy, dirty, unventilated rooms, performing dangerous tasks, unprotected from machinery and prey to various occupational diseases; they might have to furnish coal for the company's stoves. Workers were fired at 40 or 50; reformers risked their jobs when they earned reputations as troublemakers. Female workers often lost their jobs when they married or became pregnant.

These problems tarnished hopes generated by advances in technology, education, and law. In spite of increased salaries and reduced hours, the cost of living rose with the standard of living, so that real income declined, undercutting beliefs about work. While expansion at home and abroad led to full employment and new jobs in industry, manufacture, trade, and commerce, it also brought confusion and risk. Farm prices declined; crafts became obsolete. Bank failures and reports of corruption increased political agitation and labor unrest.

The resulting reform efforts gradually regulated children's employment, hours, and health and safety standards, and provided the respite of official holidays. But few of these changes applied to all factories, fewer still to shops, and virtually none to domestic servants or governesses. The jobs least regulated were those open to women. Clerks could work 12 hours, seamstresses 16, and the whims of mistress or master governed a servant's life. Bakers', butchers', and grocers' assistants prepared the shop at 7 A.M. and cleaned up at 9 or 10 P.M.. Working 80 or 90 hours a week, laborers had few holidays, and a half day on Saturday might require making up tasks in advance; perhaps in retaliation, Monday illnesses were common. The job market and inadequate law enforcement gave tremendous power to employers, mostly middle- and upper-middle-class men.

The popular doctrine of self-reliance implied that workers could rise through their efforts, and some did: a shop assistant—in time, even a female worker—might buy a small store, or a clerk become a partner in a business. On the other hand, the lack of jobs and potential advancement inspired the employing class, especially women, to pursue both charity and reform. Public and private groups financed and ran schools, almshouses, and hospitals. "Good works" provided respectable occupation for genteel ladies and kept them from seeking paid employment. While charity reinforced the subservience of those needing help, some feared it might demoralize them, further detracting from the ideal of self-help. The middle class felt a paternalistic responsibility for the workers' behavior, drinking, morality, and industriousness. Henry Mayhew's famous *London Labour and the London Poor* was just one study designed, according to the *Morning Chronicle*, where it first appeared, to show readers the disparities between the lives of the middle class and the industrial poor.[4] It succeeded, influencing both reformers and authors.

But even in novels of social reform, few characters do as Felix Holt did, voluntarily taking a step down the social ladder by his choice of job. Those who do have some special reason. Religion motivates the title character of Eliot's *Adam Bede*, who works as a carpenter. Besides, the narrator observes, at that earlier time "there was no rigid demarcation of rank between the farmer and the respectable artisan" (90), especially when the artisan, like Adam, would someday be his own master. Independence from an employer's will for income, working conditions, or hours improves Adam's situation.

In contrast to Felix and Adam, most characters seek jobs that, in rank and money, might make possible a "high door-step and a brass knocker." For the tenant farmer with no hope of seeing his children's lots improve, emigration may provide an answer. That is the desire of Angel Clare, a parson's son who takes up farming (Hardy, *Tess*). More commonly, characters try to escape farming, noting that a "clerk in one of the public offices" achieves higher income and rank (Helme, *Farmer*, 23). Proposing to Bathsheba, Gabriel Oak says, "I can make you happy," and lists what he can offer: a newspaper announcement of the marriage; a piano ("and I'll practice up the flute right well to play with you in the evenings"); "and a frame for cucumbers—like a gentleman and lady" (Hardy, *Crowd*, 39). His assumption that upward mobility is appealing may be false, but his assumption that his wife's status will depend on his is surely correct.

The family of estate owners of greater wealth or position find that certain responsibilities attend their privileges. In Eliot's *Middlemarch*, Dorothea and Celia share "the pride of being ladies," for "the Brooke connections though not exactly aristocratic, were unquestionably 'good:' if you inquired backward for a generation or two, you would not find any yard-measuring or parcel-tying forefathers" (5). Dorothea hopes to use her money to improve the living conditions of her uncle's "uncomfortable" laborers. Eliot gently mocks Dorothea as a representative of certain female middle-class reformers, for her vision is flawed and she lacks the strength or freedom to make that vision come true.

Rank and comfort also depend on the characters' behavior and the author's themes. Hardy's Jude is a stonemason who serves an apprenticeship, educates himself, and attends night school; but his nature and fate trap him. In contrast, the blacksmith William Stanfield in Oliphant's *Agnes* lives above the smithy but behaves so that people "respected and looked up to" him (3). The cart-driver hero of Craik's *John Halifax, Gentleman* seems genteel. This virtuous, hardworking, self-educated son of a scholarly gentleman must save the tanyard during a flood and quell a riot before the prosperous owner makes him first an apprentice and then a partner. When John attains his dream of owning a mill, he moves from a farmhouse to the fancier Beechwood Hall. Idealistically, he says, "I would like to be anything that was honest and honorable. It's a notion of mine, that whatever a man may be his trade does not make him; he makes his trade" (35).

Gradually John's vision gained more the ring of truth. Novels written around World War I but describing the turn of the century reflect far greater social and job mobility. The daughters as well as the sons of miners, laborers, and farmers in Lawrence's *Sons and Lovers*, *The Rainbow*, and *Women in Love* become artists, teachers, office workers, and engineers. Gudrun and Ursula attend parties of the estate and mine owners who employed their ancestors. Yet people note their odd position. Rising from the "uncomfortable" laboring class, they discover the discomforts of life in a changing, competitive, and complex world with new rules and expectations.

Many middle-class women reading about Gudrun and Ursula would envy their freedom—even while castigating their morals; working-class women, had they read Lawrence's novels, would envy Gudrun and Ursula their jobs. Real lower-class women held the same or equivalent jobs as men, working in fields or tending poultry and dairy. In factories and mines they might perform tasks suiting their greater dexterity and smaller size, executing a delicate machine operation or hauling coal through a shaft too narrow for a horse. Women laboring unofficially beside their husbands in making such products as jewelry, fans, lace, buttons, and hats, automatically combined career and marriage; widowed, they might take over the trade. As work moved out of the home, the age at marriage rose, perhaps because toiling 12 hours a day plus commuting left a woman no time for husband or children. Numerous reports of working girls' ignorance about hygiene, nutrition, child care, even cooking and cleaning, attest to the problem. Entering factories as children, women had little chance to learn domestic skills, and no time or energy to perform any they might learn. Poor food and housing, lack of care, inadequate baby nurses, and liberal use of "soothing" opiates led to high infant mortality rates among workers.

Given this situation and believing immorality ran rampant among factory women (lack of proof never injured the popularity of this literary theme), people felt driven to act. Private effort and then state intervention led to day nurseries and other reforms. Others in the middle class—and the women's movement was essentially a middle-class phenomenon—focused on concerns about women. They questioned not only the disparity of wages and opportunities for working women but also the fundamental issues of women's options, rights, and needs. The nature of the questions asked and the jobs sought differentiates working women of the lower middle class from those in higher social strata. No one looking at Gudrun or Ursula would mistake them for laborers.

Gentility, Work, and Women

Feminists considered advances in job conditions, wages, and opportunities an appropriate part of the redefinition of women's roles and rights. But in literature and society, people voiced concerns about the rightness and effects of women working outside the home and for pay. The very idea offered a fundamental challenge to contemporary sex roles and led to opposition on both philosophical and practical fronts. Conservatives asked: Should women work? Could women continue to be subservient to their fathers and husbands if they worked? Should they be? Could they work without destroying the sanctity of womanhood or the home? And the feminists' questions show the profound conflict: Why raise the issue of gentility at all? Why should motherhood bar a woman from a career when fatherhood doesn't bar a man? Why are women often prevented from performing the same jobs as men? And when they do the same jobs why are they paid less? Why should women be treated at all differently in the job market?

In that many authors recognize and confront the issue of women's needing or wanting to work, literature is less conservative on this controversy than on education or marriage. Still, very few women characters seek jobs, and most of those who do, work only as a stopgap until marriage. Far fewer fictional women work outside the home for pay than their sisters in reality. Even in representative fiction of the 1890s, three-fourths of women fit what government reports call the "dependent" class, although a noticeable shift occurs in literature published from 1900 to 1920, describing the last decades of the century. Literature changed more slowly than reality, but it almost certainly influenced the evolution; poems and novels alike forced readers to consider how women could support themselves and how they could achieve a satisfying life. Perhaps because women authors had to cope with the enormous stresses of trying to write in the face of profound objections, perhaps because they knew firsthand what it meant to try to combine work and marriage, or retain femininity and gentility while working, or work because they absolutely could not live without working, they present the issue with great sensitivity and emotion. Elizabeth Oakes-Smith, in "Unattained," from the sonnet-sequence *The Poet's Life*, expresses the frustration of many women when she asks, "And this is life? And we are born for this?"

In reality, men who worked could maintain their gentility and even achieve social and economic progress. Salesmen could become shopkeepers, foremen could take over factories, and their sons might become doctors or engineers. Working in less-cramped and better-lighted rooms, perhaps commuting by carriage instead of on foot, moving into a larger house, these men could establish a life of genteel ease for their wives.

Their daughters saw the changes, but contemporary attitudes blocked their reaping the direct benefits in the marketplace. American pioneer women, laboring beside their husbands in shops or fields, cherished their symbols of gentility—a fancy clock or a few precious pieces of china—but felt no less womanly for their difficult work. Running newspapers, inns, schools, and plantations, women played an active role in the nation's business beyond home and family. But by midcentury, first in Europe and then in America, the cult of femininity took over, as an ideal to coexist in conflict with the reality of rural and factory life, and as a goal to strive for elsewhere. Domestic chores lost value, and women, barred from additional work, were taught to be subservient and dependent—to please, support, and care for others. Family size decreased, and as government began to care for the poor, tend the elderly, and teach young children, women's roles diminished further.

Women who considered working outside the home faced tremendous problems. The first question asked by reformers and in literature was the basic one: should women work at all? Some authors, simply acknowledging that women did toil, wrote about the reality of their lives. Novelist Elizabeth Stuart Phelps used data from government reports to describe how industry (run by men) controlled workers (especially women), in *Hedged In* (1870), *The Silent Partner* (1871), and the Gates series (*The Gates Ajar* [1868], *Beyond the Gates* [1883], *The Gates Between* [1887]). In truth, poorly educated even for the only "suitable" career of marriage, girls lacked preparation for any other job. Most women in literature never consider work, or work only until they become wise to reality—or fall in love. Even satirizing the norm, Grand reveals its power: "At that time marriage was the only career open to a gentlewoman" (*Beth*, 318). Yet nearly all women from laboring and farming families worked from childhood through marriage and often while raising children. In the middle or upper classes, new widows or orphaned daughters could abruptly plunge to the level of artisan or laborer.

Desperate for work, these women had few options other than living with a relative in exchange for nursing or housekeeping duties, making crafts, struggling to run a shop left by father or husband, or becoming a governess or needleworker. The available jobs rarely maintained both soul and body.

Most literature supports the rule that women will marry and only those who fail to marry will work. One character says of a new employee, "Being a woman, it's ill troubling her with a partnership; better give her a fixed salary till such time as she marries" (Gaskell, *Sylvia's Lovers*, 187). Accurately reflecting reality, this attitude meant that women had less opportunity than men. Making matters even worse, women outnumbered men throughout the period, and people tended to marry later: after the 1850s, nearly one-fourth of women in their thirties were single. More women faced long solo years, even if they did eventually marry. While a single man, prepared by education and expectations, could fill his life with work, women confronted the painful disparities between social and personal assumptions and the true situation. As Beth well knows, "a woman was expected at that time to earn her livelihood by marrying a man and bringing up a family" (Grand, *Beth*, 119). Given this view, the talented Beth must hide her work and income from her husband.

The conflict between this reality and the ideal of an innocent goddess presiding over and sheltered within a protected home intensified the long struggle for change. Reformers argued that lacking appropriate education and job opportunities jeopardized a woman's happiness, even her life. Conservatives answered that work would make women unfeminine and destroy the sanctity of the home. Because supporting an "idle" wife demonstrated a man's success, women's interest in work threatened men's roles and power as well as the family's gentility.

Speaking for the conservative majority and believing women's physiological differences (such as their generally smaller skulls) indicated or determined their inherent intellectual and moral differences, Alexander Walker, in *Women Physiologically Considered*, argued for different occupations, as well. He felt women's inferior intellect and superior instinct suited them to be wives and mothers. Walker quoted Wollstonecraft's argument that "men, in their youth, are prepared for professions, and marriage is not considered as the grand feature in their lives; whilst women, on the contrary, have no other scheme to sharpen their faculties"; but he defended the appropriateness of the situation she deplored: "Well, indeed, may this be the case, when the consequences of marriage must necessarily, and almost incessantly, employ every faculty they possess" (139). Continuing his denigration, he suggests the importance of biology: woman's "mental system has no power to rise above the instinctive influence of her vital system, but on the contrary contributes to aid it" (6). Even her body is "fit only for sedentary occupations," so that she must stay inside the house, where her "chief duties" are necessarily performed (140). Given this perfect match between women's mental and physical equipment and their role, Walker predicts only harm in changing their education or jobs.

Although other conservatives asserted that the likelihood of marriage made jobs and education for women unnecessary and wasteful, if not detrimental, feminists countered that many women needed to work and that the underlying assumptions about women's "sphere" could be questioned. A talk on "Work as a Necessity for Women" reveals the fears of single women: they "can but feel themselves a burden and a drag on the hard-won earnings of their fathers, they must know—if they allow themselves to think at all—that they are a constant cause of anxiety, and that should they not get married, there is every probability of their being, sooner or later, obliged to enter the battle of life utterly unprepared and unfitted for the fight."[5]

At the moderate end of the reform spectrum stood many who recognized this painful situation. Subtly opposing the norm, literature may present an unmarried woman confronting her restricted life. In Carey's *Aunt Diana*, when Alison's family needs her, she must return home, since "a daughter's place is with her widowed father" (20–22). Yet the same book presents another view, for, although Aunt Diana does not support herself through art, she considers painting essential to life: "I hope to do something good before I die, and if I do not succeed, well, my life will have been happier for trying" (36). Sketching the "deplorable sight" of real women "turning into old maids" and suffering a decline, the contemporary reformer Edward Wakefield uses truth, pathos, and hyperbole to show the need for change. After "reaching the bloom of beauty, full of health, spirits, and tenderness," women are seen "striving anxiously, aided by their mother, to become honoured and happy wives." Failing this goal leaves them no other: "then, fretting, growing thin, pale, listless, and cross," they "go mad or die of consumption," or perhaps find solace "in the belief of an approaching millennium, or in the single pursuit of happiness in another world, which this world has denied to them" (73). Carey's Diana found a solution in a natural vocation; if unpaid, her labor still gave meaning to her life.

Writers in reality as well as literature heed Diana's advice to Alison, that women should plan for the possibility of an independent life. In her nonfiction, popular novelist Dinah Mulock Craik contended that single women most need "something to do" (A *Woman's Thoughts about Women*, 1).

Insisting that their profound differences from men require women to seek specifically feminine occupations, Craik offered a conservative solution: a woman should first look for nearby appropriate work such as remedying a sloppy household, teaching a child, or caring for an elderly parent. If these are unavailable, she may "extend her service out of the home into the world" through one of the "female professions," such as "the instruction of youth, painting or art, literature, and the vocation of public entertainment, including actresses, singers, musicians, and the like" (3, 12, 33).

Suggesting women choose work allied to the traditional roles of nurturer and child-rearer or performed in the safety of the home, Craik warned how much women risked to "quit the kindly shelter and safe negativeness of a private life" (49). She barred women from jobs in government, law courts, or colleges, though she excepted from her restrictions the "rare and peculiar" writers and artists whose work may "spring from an irresistible impulse" and the "heroic" and "self-sacrificing" doctors, missionaries, scientists, and travellers (14, 16). Craik appealed to conservatives by explaining that work might prevent women from unhappy idleness *and* feminist agitation. Yet, while insisting that men's and women's work differ fundamentally ("one is abroad, the other at home: one external, the other internal: one active, the other passive"), she also said both are "honorable" and "difficult" (11). She believed a woman could sing, act, paint, or sculpt and still be both moral and a good housekeeper; she believed jobs involving handiwork (watchmaking, serving as a draper's assistant) or new skills (bookkeeping, being a telegraph clerk) could be respectable. Pleading with society—"a great fool" in its prejudices—not to make it impossible for a woman needing work to "fulfill her lot" (53), she offered a moderate and respected voice on the side of expanding opportunities.

Literature had no problem with the first of Craik's ideas, the propriety of selected volunteer activities, but that raises the issue of the value of women's unpaid labor. When Nettie in Oliphant's *The Doctor's Family* realizes her sister's family needs her help, she finds lodgings for them, sews the children's clothes, and fills the parental role abdicated by her sister and brother-in-law. Twice rejecting proposals, she fights against bitterness with "self-contempt and reproach." Although she answers the "simplest duty and necessity," not even "the natural generosity of her mind . . . could blind her eyes to the fact that she *had* given up her own happiness." Sympathizing with her plight, the narrator recognizes the "dark and perplexing shades" cast upon Nettie "as upon all other wayfarers in these complex paths" (218–20). The paths grow more complex as "natural duty" changes in ways Nettie might consider selfish, and women question sacrificing their lives and dreams for others.

Women who need to work fit a different mold from those who choose to work. Faithfully reflecting reality, Gaskell's *Cranford* asks the basic question: what job can Matty find that will support her and let her maintain gentility? Jessie, in the same novel, can choose among sewing, nursing, housekeeping, or working in a shop if she does not marry; naturally, she marries. Brontë's *Jane Eyre* presents a similar list for women of a slightly higher class: governess, seamstress, servant, nurse; "it can be no better" (331). Eliot's Gwendolyn in *Daniel Deronda* adds acting and singing to the list, though many would consider these ungenteel professions; lacking talent, she knows she must be a governess or wife, and end up a wife. Agnes in Dickens's *David Copperfield*, a talented and decent teacher, keeps a school for young girls in her home. In time she, too, marries. Julie in Ward's *Lady Rose's Daughter* selects another respectable option, becoming a paid companion—reading, writing letters, running errands, walking the dogs, and handling the social arrangements for an aristocrat. Some women occasionally even receive respect for working, not only in literature written by feminists like Stowe and Grand, but also in the works of more gentle reformers like Alcott and Charlotte Brontë. *Villette's* Lucy Snowe, who teaches out of financial need, encounters the common divided reactions: Polly Home pitying her and Polly's father respecting her courage and enterprise.

A conversation in Howells's *Silas Lapham* nicely summarizes the situation. The male secretary begins, "I suppose a great many pretty girls have to earn their living," and the bookkeeper responds. "Don't any of 'em like to do it. . . . They think it's a hardship, and I don't blame 'em. They have got a right to get married" (97). Yes, but increasingly, women asked in literature as in life: don't we also have the right to work?

Educational reformer Emily Davies saw the incongruity between a cult of work, which made a woman feel useless ("everywhere we hear that true happiness is to be found in work"), and the opposing cult of the ideal, idle woman, which forbade her working.[6] Watching his daughter fill her days with gardening and letter writing while awaiting a marriage that might never come, an overworked father might consider her lack of responsibilities pleasurable. But Davies insisted the girl had every right to be "discontent" in "an age in which idleness is accounted disgraceful." Perhaps the local laborers do not need charity and the village children have a good teacher; perhaps the young woman must later support herself; perhaps she simply wants to work. Davies knew that some women, "driven" to do more, had managed with great difficulty, but she felt "there must be something wrong in social regulations which make a demand for exceptional wisdom and strength on the part of any particular class." Instead, education should help women plan for a career other than or in addition to marriage, with a wide range of jobs, from factory overseer to workhouse chaplain. If she subsequently marries, her education and job experience would make her better able to raise her children, talk with her husband, sympathize with his work, and function responsibly in society. Saying that an educated, organized woman with good servants could do her housework in an hour a day, Davies pointed to married women who teach or write, and to clergymen's wives, who "notoriously undertake a large share of extra-domestic work" without neglecting spouses or children. Training young women would be a kind of "insurance—the provision of a resource in case of widowhood or other misfortune, which it is well to have in reserve."

As philosophical issues were addressed by social reformers, practical actions met practical needs. For example, when the reformers who tried to gather petitions in support of the Married Woman's Property Bill in 1855 realized the legislation would not pass then, they founded the Society for Promoting the Employment of Women. The society shared a building with the *English Woman's Journal*, the first real forum to publicize and debate women's situation. Such groups fought a hard battle against much resistance. Only rare reformers like Antoinette Brown Blackwell and her sister-in-law, Lucy Stone, argued that even married women with children should join the work force if they wished. Blackwell, who worked as a minister after marriage, suggested the revolutionary idea that mothers and fathers share child care. To these women, work was natural.

Like such powerful reformers, John Stuart Mill stunned, frightened, and angered readers of *The Subjection of Women* by boldly confronting the underlying objections to women's changing roles. He insisted that the sexes were inherently equal ("any of the mental differences supposed to exist between women and men are but the natural effect of the differences in their education and circumstance"), that women's subordination had political rather than innate causes, and that women's supposed "disabilities" are "clung to" in order to justify and maintain that subordination. "The generality of the male sex cannot yet tolerate the idea of living with an equal," for they would have to "admit the injustice of excluding half the human race" from the best jobs (perhaps to protect these positions for men), while "ordaining from their birth either that they are not, and cannot by any possibility become, fit for employments which are legally open to the stupidest and basest of the other sex" (chapter 3). Though others agreed with Mill and strove for change, few spoke with so clear a challenge to basic convictions or so direct a confrontation to sexual fears.

Unmarried and discontent, married and bored, or simply needing money, more women sought work after an unusual period of imposed idleness. Harriet Martineau succinctly summarized: "the conditions of female life have sustained as much alteration as the fortunes of other classes by the progress of civilisation"; the numbers of women available to work drastically increased, but attitudes had not changed.[7] She challenged people to admit it is "false . . . that every woman is supported (as the law supposes her to be represented) by her father, her brother, or her husband." She notes "we are only beginning to think of the claim of all workers—that their work should be paid for by its quality, and its place in the market." She pointed to a basic discrepancy: "A social organisation framed for a community of which half stayed at home, while the other half went out to work, cannot answer the purposes of a society, of which a quarter remains at home while three-quarters go out to work."

Though speaking more gently than Martineau, Alcott represents her conviction that women should have the right to work and that society should not hinder but help them. Jo, the most appealing of the "little women," works for money, but also for fulfillment; she reflects her creator, who worked to help her family but could never stop writing. In *Little Men* and *Jo's Boys*, Jo combines marriage, a family, and the double career of helping to run a school and writing literature. Not surprisingly, the school and college she fosters attract young women who "were hungry for whatever could fit them to face the world and earn a living, being driven by necessity, the urgency of some half-unconscious talent, or the restlessness of strong young natures to break away from the narrow life which no longer satisfied" (*Boys*, 222). Reflecting Alcott, Jo sometimes reverses the rule: of Nan, a future doctor, Jo says she "shall earn her place first, and prove that she can fill it; then she may marry if she likes, and can find a man worthy of her" (123).

Work, originally called *Success*, contains Alcott's most direct attack on society's treatment of working women, and its heroine illustrates women's growing consciousness. Christie toils as maid, actress, seamstress (first in a factory, then doing piecework at home), and again as housekeeper, but in a supportive environment. Thus, she learns the misery of dependence and the limited opportunities for women. Finally she joins an association of working women, even speaking publicly. Alcott knew what she was discussing, having sewn dolls' clothes for neighbors at 13 and worked as a paid companion at 16. Even after beginning to sell her stories, Alcott toiled as governess, seamstress, laundress, housekeeper, servant, nurse, and companion to support her mother, her younger sister May (model for Amy), and the family of her widowed sister Anna (model for Meg). Not surprisingly, she said her many responsibilities kept her from concentrating on writing. She was dissatisfied with *Work*, into which she poured her consciousness of social reform: education, jobs, abolition, suffrage, and the need for new social and moral ideals.

Even in romantic novels clearly not heeding issues of reform, similar ideas occur. Women characters know their lives preclude fulfilling their potential. Though Lucilla is active in politics, "her capabilities were greater than her work" (Oliphant, *Marjoribanks*, 107). Others worry specifically about their future if they do not wed. One heroine decides that if she remains single it would be "impossible" to "live on in this rose-scented stillness of the old house and garden . . . while the agony of the world rang in her ears"; "she must take her life in her hands, offering it day by day to this hungry human need" (Ward, *Diana*, 501–2). So too, as late as Woolf's *Night and Day*, Mary and Katharine see work as a substitute for marriage. Gillian, in Broughton's *Second Thoughts*, wants to continue her temperance work in the city to help others and to give her life value. But her guardian, Dr. Burnet, worries for her safety among the rough townsfolk. While he may be correct, he offensively jokes that the idea would have merit if she were "fifty" and "slightly humpbacked." She berates his seeming "incredulous" when she speaks of her "former usefulness" in running a house, working in the village schools and temperance room; but surely "even" he should "understand what it must be to a woman with an active head, capable hands, and God knows, a willing heart, to be kept in enforced idleness for six whole months of her life; and, if she makes an effort to break from her bondage of sloth, to be sent back to it with a sneer and a smile" (22).

Gillian's attitude, ever more common, appears most often in literature by women. Charlotte Brontë strongly supports women's right to work, even seeing it as a duty they owe themselves. In *Shirley*, as in her other literary forums for social reform, Brontë rejects the idea that "virtue" might "lie in abnegation of self," and ponders, "Is this enough? Is it to live?" (158). Shirley asks Caroline the customary question, "Don't you wish you had a profession—a trade?" Her friend quickly answers, "I wish it fifty times a day. As it is, I often wonder what I came into the world for." Saying work gives women something worth doing, she reinforces several stereotypes when she argues that even if work makes women "masculine, coarse, unwomanly," as Shirley fears, it does not "signify" for unmarried women, so long as they are "decent, decorous, and neat" (203).

Further discussing the dilemma of "old maids" lets Brontë justify the value of work in itself, and to do so in powerful language. One character notes that unmarried men always "have something to do," while "their sisters have no earthly employment, but household work and sewing; no earthly pleasure, but an unprofitable visiting; and no hope, in all their life to come, of any thing better." Reflecting society's dream and reality, he expounds that all women wish to marry but many will not, for "the matrimonial market is overstocked." Fathers expect their daughters to stay home with nothing significant to do, "contentedly, regularly, uncomplainingly, all their lives long, as if they had no germs of faculties for any thing else: a doctrine as reasonable to hold as it would be that the fathers have no faculties but for eating what their daughters cook, or for wearing what they sew." In sympathy with the women's movement, the speaker concludes with some telling questions: "Could men live so themselves? Would they not be weary? And when there came no relief to their weariness, but only reproaches at its slightest manifestation, would not their weariness ferment in time to frenzy?" (348–49).

Brontë supports combining marriage and a career. In *The Professor*, when William Crimsworth and Frances Henri marry, their common profession as teachers enriches their relationship. At first William asks Frances to quit work after marriage, with an explanation reminiscent of the hierarchy in Bradstreet's poem two centuries before: God takes care of man, who takes care of woman. William says, "there is something flattering to a man's strength, something consonant to his honourable pride in the idea of becoming the providence of what he loves—feeding and clothing it, as God does the lilies of the field." But Frances objects, "Think of my marrying you to be kept by you." Rather, she as an individual and they as a couple will be better off if she works: her days would otherwise be "dull"; "I should get depressed and sullen, and you would soon tire of me"; "people who are only in each other's company for amusement, never really like each other so well, or esteem each other so fully, as those who work together, and perhaps suffer together." He accepts this as "God's truth," a truth many contemporaries could not concede (199–200). Brontë had fallen in love as a pupil-teacher, and Frances and William undoubtedly act out her dream, but she did not dream alone: many women wished for the fulfillment of work and marriage. In other works by reformers, such as Stowe's *My Wife and I*, that dream also comes true.

To an ardent feminist like Grand, women's right to work becomes a new norm, although generating much heated debate. In *The Heavenly Twins*, a minister objects to the women's movement, contending that "the way in which women are putting themselves forward just now on any subject which happens to attract their attention is quite deplorable, I think; and pushing themselves into the professions, too, and entering into rivalry with men generally." A second man disagrees that this is "unwomanly," alleging that women want "to earn their bread honestly; but there is no doubt that the majority of men would rather see them on the streets" (194). The title character in *Ideala* consistently lobbies for the "many thousands of us" who "have no object in life," whose household duties take "on the average, half an hour a day" and social duties not much more. Unhappily married and childless, Ideala loses credibility with her critics. Still, anticipating Gilman's optimistic credo quoted at the head of this chapter, she says, "My function is not to do, but to be. . . . I am one of the weary women of the nineteenth century. No other age could have produced me" (15).

Babs the Impossible vindicates the New Woman in all her frightening and exciting differences. One character speaks of the "cruel ache of expectancy" that, in the absence of alternatives, leads a woman to "succumb to the first who held his arms out to her" (115). University graduate and tutoress Barbara Land undercuts the traditional argument about women's inferiority by observing "a subjected race produces no great work of art"; once women are no longer "the thrall of law and custom . . . they will succeed" (345). Sir Owen reminds Babs that confusion and fear accompany change: "The Old Woman . . . would give anything to have done what the New Woman has done, to be what the New Woman is, but cannot forgive her for what she has done and is." Fear or jealousy lead "gross men" and "ill-conditioned women" at first to castigate reformers they later admire, like Florence Nightingale (336). To Grand, the Florence Nightingales of the world prove Barbara Land's point: once set free, women can do anything. And increasingly, they gain their freedom. As Babs notes, thanks to social change the "New Woman has aspirations and ideals" she can hope to fulfill, unlike the "Old Woman," who dreamed but was doomed to frustration and emptiness (381).

By the end of the period, authors like Grand could suggest that women had the right to work not just for money but for fulfillment; they even had the right and ability to combine marriage and work. Gissing could write *The Odd Women* about unmarried working heroines who may be "odd," but whose story he tells sympathetically. Still, the questions had not been answered to everyone's satisfaction.

Even at the turn of the century, Charlotte Perkins Gilman continued to fight for the feminist minority. Although conditions had improved by the time she wrote *Women and Economics*, she still saw disparities between men's and women's opportunities, and the injustice and waste—for women and for society—rankled. She argued that society cruelly barred women from employment while valuing people for what they do. Quoting the proverb, "the woman, the cat, and the chimney should never leave the house" (65), she observed that confinement precludes women's developing their talents or minds, preventing them from as yet assuming men's jobs. She countered the familiar argument that women's economic independence injures the family by saying that people who marry for reasons other than finance can achieve the best relationships, free of dominance and fully democratic. And she insisted that both women and men grow and become fully human through work.

Such a revolutionary concept would have stunned society in 1800 and was still unpopular in 1900. In literature as in life, people tried to keep the status quo; change, whether from economic necessity or from philosophical development, causes discomfort. Yet, society was altered, by world economics and technological development as well as the efforts of feminist reformers. Whatever people desired as an ideal, the fact was that employment changed dramatically for women, and as it did, so did their image and their roles. Still, those who accepted the idea of women working, even those who applauded it, still wondered: could or should women work in shops or factories? could or should they be judges, doctors, or government officials? The problem of the job market remained.

Professions and Professionalism

Early on, the sons of the middle class found the door to the traditional professions shut; daughters found it locked. As education replaced patronage and occupational groups felt uniquely qualified, jobs in medicine, law, and teaching became professions, carrying a certain mystique and fitting the ideal of effort leading to success. Truthfully reflecting reality, literature depicts virtually no women entering the traditional professions of the church, government, law, or military, and none become architects or engineers. In contrast, throughout the century roughly one in ten male characters served in the military, about the same percentage in law; clergymen reached a high of nearly one in five at midcentury, five times the ratio as at the beginning or end of the period, and government service was even more popular. Lagging behind society in enlarging job options, literature shows very few men and no women in new professions such as architecture and engineering, none at all before midcentury. As teaching offered the most opportunities for real women, so it is most popular for female characters, but literature virtually ignores women's role in revolutionizing nursing. Male characters nearly always obtain the jobs they want, usually in the traditional professions; women rarely want jobs at all.

In the real world, qualifying exams slowly unlocked the civil service; abolishing the purchase of commissions eased military promotions. Although women could not enlist in the military, some served in the century's bloodiest conflict, the American Civil War, disguised as men or working behind the scenes as spies. As army nurses, they revolutionized medicine until dysentery and sepsis no longer caused more deaths than wounds did.

Impressment, the debauched life of bachelor soldiers, and the trauma of a woman's separation from her beloved soldier or sailor are minor literary themes. Novels display the impact of military life on women as wives or daughters. To Becky Sharpe in Thackeray's *Vanity Fair* (1848), the army means a life of travel and socializing, for she ignores the misery of war. Less naive, Godwin opposes his son's joining the army despite the social advantage (Helme, *Farmer*). The upper class considers the military an attractive option, especially for younger sons; here literature is accurate, if conservative. Marcus Hill contemplates three commonplace occupations: the army, government, or managing his future wife's estate (Clay, *Heiress*).

In England, to keep the "wrong" people out of the legal profession, potential barristers had to pass an examination mirroring an upper-class education, then gain acceptance at the Inns of Court. This required fees, a deposit (except for graduates of Oxford, Cambridge, London, or Dublin universities), and an introduction. Since even the more accessible branches of the law in both nations demanded apprenticeships, money, and influence, middle-class men often became law clerks, copyists, or law writers, paid on a piecework basis. But if men found the law less accessible than medicine or teaching, women found it virtually impenetrable. In England, to the end of the century, there were no women barristers, solicitors, or even law students, and male clerks outnumbered females by 250 to 1. The situation was slightly better in America, where each state had its own code. By the 1860s, women petitioned several states for admission to the bar; gradually, starting in the west, states permitted women to practice law; by 1900, women attended law schools.

In literature, all lawyers are male. Some actively practice (Trollope, *Orley*; Carey, *Herb*), some use their training indirectly (Oliver Markham, an M.P. in Ward's *Diana*), some quit the field entirely (Thackeray, *Pendennis*).

Literature's law clerks (Dickens, *Pickwick Papers* [1837]; Egan, *Flower*) reveal the meager chance of rising through hard work: Charley was "doing his best to fit himself either for the bar, if he could raise the necessary funds to be called to it, or to be a first-class solicitor" (Egan, 1:49).

Real university graduates retained the prestigious positions of government administrators and department heads, while other men and increasing numbers of women served as clerks, secretaries, or telegraphers. Government service often gave women entry to further jobs. From 1841 to 1891 the number of Englishmen in government quintupled; the number of women, though still far less than men, multiplied nearly 40 times (Booth, cited in Wrigley, 253–58). By 1911, women held over one-fourth of the jobs in the British Central Government (Holcombe, 212).

Government hired women partly because they cost less than equivalently trained men. Women worked as clerks, typists, telephone and telegraph operators, supervisors, factory inspectors, and postmistresses, attracted to these jobs for their comparative security, steady employment, shorter work weeks, better sick leave, vacations, and pensions. But women earned half or less of a man's salary and had less chance of promotion. Only widows or single women could hold certain jobs, which forced them to retire if they married.

Especially conservative about government, literature fails even to acknowledge female clerks. Many male characters serve in Congress or Parliament, from Adams's *Democracy* to Disraeli's *Coningsby, Sybil, Tancred,* and *Vivian Grey* (though the hero of the last rejects politics—as well as the law, church, and army—to become a wanderer). Doctor Bold, in Trollope's *The Warden,* serves as a town councilman out of an interest in reform. Eden rather unsympathetically outlines the daily life of government clerks and their families: the men's parents supplement their salaries so they can live at the standards of gentility their wives desire (*Couple*). In these works, women are wives, daughters, or mothers; at most, they serve peripherally and unofficially. Mrs. Lee in *Democracy* becomes involved in politics in the orthodox feminine way of quiet, private machinations. One heroine openly helps her friend in his campaign, even though women can't "be on the committee" (Oliphant, *Marjoribanks,* 16). A very few stories of social and political activism, like Eliot's *Felix Holt* or Gaskell's *North and South* and *Mary Barton,* allow women direct involvement, not holding office but assisting in reform. Political activists like abolitionists or feminists rarely appear.

Real women seeking careers in religion became "missionaries" or "service readers," visiting the poor and engaging in charity, but almost none became ministers, certainly not in major religions. A clergyman's hours and salary—and thus, his wife's position—depended on whether he served as vicar (and often the only educated man) in a small village, or as schoolteacher or perhaps curate in a large city parish. When Antoinette Brown Blackwell attended Oberlin College, hoping to become an ordained minister, most men rejected the idea, but in 1853 she reached her goal; by 1900, more than a dozen denominations allowed women to preach, usually without ordination (Firor, 44, 47, 134–35).

In most literature presenting the clergy, women serve passive roles—wives and daughters whose lives are fashioned by the ministers in the family. Gaskell's *North and South* presents a minister who decides to leave the church because he doubts his fitness to serve, moving his family to a factory town. Eden's *Semi-Detached House* shows a curate who seeks a vicar's position to gain the money needed for marriage. Other characters raise their wives' status as they advance through the church (Gore, *Mothers*; Cholmondeley, *Red Pottage* [1899]).

In novels like *The Warden* (1855), *Barchester Towers*, and *Framley Parsonage*, Trollope concentrates on his clergymen's human side, believing, as he writes in *The Last Chronicle of Barset*, that they have a great indirect influence as role models. Not everyone succeeds in the church. Witness Eliot's Casaubon in *Middlemarch* or one of Oliphant's many clergymen, Proctor of *The Rector*: too learned and cold for his new community or a minister's life, Proctor accepts a fellowship to Oxford. Dissenting ministers, coming from and ministering to the lower classes, lacking in education and social polish, face far more difficult times. The impact on their wives—obvious in Oliphant's *Salem Chapel*, and in Gaskell's *Ruth* and *Cousin Phyllis*—is poignantly described in Eliot's *Scenes from Clerical Life*, where Reverend Barton's wife, weakened by repeated pregnancies, never stops working, and the family struggles to remain genteel on a too-small salary.

A woman could serve as a minister only outside the mainstream churches. Dinah, of Eliot's *Adam Bede*, though lacking Antoinette Brown Blackwell's education or social background, shares her motivation and commitment. A mill-hand, Dinah preaches as an itinerant Methodist minister. She agrees to marry Adam only after he promises he will not hinder her work with the poor or her preaching. But Dinah is exceptional in many ways, not only in being the rare female minister.

Literature virtually ignores real women's small but significant steps in fields like law and religion. In failing to include women engineers, scientists, and architects, however, literature truly reflects society. Yet the goal is not verisimilitude, for literature also discounts these fields for men, instead creating an idealized world appealing to readers. Real technological advances led former artisans to become engineers, engineers to become civil or mechanical or railway or hydraulic or electrical engineers, and engineering to go large- scale, with hundreds of firms employing 10 or more people; almost no women became engineers. Other jobs, while not professions, suggest the new range of employment options and specialization: copyists convert to clerks, then bookkeepers, abstractors, even accountants; women become typists, telegraph operators, telephone supervisors. By 1900, there were a few women accountants, as well as printers, social workers, bank tellers, and overseers of factories, workhouses, and reformatories. Based on traditional female roles and thus especially fitting, social work turned volunteer work into paid employment.

A handful of male characters late in the period consider the newest professions, usually with reluctance, unless they come from the lower or lower-middle classes. Then, realistically, jobs like engineering offer social advance: thus, Paul Manning moves from clerk to railroad engineer, while the engineer Edward Holdsworth receives a promotion when he goes to Canada to supervise the beginning of a new line (Gaskell, *Cousin*). More typically and conservatively, an architect (Galsworthy, *Man*) and scientists (Wells, *Tono-Bungay, Ann-Veronica*) fall into social limbo. Lucius in Trollope's *Orley Farm* considers engineering beneath him and ends up a gentleman farmer, also the fate of John in Hungerford's *Molly Bawn*, who works as an engineer until he inherits money. The new professions clearly had something of a taint, according to literature. If fictional men enter the traditional professions, the women stay home. Medicine receives some attention, but literature accords only three fields, two of which are professions, a consideration for women that matches reality: teaching, the arts, and needlework.

Medicine

It took the introduction of professional education, qualifying exams, and licensing, as well as changes in attitude, to open medicine to women. Scientific advances such as the use of ether anesthesia in the 1840s, the beginning of immunizations after the 1850s, and the introduction of antiseptic methods in the 1860s enhanced the need for education and the prestige associated with medicine. A man might be a well-paid and highly respected surgeon, a medical health officer, a druggist, or an ointment maker. In the last decades of the century, women received doctorates in science in America and developed the research field of food science and nutrition. A few became medical doctors, and many more entered related fields such as nursing and pharmacy.

The greatest challenges to female physicians came from the cult of femininity and the determination of men to prevent women from sullying themselves—or taking men's jobs. Martineau wrote of barriers erected by the "jealousy of the medical profession" (*ER*, 331). Jealousy mingled with patronization when the *Lancet*, a respected medical journal, suggested that "those ladies of restless energy who now besiege the portals of our profession" might supervise day nurseries (Hewitt, 164).

Although men's presence during childbirth had once been considered indecorous, when midwifery gave way to technologically advanced obstetrics, women had to yield to men. But gradually women succeeded in besieging the portals, as discussed in chapter 2. By 1900, several hundred women physicians practiced in both nations, and women comprised one out of five students in major American medical schools. In the mid-nineteenth century there were fewer than 200 women doctors in America; a century later there were nearly 30,000. Still, male doctors outnumbered females by 200 to 1 at the end of the era. In 1918 Alice Hamilton was an anomaly on the Harvard Medical School faculty; she could not march with her colleagues at commencement, nor could she enter the Harvard Club (Firor, 53–55).

Women made the greatest strides in nursing, a job fitting their traditional nurturing role.[8] At first, hospital nurses—often drunk, rowdy, or promiscuous—spent long hours performing routine tasks of physical drudgery; private nurses cared for middle- and upper-class patients in their homes. Pupils in the new nursing schools learned how to behave appropriately as well as how to maintain antiseptic procedures, use innovative devices like thermometers and syringes, and keep medical charts and records. Nightingale established a separate program for "lady pupils," freeing them from the matron's patronizing watch, night duty, and routine tasks, and leading them to supervisory positions. Physicians did not always welcome these more qualified nurses, who might question their orders, and the regular students objected to the "ladies'" special treatment, even though the former were paid during training while the latter paid their own way. By the time the programs merged, nursing had become a respectable profession and a significant aspect of health care delivery.

Working conditions did not match new qualifications. Nurses averaged 15-hour days at salaries comparable to better-paid domestic servants. Competition increased as the number of nurses multiplied more than 200 times by the early 1900s. Nursing gave women a chance to use their minds and education in a job with increasingly high standards and recognition; it made them independent and productive without sacrificing gentility or femininity. But doctors, primarily men, earned both prestige and high salaries; nurses remained secondary to doctors, and they were primarily women.

Literature rightly reflects the very small number of women physicians but downplays the number of male doctors or female nurses. Representative fiction suggests that men avoided medicine: no more than 1 in 10 become doctors. Still, that is 20 times the number of female doctors. Even as the numbers of female nurses and midwives triples to about 1 in 30 at the end of the period, men still outnumber women by 3 to 1. But the rare women characters who enter medicine receive much consideration by their authors, usually appearing for both social commentary and literary reasons.

Typically, literature dealing with doctors places women in secondary roles, showing how a husband's or father's practice affects a woman's life: for example, Gibson marries a widow with a daughter because he cannot manage his house, daughter, and medical practice after his wife's death (Gaskell, *Wives*). The kind of medicine a man practices also determines his family's life-style. Philip Carey attends school part-time, works as an apprentice, and finally enters medical school at 23, eventually settling as a country doctor with the good Sally (Maugham, *Bondage*). In contrast, the wealthy Dr. May in Yonge's *The Daisy Chain*, educated in London and Paris, maintains a country house with many servants for his family of 11 children. His daughters have a governess, then stay at home or marry; his sons attend Eton and Oxford, then enter the military, church, or medicine.

Though trained as a surgeon, John Bold has more interest in social reform (Trollope, *Warden*). In contrast, Dr. Galbraith becomes a doctor from financial need, but "continues to practice for the love of science, and also for philanthropic motives" (Grand, *Twins*, 42). In Kingsley's *Two Years Ago*, village physician Tom Thurnall faces a cholera epidemic that taxes his ability and patience: in their "ignorance, pride, laziness, and superstition," the villagers brand Tom "very silly" and "impertinent" for suggesting that overcrowding spreads disease (238). Women help Tom as nurses during the epidemic, taking on many unpleasant and even dangerous tasks.

In that unofficial way, heroines care for a sick child or elderly parent, visit poor families in the village, or assist at local charitable institutions. This important work brings no income and little recognition. Dr. Thorne faces the problem that, as a bachelor, he is unsure how to talk about "Matilda's stomach, and the growing pains in Fanny's legs" (Trollope, *Thorne*, 29). But few characters or authors accept the solution of female doctors. On the contrary, the unpleasant Dr. Maclure exemplifies current views in suggesting that Beth's sense of medicine's great "responsibilities" proves it would be a "folly" for sentimental, emotional women to become doctors (Grand, *Beth*, 326–27).

Perhaps women physicians outnumber nurses in literature because being a doctor has the potential for both glamour and thematic conflict. Dr. Prance, a minor character in James's *The Bostonians*, in part a study of lesbianism, appears almost asexual, but is very professional. A more complex situation occurs in Howells's *Dr. Breene's Practice* (1881), where the lonely, insecure, but feminine heroine becomes a doctor after being jilted and thus failing at woman's usual role. Grace blushes, cries, worries about her patients' and her own respectability, and is defined by her relationships with men, not by her profession. She rightly observes two problems women doctors face: lack of experience and lack of patient trust. Initially abandoning medicine upon marriage, she later finds a perfect solution in ministering to the children of her husband's employees. Dr. Zaidee Atalanta Lloyd, heroine of Phelps's *Dr. Zay* (1882), establishes her career before falling in love. Although Phelps implies Dr. Zay will continue to practice after marriage, she conveniently ends the story to avoid having to examine the outcome.

In Alcott's *Little Men*, Nan likes to care for the other children's injuries and has no interest in marriage. Jo tells her husband that if Nan cannot find "something to live for" she may become "one of the sharp, strong, discontented women." Besides, both recognize Nan "will make a capital doctor, for she has courage, strong nerves, a tender heart, and an intense love and pity for the weak and suffering." Determined not to shut any doors just "because she was a little woman," they agree to "persuade her father to let her study medicine" (216–17). In *Jo's Boys* Nan is "a busy, cheerful, independent spinster" who "dedicated her life to her suffering sisters and their children, in which true woman's work she found abiding happiness" (285). Exceptional among women characters, Nan would have been very lucky to have found people as supportive as Jo and Fritz Bhaer had she lived in the real world. Medicine remained a field for men in literature even more than in reality, but once again, writers gently point the way toward change.

Teaching

Like nursing, in which women also made tremendous progress for themselves and the profession, teaching conformed to the feminine ideal of nurturer and social servant. At first, no training was needed to teach young children, a job seen as merely expanding women's natural duties. As higher education opened for women students and teachers, however, the job changed from an economic necessity to a genteel profession.

The governess's occupation maintained her respectability but offered social and financial stresses. Incompetence abounded as desperate women fell into the job after the death of a father or husband, and as 17-year-olds tried to teach children only a few years younger. Neither servant nor family member, allowed no visitors and little free time, the governess inhabited a social limbo. Rather than job security, she faced the natural end of her position as her charges grew up, certain that in old age she would find only destitution, not jobs. Magazine articles and books counseled parents (chiefly mothers) to visit their children's schoolrooms, support and respect the governess, and pay her more. The flood of requests to organizations like the Governesses' Benevolent Institution confirms the gravity of the situation: five or six times as many candidates applied for annuities as were available; over 3,000 used the home between jobs; and some 14,000 found positions through the registry (Neff, 176–77).

Martineau compares governesses to "the hand-loom weavers, and the slop-makers, with the aggravation that the sufferers are, generally speaking, gentlewomen by birth, and universally accustomed to the comforts, and many of the luxuries, of life." No longer "supported by father, brother or husband," they "reversed the old rule of woman's destiny" and paid the man's debts or covered his "vices" or "shiftlessness." Martineau felt "sheer pain" at seeing "old age, or impaired health in middle age, amidst perfect destitution; failing sight, paralysed limbs, over-wrought brain, and no resource or prospect whatever; though (or because) the sufferers have supported orphans, saved a father from bankruptcy, educated brothers, or kept infirm and helpless relatives off the rates. We need not go on. The evil is "plain enough" (*ER*, 331).

Private schools offered more chance for promotion than state schools but paid less—sometimes what a shop assistant might earn, and sometimes no more than room and board. The exceptional prestigious position at a fine preparatory school remained the right of upper-class male university graduates. Salaries gradually improved, though women still earned less than men even for the same job. As the percentage of teachers with college degrees or specialized training increased, more men than women earned university degrees. Men headed all boys' schools, nearly all coeducational schools, and many girls' schools, as well. Virtually all schools forced women to resign if they married and certainly if they became pregnant. The rare female members of a university faculty tended to be lecturers or assistants rather than professors, except at women's colleges.

By the 1860s professional organizations strove for better training, reduced class size, higher salaries, pensions, relief funds, regulations involving tenure, and government support for secondary education. Some groups focused on specialized fields such as physical education, working with the deaf or blind, and vocational education; some included both professionals and interested amateurs. As university education departments made professional training more respectable, men joined women in such organizations and founded their own.

Women flocked to teaching, more than five times as many in 1900 as in 1800. Once able to join only the Ladies' Committees of England's National Union of Teachers, by 1914 women accounted for 80 percent of the union's certified teachers (Holcombe, 38). More than half the American schoolteachers in 1900 were women, with northern and western states in the lead. In the 1890s, 314 English school inspectors were men paid between £80 and £100 a year, but there were also 7 female visitors, earning from £50 to £85 (Booth, 2d ser. 187). Granting the disparity in numbers and salaries, this represented one more barrier women had overturned.

When Sophia Jex-Blake tutored at Queen's, her father refused to let her accept a salary usually associated with a lower social class, so she worked without pay. By the end of the period, middle-class women could teach knowing they would be paid (if not well paid) and could accept job and salary without loss of status.

At least in literature, teaching offers opportunities to meet people and maybe find a husband. Impoverished heroines could teach without loss of gentility and without any special talent. Whether because of authors' personal experience with education, or because of the options teachers provide to plot and theme, or because of interest in women's changing roles, more women in representative fiction work as teachers than in any other paid profession. Prior to the 1830s, virtually no male characters and only a handful of women serve as schoolteachers, none serve as tutors, no men and essentially no women as governesses. Then the number of male teachers steadily increases, mostly in schools rather than as tutors: the accurate rise masks unrealistically low percentages, only 1 in 10 at the highest. Less accurate about women, literature shows a steady percentage of schoolteachers at about 1 in 20 and about the same number of governesses at midcentury; the percentage of governesses slips to 1 in 100 by the end of the era.

Idealistically, Brontë's *The Professor* presents a couple who enjoy teaching, found a school, and work together after marriage. But for essentially all other women, teaching is a stopgap, a financial necessity, not a calling or special interest. Unlike Reverend Hale in Gaskell's *North and South*, who becomes a private tutor after leaving the church, most women lack appropriate education to teach; but like him, they need an income. Routinely, love as well as financial need motivates action. In Carey's *The Mistress of Brae Farm*, Lorraine takes a job as a governess to flee a man she loves unrequitedly. In contrast, Sophia of Bennett's *The Old Wives' Tale* leaves her teaching job to be near Gerald, a salesman with whom she later elopes.

While teaching may not provide adequate income or comfortable status, it offers job opportunities partly by requiring little preparation. Unlike women, male tutors and teachers usually have university educations. But realistically, lack of regulations or high expectations permits unsuitable teachers to find jobs, as does the unqualified schoolmistress Maria Albany (Hofland, *Daughter*). Cynthia in Howells's *The Landlord at Lion's Head* teaches during the school year, but by working as a housekeeper in the summer, she loses face with the inn's female guests. Sue Bridehead in Hardy's *Jude the Obscure* and Brontë's Jane Eyre receive some training before seeking work, Sue in a day school, Jane as governess and teacher. Describing Tom's schoolmaster in *The Mill on the Floss*, Eliot says Mr. Stelling was like many clergymen with "narrow intellects and large wants" and an "income . . . proportioned not to their wants but to their intellect"; still, "education was almost entirely a matter of luck—usually of ill-luck—in those distant days," and Tom was "not so very unlucky" (149–51). If he doesn't teach his pupils well, Mr. Stelling at least feeds them well, unlike Squeers in Dickens's *Nicholas Nickleby*. In that novel and in Reynolds's *The Soldier's Wife*, headmasters freely advertise to attract pupils and faculty to schools little resembling the ones in the fliers; as Hughes's *Tom Brown's Schooldays* says, schools range tremendously in nature, philosophy, and quality.

Requiring even less training than teachers, governesses were more dependent on their employers, making it easy for authors to plunge heroines into situations of conflict and tension. Contrasting teachers and governesses, Carey naturally uses a man in the first role, a woman in the second. Mr. Royston, the local schoolmaster, is an Oxford graduate who wears a cap and gown to work. Miss Osborne, an experienced governess who can teach music, drawing, French, and even German, can be choosy about a new job after her pupil marries. Determined not to live in, she finds a position with that "moderate degree of freedom" (*Men*, 215). Brontë's Jane Eyre, not quite 18, is less demanding when advertising: "A young lady accustomed to tuition . . . is desirous of meeting with a situation in a private family where the children are under fourteen. . . . She is qualified to teach the usual branches of a good English education, together with French, Drawing, and Music." The narrator reminds us, "In those days, reader, this now narrow catalogue of accomplishments, would have been held tolerably comprehensive" (84).

Literature often bemoans the governess's plight. Marryat's *Too Good for Him* presents an ex-governess who struggles to subsist on translations and help from a former pupil. In contrast, an unusually blessed governess receives a pension when her pupil outgrows her services (Gore, *Progress*). More characteristically, a cook declares governesses "ain't near as well off as we servants. We get our work done and then sit down to a nice bit of supper, and have some fun, for we're all equals"; but in the governess's rare free minutes, she "sits all alone in the schoolroom . . . with no one to speak to, and nothing to think on but the better days as are gone and the worser days is coming" (Guyton, *Married*, 23–24). Hugh Sutherland "would have disliked the thought of being a tutor all his days, occupying a kind of neutral territory between the position of a gentleman and that of a menial" (MacDonald, *David*, 210). Unlike governesses, Hugh can expect to escape his job if he wants.

Anne Brontë suggests the ideal in *Agnes Grey*, whose heroine remarkably regards her career with joy. At 19, Agnes thinks it would be "delightful" to be a governess, "to go out into the world; to enter a new life; to act for myself; to exercise my unused faculties; to try my unknown powers; to earn my own maintenance, and something to comfort and help my father, mother, and sister" (10). When her first job fails to match her dream—the family undercuts her authority, lets the older children bully her, and moves the baby's crib into her room so she can double as nursemaid—she chooses her next position more carefully. At 20, Agnes works for a family of four spoiled children and stays with them until the youngest outgrows a governess. Returning home, she and her mother open a small, orderly school. Finally, she fulfills the dream of many a governess in life and literature: having proven herself and achieved independence, she marries the man she loves; her mother hires an assistant for the school, and Agnes teaches her own three children.

Unlike a schoolteacher, a governess working in a home can only "stand between the children and the faults of the people about them" (Martineau, *Deerbrook* [1839]). Although Agnes Grey and others can attest to that truth and to what another character calls the "evils" of the governess's anomalous social position, Martineau's proselytizing novel blames women's expectations as well: to be content, women must know what to expect and renounce false dreams of happiness (20–22).

Maybe so, but social and literary realities justify the high level of discontent. Most female characters teach because they have to, serve as governesses rather than in schools, and lack preparation for or interest in the field. Teaching may keep them fed, housed, and genteel; but it rarely keeps them content, fitting both romantic images of woman's idealized role and new ideas of transforming that role. Largely ignoring changes in the profession or in attitudes toward teaching, authors choose this career to describe the glory of the virtuous ingenue who teaches until she finds her true vocation and reaps her reward in marriage, or to lament the misery of the trapped spinster whose limited options symbolize the need for reform.

The Arts

To serve as muse for a male artist, inspiring him through physical beauty that symbolized inner purity, fit woman's idealized role; to heed the muse and create art of her own was another story. Artists and writers—especially women—hovered on the fringes of respectability. Although some people, accepting the passion of artists, writers, or actors, absolved them from the usual social constraints, others frowned on them as bohemian. It took unusual talent to succeed in the arts but little talent to try, so leisured men and women occasionally wielded paintbrush or pen in pursuit of creativity, if not a living. While some women turned hobbies such as painting on glass into new trades, the most popular and acceptable pursuits for women were writing in general and novel writing in particular.

Women writers tended to be classed by themselves, and not positively, despite the tremendous popularity of individuals like Harriet Beecher Stowe in America and Charlotte Yonge in England. Thus Emerson described Helen Hunt Jackson as the best *woman* poet of her time. Critics who thought the novels of "Currer, Acton, and Ellis Bell" were unique and powerful reclassified the books as minor women's novels after identifying the authors as Charlotte, Anne, and Emily Brontë. The British poet Felicia Hemans exemplified the popular and influential authors who saw themselves as part of a line stretching back to Sappho but faced critics who denigrated their work as overly emotional, melancholy, and trivial. Society warned women that writing could unsex them, that it was self-centered and narcissistic. Even those who believed women could be poets denigrated them by downplaying the profession itself: poetry taps into feminine sensibilities and emotions, requires no facts or knowledge, can be written in brief periods of respite from household chores, and can focus on "women's" topics like love and marriage. And women tended to write on traditional topics like love (Elizabeth Barrett Browning, *Sonnets from the Portuguese*) and religion (Sarah Flower Adams, "Nearer My God to Thee"). But some defied the stereotypes—either openly, like feminist Ella Wheeler Wilcox, author of the passionate poems in *Men, Women, and Emotions* (1893); or privately, like Emily Dickinson, whose poems broke the rules of meter, rhyme, and grammar, and challenged many rules of feminine interests and attitudes.

Women artists and writers braved special conflicts. The love story of two writers, Robert and Elizabeth Barrett Browning, is unique; the happily married author, like Elizabeth Gaskell, is almost as rare. Dickinson renounced marriage, perhaps in order to write. Alcott and the Brontës create characters who enact the authors' dream of combining marriage and career. Other writers, including Julia Ward Howe, Sarah Grand, Lydia Sigourney, Elizabeth Oakes-Smith, Maria Brooks, Frances Harper, Olive Schreiner, and Frances Osgood, had mixed success in combining marriage with writing. Obviously of special interest for women writers, who faced all the joys and traumas of creation intensified by the fact that women who worked were anomalies, the female artist is very popular in nineteenth-century literature.

Women writers naturally create many women musicians, actors, painters, sculptors, and especially other writers. Here literature surpasses reality, reflecting the authors' intimate knowledge and concern, and the literary convenience and significance of the artist-heroine. Early in the period few male characters work in any of the arts, but after midcentury there are more artists, dancers, actors, and musicians than teachers, and even more writers. Roughly 1 out of 20 male characters is an artist in representative fiction just after midcentury. For women, the figures are equally startling: nearly 1 in 10 female characters works in the arts early in the century, more than 1 in 6 in the second half of the century. A comparison with other fields reinforces the importance of artists to their creators, for personal or artistic reasons. At virtually any time, fictional women artists and writers outnumber teachers and governesses: in the 1850s to 1870s, there are as many writers as schoolteachers, and more than four times as many writers, artists, dancers, actors, and musicians as governesses. The result, while reiterating how carefully literature must be used as a source of knowledge about past times, makes a fascinating series of works focusing on the plight of the woman who tries to fulfill herself through art.

Mary Garth in Eliot's *Middlemarch* suggests that women can honorably choose between only two professions—teaching and writing. Hawthorne echoes this idea, suggesting there was no "fitter avenue" for Zenobia's talents than to become a writer (*Blithedale*, 368). The widow Susan Stringham loses no status supporting herself through fiction (James, *Wings*). Another widow, Diana Warwick, supports herself through journalism and fiction and knows the joy of earning money "by the labour we delight in" (Meredith, *Diana*, 183). Significantly, these two exceptions are widows, considered safely beyond the bounds of sexual interest; since they are un-marriageable, their work in the arts matters less. Writing for newspapers, virtually unknown among women, is sometimes even a quandary for men. To Forster, stuffy standard-bearers of morality like the lawyer Philip in *Where Angels Fear to Tread* (1905) oppose slightly risqué journalists like Emerson in *A Room with a View* (1908). However, most male journalists or best-selling novelists risk neither position nor prestige, as evidenced by the title characters of Thackeray's *Pendennis* and Linton's *Christopher Kirkland*. This was not the case for women.

Characters seem as unsure as real people about the respectability of the arts, especially for women. Noemie, in James's *The American*, in doubtful gentility supplements her father's income by copying great paintings in France. A singer is filled "with a terrible sense of shame" when her future husband sees her on stage, even though she works to support her widowed sister-in-law's children (Hungerford, *Molly*, 345). She and the violinist Joyce face the problem that people routinely question the artist's virtue. No wonder the narrator describes Joyce as "an artist to her heart's core, although, happily for herself, dear child, she is destined to lead the life of any ordinary woman" (Edwards, *Ballroom Repentance* [1882], 62). This attitude may explain why Sinclair's *The Three Sisters*, based on the Brontës, makes none of its heroines authors. Sinclair's biography, *The Three Brontës*, was followed by this sensitive novel with fairly obvious parallels to the writers, including the title, a minister father, and life on the moors. Her three characters may have artistic talent, but it remains stifled, and they find outlets for neither their abilities nor their emotional and sexual frustrations.

Most artists, like those in Gissing's *The Emancipated* and Du Maurier's *Trilby*, must defy the rules of society and their family. Dedicated to art, they often also dedicate themselves to drink and sexual freedom. Will in Eliot's *Middlemarch*, Cyril in Bennett's *The Old Wives' Tale*, Jo in Galsworthy's *The Man of Property* and *In Chancery*, and Gudrun in Lawrence's *Women in Love* represent the offbeat, bohemian, self-centered, and usually unre-spectable artist. Yet sympathetically, Hawthorne says Hilda in *The Marble Faun* (1860) exemplifies "the freedom of life which it is possible for a female artist to enjoy at Rome," where customs "bestow such liberty upon the sex, which is elsewhere restricted within so much narrower limits." He endorses more freedom for women, especially artists: "whenever we admit woman to a wider scope of pursuits and professions, we must also remove the shackles of our present conventional rules" (55).

But others find this view dangerous proof that women should not quit their accustomed sphere. When the title character in Phelps's *The Story of Avis* (1877) tells her father she will be an artist, he responds, "I can't have you filling your head with any of these womanish apings of a man's affairs, like a monkey playing tunes on a hand-organ" (59). She learns not to quote *Aurora Leigh* or reveal her talent, but manages to study in Europe. There she not only sells her work but receives serious critical praise. Returning home, she is dismayed to fall in love: saying "it is civil war" (192), an image an American in the 1860s would not use lightly, she reveals a basic conflict for the female artist. She warns her suitor that while "it is quite right for other women to become wives . . . I am not like that: I am different. And God did it" (195). Later, having "bowed to the great and awful law of married story" (325), she focuses her attention on her family, tacitly acquiescing in her husband's objections to her work. But she tells her former teacher that "life is behind me" (374). Abandoning creativity, she teaches painting to support her husband and children. He deserts his family and spends years in Europe to recover from an "illness" derived of his professional disappointments. Yet contemporary critics castigated Avis as selfish, her view of herself as hubristic, and the suggestion that talented women avoid marriage unhealthy and morbid.

Add to this background the special onus against the theater, and the reluctance of Braddon's hero in *Ishmael* (1884) to see Paquerette on the stage makes sense, even though his mother had acted. Rejecting trades from artificial flower making to tailoring, Ishmael chooses for Paquerette an unhappy marriage over the disreputable theater. Alcott shows her liberalism in *Jo's Boys* when the family accepts Meg's daughter Josie's going on stage. Her brother says, "Why not have a great actress of our name, as well as an authoress, a minister, and an eminent publisher? We don't choose our talents; but we needn't hide them in a napkin because they are not just what we want" (154). Guided by a successful, genteel actress, Josie achieves her dream *and* her mother's, becoming a fine, virtuous performer and marrying a good man. Yet in *Work*, when Christie quits the stage, fearing she's "not wise enough to keep steady there" and seeks a governess's post, a pragmatic friend warns, "don't mention you've been an actress or it will be all up with you" (58–59).

Although many accept that writing, especially done in the sanctity of the home, can offer a safe and potentially lucrative career for women, they question the propriety or even the possibility of combining marriage or family with authorship. Browning's successful poet, Aurora Leigh, ultimately gives up writing, learning that "art is much, but love is more." One man tells a young girl, "Be anything you like except a writer of prose or verse. The popular idea of an authoress brings before us an extraordinary individual whose hair is always dishevelled, whose fingers are always blackened with ink, who takes snuff, and sometimes, inadvertently, uses her nightcap as a pocket-handkerchief; who talks very tragically about nothing, and has an uncommon opinion of herself; and who, altogether, is not to be tolerated under any circumstances" (Gore, *Women*, 180–84). To his niece he adds that even if some fool weds her, society will blame her for problems in the marriage or with her children. Emphasizing how unwomanly the future writers will become, he does not consider that talent or necessity might drive them. Yet Amy must write, in part to support herself and her father, and she eventually marries.

Women writers thus defeat society, more often in literature than in life, but success requires a formidable struggle. Typically, Hester in *Red Pottage* by Cholmondeley, suffers for her art. A clergyman reads one of her manuscripts without her permission, then tries to burn it. Later, as a best-selling author, Hester writes four hours a day before anyone awakens, because her family neither appreciates her work nor even considers it work. Fanny Fern's title character in *Ruth Hall* (1854) turns first to sewing and then to writing when her father, husband, and father-in-law all die or desert her, leaving her to support herself and two children. Several unscrupulous editors treat her badly before she earns fame and fortune. Ruth typifies the reluctant artist who finds her talent out of necessity and struggles to remain womanly while grappling for a living.

The heroine of Grand's autobiographical *The Beth Book* marries at 18, still confusedly seeking a purpose in life. Before her marriage sours, she starts writing and anticipates Woolf by creating "a room of her own" in a hidden alcove. Even in childhood, when a young man asserts a woman can only care for husband and child or, if single, fill her life with the "little things a woman can do," Beth retorts, "Supposing little things don't satisfy her, and she has power to follow some big pursuit?" He insists "it's too rare to be taken into account—talent in women." Beth responds like an incipient feminist: "Robbing women of the means to develop their talents doesn't prove they haven't any" (246–47). Beth has more than talent; she has genius, although how she will express it is unclear. Her unsympathetic husband dismissively avows, "little heads like hers can't contain books," though "it's all very well to scribble a little for pastime." When Beth notes the many successful women authors, he scoffs that she is not one of the "exceptional women . . . coarse and masculine" (366). Fortunately, Angelica, Ideala, and Dr. Galbraith, liberal characters reappearing from other of Grand's novels, encourage Beth to write and later, learning of her husband's evil, to strike out on her own. Still, she almost starves before achieving success and satisfaction as a writer and lecturer about women's rights.

Beth becomes a professional, not one of the "scribbling women" Haw-thorne detests and Twain mocks through Emmeline Grangerford (*Huck*), writing sentimental nonsense in badly rhymed verse. Like many women characters who try to write, Beth ultimately fulfills her desire. The number of successful, even happy, women writers in literature by women suggests that for the real authors, literature provided a chance to live out a dream they could only approximate in their own lives.

Industry and Trade

The growth of commerce, industry, and specialization altered jobs and heightened distinctions between owners and assistants. Men might rise to the new class of managers or run ship and construction companies, mines and railroads, factories, or department stores. Some wealthy and powerful Englishmen, like the "Beer Barons," Arthur and Edward Guinness, received peerages, while the American "Robber Barons" (Gould, Rockefeller, Carnegie) made their mark in banking, industry, railroads, and politics. The wives of managers, foremen, and industrial leaders joined the "idle" nou-veaux riches. But other women, especially from the middle and lower-middle classes, found that opportunities for new jobs abounded.

In factories, women performed tasks once done in cottage industries by craftsmen. They found jobs as shop assistants, positions once held by trades-men's apprentices. In England from 1841 to 1891, the number of men involved in clothing manufacture remained at around 160,000, while the ranks of women swelled to 5 times that figure; the number of men involved in retailing multiplied by 2, women by 15 (Booth, cited in Wrigley, 253–58). In 1900, one-fourth of the five million American women who held jobs worked in factories (Ryan, 195). Representing the impact of techno-logical change, the typewriter alone provided a whole new field for women. As the job of office assistant became more mechanical and less prestigious, it was no longer restricted to male university graduates: then, employers preferred hiring respectable, educated middle-class women rather than less prepared, less genteel working men. In the last half-century, the number of male clerks multiplied about 10 times, female clerks about 600 times (Holcombe, 211).

Gender often determined job description and pay. Women always earned less than men—sometimes only half—even if salaried and performing the same tasks. In many fields, women were paid by piecework and faced the vagaries of seasonal employment. Most unions refused to represent or even include women, considering them part-time workers. Yet women joined picket lines and took part in the movement to increase safety, shorten work hours, establish a minimum wage, allow shop assistants to sit down during the day, outlaw deducting fines, and abolish the requirement of "living-in" (residing in dormitories or selected boarding houses and eating meals the employer provided for a fee).

Reformers urged women to prepare for the new opportunities and castigated society for impeding women's efforts. Arguing that a lack of practical business skills hampered women, Martineau exclaimed that English widows who take over their husbands' shops often "decline in fortune" or "hand over the business to men," while similarly situated American women "prosper at least as well as men" (ER, 311). Compared to factory hands, assistants in commercial offices and retail shops, bankers, cashiers, and secretaries all earned more under better conditions: for example, by 1900 clerks began their eight- or nine-hour day no earlier than 9 A.M. and often dined in restaurants. A clerk who could type or do bookkeeping and knew a foreign language outearned a general office worker, again emphasizing women's need for education.

Reformers also confronted philosophical strictures against women working, especially in certain jobs. Emily Davies hopelessly insisted, "it is vain to say that a factory is not a fit place for a lady" or, "if it is not, it ought to be made so," for it would give higher-class women "larger sympathies, more living interests, increased aptitude for affairs, and an exhilarating sense of usefulness" and the lower-class women contact with real "refinement" (93–95). Martineau cited a sadly illustrative tale of a shop owner who employed experienced, reputable women "in a suitable department," but discovered business declined "because there were only women behind the counter." Forced to "introduce some shopmen, to reassure the ladies who could not trust the ability of their own sex," the owner found the two men "were worked off their feet, while the shopwomen stood idle; for the ladies had no faith in female ability, even behind the counter" (ER, 312). Some contemporaries resorted to ridicule: "As for finance, in its various branches—if you pause to consider the extreme difficulty there always is in balancing Mrs.

Smith's housekeeping-book, or Miss Smith's quarterly allowance, I think, my dear Paternal Smith, you need not be much afraid lest this loud acclaim for 'women's rights' should ever end in pushing you from your stools, in counting-house, college, or elsewhere" (Craik, 5). But B. L. Smith (Mrs. Bodichon) in *Women and Work* argued poignantly that "many trades" are "open to women with good training in bookkeeping and knowledge of some special branch of business, not difficult to acquire, if fathers would help their daughters as they help their sons" (quoted by Martineau, *ER*, 313).

As prejudices shifted, the less prestigious jobs in shops and offices became "women's work." Business colleges and commercial schools helped women prepare for office jobs. The fact that shop assistants no longer expected to take over a business ended one objection to hiring women. Women were barred from certain jobs—apprenticeships in chemists' shops and drug-stores, rough work in butchers' or furnishers' shops; but "women's" stores (milliners, florists, bakeries, lingerie shops) eventually came to prefer female employees. There were still "women's" and "men's" jobs in 1900, and the latter always paid better. But at least women could work in most stores or offices and be paid for their efforts.

Representative literature downplays the number of factory hands, who tend to be minor characters even in novels of social reform. Surprisingly, nearly as many women as men own shops at midcentury, though virtually no women hold these jobs before or after. Fiction noticeably underrepresents the real numbers of male shop, mill, and factory owners, especially late in the century. Hofland's *Patience* offers glimpses of life in Liverpool, a manufacturing town; Disraeli's *Sybil* shows how Gerald rises from mill-hand to overseer; Dickens's *Hard Times* discusses factory owners and workers; Howells's *Silas Lapham* depicts the archetypal self-made American manufacturing his discovery. Still, only rare novels like Gaskell's *Mary Barton* or *North and South* or poems like Barrett Browning's "Cry of the Children" actually focus on the issues raised by numerous government reports and newspaper articles on the power of owners and the plight of workers.

In *North and South*, Margaret looks down at manufacturers and fears workers. "A deep lead-coloured cloud" hangs over the town, and "the air had a faint taste and smell of smoke; perhaps, after all, more a loss of the fragrance of grass and herbage." In the "long, straight, hopeless streets of regularly-built houses, all small and of brick . . . here and there a great oblong many-windowed factory stood up, like a hen among her chickens," emitting foul black smoke (59). But Margaret learns that wealthy, self-educated John Thornton seeks gentility for himself and progress for his workers. Through the family of union leader Nicholas Higgins, she gains sympathy for the hard lives of the rough-mannered workers. Bessie Higgins, dying from lung disease, is determined to save her youngest sister from the factory by finding her work as a servant.

Thornton tries to help the workers and the town, even reducing pollution from his company's furnaces before the Town Improvement Causes Act required the change. But the masters cut wages as business declines, offering no explanation to workers, whom they regard as children. When the desperate workers strike, the owners bring in strikebreakers; rioters attack Thornton's house, and the masters call out soldiers. Arrests follow, and Higgins, among others, loses his job. Later, Margaret overhears Thornton seeking to work directly with the laborers, so that all share the desire for success "as all had borne a part" (432). The novel ends with the hope that this might reduce misunderstanding and improve relations between workers and owner. And, of course, Margaret and Thornton will marry.

In *Mary Barton*, John joins a delegation of workers fruitlessly seeking government aid for jobs. His daughter Mary, a dressmaker, hopes to escape the working class by marrying the factory owner, Carson, but is loved by a mechanic, Jem. John murders Carson, Jem is accused of the murder, and Mary pursues a solution with the help of many people, including her aunt, a prostitute. Jem is acquitted, John dies, and Mary and Jem start fresh in Canada. Thanks to this experience, Carson's father negotiates with his workers, and the narrator credits those talks with "many of the improvements now in practice in the system of employment in Manchester" (376).

The notion expressed in *Mary Barton* that "machines is th' ruin of poor folk" (81) reappears in works like Brontë's *Shirley*. Here problems develop when mill owner Robert Moore buys new machinery, favoring progress over people. Riots result, Robert has the rioters jailed, and they attack him in retaliation. Finally, Robert's beloved Caroline helps him to cooperate with the mill-hands. Caroline joins Mary and Margaret in the standard secondary role. Women marry or are the children of factory owners or factory workers; they may help inspire social reform; but only minor female characters work in mill or factory, and women almost never own the company.

The situation is similar for commercial and office work, but not for shopkeepers and shop workers. Few female characters work in business. The percentages of men in businesses, banks, or other offices more than doubles by midcentury (up to one in four characters), a fairly accurate reflection of social change; but the number is halved in the 1880s and 1890s, opposing reality. For women, literature begins accurately—2 percent are in business in the first decades, 10 percent at midcentury; but again, the numbers later drop at a time real women flooded the market. One problem is that the business world has questionable gentility. An enterprising American businesswoman, Mrs. Newsome leads a full life supervising "a roaring trade . . . a workshop; a great production; a great industry" whose product Strether quietly refuses to identify, implying there might be something "vulgar" about her work (James, *Ambassadors*, 53).

While women shopkeepers are not more numerous than women factory workers, they more frequently serve as major characters. After the 1820s, at least some characters worked in shops at all times, up to about 1 in 14 women and 1 in 16 men at midcentury. Whether in England (Gaskell, *Cranford*) or America (Hawthorne, *Seven Gables*), opening a shop provides potentially genteel work and at least the hope of an income for many an impoverished widow or unmarried daughter, so that shopkeeping fits plot requirements and may permit a comment on the need to redefine women's roles. When Hepzibah Pyncheon must earn money, Hawthorne sympathizes with her plight even as he gently mocks her. She is too nearsighted and arthritic to sew, insufficiently educated to open a school now that "the very A B C has become a science." Hepzibah believes "a lady's hand soils itself irremediably by doing aught for bread," yet "this business of setting up a petty shop is almost the only resource of women, in circumstances at all similar to those of our unfortunate recluse" (36–37).

Living above the store with their maid and a nurse for the baby, the Baines family in Bennett's *The Old Wives' Tale* is respectable if not genteel. Constance characteristically leaves day school at 16 to work in the shop. Mirroring social reality and ideal, her hard work leads to advancement. From dwelling above their bookstore with a maid and nurse, the Proctors in Guyton's *Married Life* move to a large town house, a definite step up. A former stonemason whose business earns vast sums buys property and becomes "Sir Roger" (Trollope, *Dr. Thorne*). Michael Henchard achieves middle-class respectability as a merchant-owner (Hardy, *Mayor*), and Bradshaw rises from clerk to junior partner in his father's business (Gaskell, *Ruth*). As a rope-maker rises through hard work to own a small business, Miller's *Gideon Giles* (1841) castigates laws that hamper workers' progress.

Gaskell describes the difference between women's and men's advance in *Sylvia's Lovers*. One man ascends from shop worker to partner, and another from shipowner's apprentice to captain, saving money to buy a ship. But the outstanding employee Hester Rose obtains promotion only because she is lucky enough to work for kind Quakers who follow their faith and defy the norm. One owner "made over to her so much of his share in the business, that she had a right to be considered as a kind of partner, and she had long been the superintendent of that department of goods which were exclusively devoted to women" (443–44). Her rise realistically depends on a kind master and a new interest in saleswomen serving other women.

Maggie in Eliot's *The Mill on the Floss* is capable of an education and the kind of office work Tom finally gets, and she would enjoy both. But because she is a woman, she must watch her brother attend school and support the family through clerical work for which he lacks interest, training, and talent. Later, ruined by her unintentional elopement with Stephen, Maggie hopes to redeem herself in the villagers' eyes and earn "enough to pay for her lodging": like many another woman, "she fell back" on the final resort, "plain sewing" (430).

The Last Resort—Needlework

Because needlework maintained respectability and required no unusual skills, the field mushroomed. And because seamstresses and shirtmakers faced lives as hard as the familiar tales implied, feminists seeking to advance women's position paid them much notice.

Farm girls and daughters of poor clergymen, retired officers, or bankrupt tradesmen turned to needlework when they could do nothing else. Nearly 100 times as many women as men worked in this field, where gentility did not preclude poverty for the family seamstress and misery reigned for the worker in a large shop or the "slopworker" sewing in her room. Fitters and milliners found steady work at rates close to shop assistants', but seamstresses and shirtmakers toiled in a firm with a thousand other women or eked out a bare subsistence with private sewing, fined for late work and erratically paid for piecework at a rate certain to lead to starvation.

Dressmaking normally required a premium for two or three years' apprenticeship, including room and board. Moving to a shop, girls worked 16 or 18 hours a day for weeks on end without regular breaks or meals during "the season," and might be fired at season's end. The demands women made when ordering clothes caused reformers to address pleas for improving seamstresses' lot to them rather than to the government or general public, sometimes using literature as the forum.

By midcentury, the burgeoning field and horrifying news stories heightened awareness of the needleworkers' plight. Besides poverty, women faced health hazards from fainting to spine problems and blindness. Girls in large shops, surrounded by unattainable luxury and denied youth's normal pleasures, were ripe for temptation. A report of a meeting of English slopworkers in 1849 revealed that most present had no underclothes, 508 had borrowed clothes to attend the meeting, 464 had sought charity in the preceding week, and 232 had been evicted when unable to pay the rent (Neff, 130). Reform organizations gradually reduced working hours, encouraged fashionable ladies to allow reasonable time for orders, and helped seamstresses find work or even emigrate, lowering competition and perhaps raising the odds of marriage. Government and private efforts could not eliminate abuses when women's job options remained meager.

In Reynolds's *The Soldier's Wife* an impoverished woman learns that to be a slopworker, she must provide a deposit as a "guarantee for the safe return of the materials when duly made up" (82); of course she has no money. Dressmaking may be a step above factory work, as Gaskell's Mary Barton and her friend know, but it is very difficult. In *Mary Barton* and other works, rich women's unreasonable last-minute orders increase the needleworkers' misery. Thus authors, primarily women, gently plead the case of the unfortunate workers.

Not all needleworkers are sympathetically portrayed. In Moore's *A Mummer's Wife*, Kate lives at her shop, has two apprentice dressmakers, and takes in lodgers to make ends meet; she also drinks and has an affair. But literature more typically arouses compassion by detailing the seamstress's life. An apprentice in a wholesale house, Lotte makes "the fronts worn inside women's bonnets. for sevenpence halfpenny per dozen. She rose at six in the morning, and worked until twelve at night, in order to complete two dozen per diem" (Egan, *Flower*, 37). Stressing her effort and virtue, the author has one character tell Lotte, "You have taught me that difference of station is levelled by human worth" (178). In *Little Dorrit*, Dickens's heroine sews twelve hours a day, symbolizing that life in a debtor's prison has not tainted her.

Even when a seamstress behaves improperly, the author may sympathize, as in Gaskell's *Ruth*. The innocence in which Ruth is raised leaves her unprepared when thrust into the life of a dressmaker's apprentice at 15. Her five-year apprenticeship in a large shop whose head provides neither fires nor food on Sundays commonly involves work until 4 or 5 A.M. or even all night on a last-minute order. Apprentices witness unattainable luxuries when they meet customers or mend dresses at a ball. It's easy to imagine the girls sitting alone on Sunday, cold and hungry, exhausted and frustrated, dreaming of a life they can never reach.

Ruth cannot quit without forfeiting her parents' premium, but she loses her job when her employer sees her naively walking with Bellingham, a wealthy man intent on seducing her. After he abducts her, Ruth gradually learns to love him, then nurses him through a severe illness, only to be banished by his mother. Alone and pregnant, Ruth is saved by a Dissenting minister and his sister. Caring for her child helps redeem Ruth, and years later when Bellingham, now in Parliament, offers to marry her because he wants their son, she rejects him, despising his values. The novel ends with her death as a respected and loved woman.

For suddenly impoverished middle-class women, needlework can maintain respectability. Kate learns this familiar lesson in Dickens's *Nicholas Nickleby*. Throughout the period, many female characters with different motives and backgrounds work as seamstresses—from a high of 1 in 10 at midcentury down to 1 in 50 around 1900, even given the many new options for women by that time. Virtually no men work in related fields. Only one job accounts for a higher percentage of women characters over the entire century, and that is the most important job of all in literature or reality: the "Angel of the House," the dependent woman who raised her family, took care of the house, guided the servants, worked in the village, nursed the elderly, and taught the young—all without pay.

"To Be" or "To Do"

Reflecting a change in society by the 1890s, in Grand's *The Beth Book*, Beth's Aunt Victoria notes that "now . . . there are women who actually go away and work for themselves, if their homes are unhappy." Willing to concede this "may be respectable," she "cannot believe it is either right or wise, and certainly it is not loyal." Later Beth escapes a bad marriage and defends women's right to realize themselves in work; but even as a child she amends her aunt's idea: "that was my father's word to me: 'be loyal.' We've got to be loyal to others; but he also said that we must be loyal to ourselves" (202).

Work might mean loyalty to an inner vision, a source of self-fulfillment, or economic survival, but none of these came easily to women in reality or literature. To the end of the period, most real women worked in just a few areas—in factories or on farms if lower class; as teachers, shop assistants, clerks, and seamstresses if middle class. They focused on social service, the lower reaches of health care, teaching, and business. Slowly, reacting to and creating a new society, reformers overcame the practical and philosophical barriers to women's fulfilling their need and desire to work. What Gilman writes about women in literature also fits real women: "They have ideas and purposes of their own; and even when, as in so many cases described by the more reactionary novelists, the efforts of the heroine are shown to be entirely futile, and she comes back with a rush to the self-effacement of marriage with economic dependence, still the efforts were there" (*Women and Economics*, 150–51). In literature and in reality, because "the efforts were there," life would never be the same. The Angel could leave the house.

ENGRAVED BY T. JOHNSON.   FROM A PHOTOGRAPH BY SARONY.

Harriet Beecher Stowe

Courtesy of the Library of Congress

CHAPTER
5

Conclusion: "To Labor for the Elevation of My Sex"

> There's going to be a new Declaration of Independence.
>
> —Alcott, *Work* (1)
>
> We hold these truths to be self-evident: that all men and women are created equal.
>
> —Declaration of Sentiments[1]

Many of the changes that transformed women's lives derive from direct political action.[2] To achieve reform in divorce and property laws, education or jobs, abolition, suffrage, and temperance, women wrote speeches, stories, and poems; they held conventions, gave public lectures, founded organizations, ran for office, petitioned Congress and Parliament, and engaged in acts of civil disobedience. Critics saw their goals and methods as disturbing and subversive. In the most specific, limited sense, this political action defines the women's movement.

In the most general sense, the movement includes *all* efforts by women to alter their lives within their homes or to take action beyond the privacy of those homes, and all those efforts involve a kind of politics. The political system ultimately specifies the rights to own property, marry or divorce, obtain an education, become a professional, or speak in public. The campaign for women's rights involved a fundamental power struggle and a re-definition of basic relationships between women and men, and between women and the state.

In this broad second sense, literature constantly deals with the reform movement. Every time a work questions women's roles or hints at dissatis-faction with either the public or the private sphere, it addresses women's struggle. Literature necessarily adheres to a particular worldview in present-ing the author's philosophy. Nineteenth-century literature, so tightly tied to reality, nearly always reflects social concerns. But not all literature overtly advocates a specific position. Relatively few works take a direct, activist role in discussing the women's movement, either to castigate or to encourage its adherents. Literature rarely deals with the first, narrower definition of the movement. But in both senses of the movement, literature reveals tremen-dous changes in the way society thought about and treated women, and in the way women thought about themselves. In turn, literature became a tool for many factions in the drive for women's rights.

Many real women dedicated a good part of their lives to improving the lot of others through direct action. Besides those who opened the doors to schools and jobs, as discussed earlier, others toiled on behalf of prisoners or the mentally ill, or organized clubs for working girls and focused attention on laborers' needs. Settlement houses gave middle-class women an appeal-ing social service based on traditional charitable roles, and taught the re-formers that those most desperate for help inevitably were women. Both blacks (Harriet Tubman, Sojourner Truth) and whites (Elizabeth Cady Stanton, Susan B. Anthony, Lucretia Mott) labored for abolition. Sarah and Angelina Grimké became feminists as they confronted the objections of other reformers to women seeking the same rights for themselves that they demanded for slaves.

Such activities proved women's abilities gleaned from the traditional sphere and taught them new organizational and political skills. The more women became involved in reform, the more they defined their primary cause. Margaret Fuller put it this way: "I believe that, at present, women are the best helpers of one another."[3] Events proved her right.

For their political efforts, activists were taunted, vilified, arrested, and jailed. Traditionally anointed the keepers of morality, women who chose to take public action on that responsibility violated the cult of femininity. They clashed against social values sustained by inertia, religion, and the prejudice of both sexes, and often reinforced by literature. They found their work difficult and the reaction of their society extremely frustrating. Yet they did not give up.

Carry Nation, ax-wielding editor of the *Smasher's Mail*, made an excellent target for cartoonists as she proselytized in Britain and America for temperance, sex education, and the homeless, and against child and wife abuse, smoking, and immodest dress. Though publicly whipped and jailed, she had an impact. So did Victoria Woodhull, newspaper publisher and champion of women's rights and free love, who ran for president in 1872, half a century before women could vote.

Far less flamboyant reformers also faced mockery and abuse. The gentle Quaker Susan B. Anthony evolved into one of the courageous women who walked through snowstorms and confronted closed doors and ridicule when seeking fair treatment for their sex. These new pioneers, as Anna Howard Shaw called her comrades, rode in uncovered wagons and spoke to huge crowds in tents. Critics regarded them as mannish and unnatural, disobedient to their duties and disloyal to their fathers and husbands.

Equally painful was the discounting of women's efforts. Dedicated female abolitionists were forbidden to take their seats as delegates to the World Anti-Slavery Convention in London in 1840. Such actions led delegates Mott and Stanton to call the first Women's Rights Convention in 1848 at Seneca Falls, New York. Rewriting the Declaration of Independence, they summarized the major goals of the movement. Adding "and women" whenever "men" appeared in the original document made clear their intent: "all men and women are created equal." Just as the Declaration of Independence listed grievances and implied the prerogatives of the American people, so the new Declaration of Sentiments outlined concrete grievances and prerogatives. Its simple, basic assertion overturned fundamental cultural beliefs: men have no right to "assign" women to "a sphere of action, when that belongs to her conscience and to her God," and women deserve the same rights as men. Abigail Adams's threat to her husband that women would rebel if not treated fairly in the framing of the Constitution had come true.

Throughout the century, feminists sought privileges and freedoms automatically granted to men. Some women abandoned crinolines and corsets, which emphasized the female shape and made physical activity difficult, for "bloomers," loose pantaloons beneath a knee-length skirt, named for reformer Amelia Bloomer. Stanton, Stone, and Anthony appreciated the practicality and significance of the outfit; critics, recognizing the symbolism, subjected its advocates to scornful abuse. Bloomers denoted a new life-style: freedom to move easily on the job or at play, freedom to travel alone to Hawaii like Isabella Bird or to climb Mont Blanc like Marie Pardis. In that new existence, women desired the same prerogatives as men in family life, education, and jobs. And they wanted to vote, to be able to frame the laws that affected them.

Many American women assumed that having fought for abolition, they would receive the vote with the newly freed slaves. Sojourner Truth insisted that race and gender be linked: "I am glad to see that men are getting their rights, but I want women to get theirs, and while the water is stirring I will step into the pool" (Lerner, 489). But in 1868 the Fourteenth Amendment introduced the word *male* into the definition of citizenship.

Still, women did not quit. In both nations, women argued they could add a purifying voice to the ballot box; they joined parades and wrote thoughtful articles appealing to humanity and reason. Between 1868 and 1872, some 400 women voted or attempted to vote in 10 states; occasionally, officials counted their votes. In 1872 Susan B. Anthony led 16 women to register and vote in Rochester, New York. Taken to court, Anthony denounced not only the irregularities of the trial (such as the judge's instructing the jury to find her guilty) but the entire suffrage issue. Ultimately fined a token $100, she refused to pay, and the court did not enforce the sentence. In 1875, the Supreme Court, in a decision which infuriated and frustrated suffragists, confirmed the government's constitutional right to deny the vote to "certain classes of males," such as "the mentally unfit, and the criminal"—and to women.

Later suffragists resorted to more violent activism than their spiritual ancestors, chaining themselves to the White House fence in America and throwing stones in England. Arrests, mistreatment, and forced feeding of hunger strikers bred mixed public reaction. In *Woman Suffrage and Politics*, activist Carrie Chapman Catt enumerates some of the efforts just in America: there were over 1,000 campaigns with state legislatures, state constitutional conventions, state party conventions, and national party conventions; 19 congresses deliberated women's right to vote. Finally England granted women the vote in 1919, America one year later. Decades of effort in the nineteenth century had led to success in the twentieth.

In literature as well, the seeds of change planted in the nineteenth century reached fruition in the twentieth. Literature consistently reflects society's interest in women's roles. Concentrated on domestic life, literature inevitably addresses the feminist debate, whether supporting the Gentle Lady and her cult of femininity or exploring the New Woman's consciousness of the stifling constraints she faced both within and outside her home. If only a few authors vehemently advocate reform, many consider women's accustomed roles and hint at problems. For every radical like Elizabeth Margaret Chandler, antislavery poet and writer for the inflammatory William Lloyd Garrison's *Liberator,* many more authors employ subtle commentary that avoids alienating their audience while still making their point about marriage or education or jobs or the reform movement. Without including a single suffragist, this kind of literature played a major role in the women's movement.

Literature's presentation of the women's movement in the broadest sense—the redefinition of women's roles at home, in education, and in jobs—has already been discussed; only a few exceptional works look at the movement in the narrower sense of political activism. Yet direct literary allusions to feminists entered into society's dialogue about the women's movement, even though ax-wielding temperance reformers, would-be politicians, army nurses heading sanitation efforts, militant suffragists and ardent abolitionists rarely appear.

While writing proved a more acceptable venture for feminists than giving speeches or petitioning governments, liberal authors paid for their efforts, as did all reformers. Earlier warned by her publishers to tone down her strong presentations of women, Chopin was condemned and ostracized for *The Awakening*; libraries removed the book from their shelves. Literature provoked such reactions because people recognized its power. Stowe's experience demonstrates that power: she engendered more reaction through *Uncle Tom's Cabin* and *Dred* (1856) than through all her speeches, articles, and travels. The novels had great impact because, though based on facts and strong in intent, they presented their antislavery message obliquely and with emotion. *Uncle Tom's Cabin* was translated into nearly two dozen languages, transformed into drama, and published in unauthorized editions worldwide (with no money paid to Stowe for most of these versions). As a measure of its effect, it led to a petition written by Lord Shaftesbury in 1853 and signed by over half a million European and English women who agreed to direct their energies against the horrors of slavery. That petition, which Stowe used during the Civil War, suggests the interaction of English and American women in the reform movement as well as the *direct* role of literature. The *indirect* influence of literature on attitude and behavior is immeasurable.

As is true of much reform literature, in *Uncle Tom's Cabin* Stowe never overtly pleads for abolition. When writers confront the women's movement, the intense and often intimate nature of their concerns—affecting women's relations with parents, children, spouses, and the state—makes the discussions potentially painful and suggestions for change inherently subversive. To many characters and authors, the right to vote symbolizes the overturning of traditional male-female roles. A female character who, like Lucy

Stone, wants "to labor for the elevation of [her] sex," generates a realistic mix of mockery, hatred, and respect from her varied audience. In more conservative works, women who seek reform are effectively silenced; they appear strident, foolish, powerless. In feminist works, they have a chance both to speak and to effect change.

Conservative authors mirror the scorn and fear with which society reacted to feminists. Even the New Woman, a far more common and certainly more welcome character, threatens to destroy the social order by valuing a career over motherhood, sexual freedom over monogamy, woman's duty to herself over her duty to others. Feminists Olive Chancellor in James's *The Bostonians* and Zenobia in Hawthorne's *The Blithedale Romance* are unscrupulous, conniving, ambitious, domineering, and destructive. Hints of lesbianism hang over their relationships with the delicate heroines of the novels. When Zenobia declaims on the injustice of keeping women from speaking freely to the world, the narrator scornfully suggests that women only become concerned about "the rights or wrongs of their sex" if they are unhappy or unloved. Another man adds that "all the separate action of women is, and ever has been, and always shall be, false, foolish, vain, destructive of her own best and holiest qualities, void of every good effect, and productive of intolerable mischief" (456–59). Neither Zenobia nor Olive appeals as a representative of the women's movement.

In *The Ways of the Hour* (1850), Cooper presents another unappealing, ineffective feminist as he decries the women's movement. Mary Monson can desert her husband because she controls her money; thus the Married Woman's Property Act of 1848 becomes the scapegoat for the shifting balance of power between men and women. Weaving an improbable plot, Cooper inveighs against a flawed justice system but even more against active women. Mary may be innocent of murder, but Cooper finds her guilty of egregious errors of judgment.

In contrast, feminist sympathizers like Grand offer strong, appealing, intelligent, effective women activists. True, as Hawthorne said, characters like Ideala and Beth develop their convictions partly in reaction to bad marriages. But Beth's values originate in childhood struggles against the biases that afford her a characteristically poor education and limited options. Knowing society's reactions to feminists, Ideala rightly warns Beth that "women who work for women in the present period of our progress . . . must resign themselves to martyrdom." While some men may "help and respect them," most will not (*Beth*, 392). Accurately reflecting society, splinter organizations result when women who share the same goals differ in approach. Angelica agrees with Beth that "the efforts of foolish people to divide the interests of men and women make me writhe" (*Beth*, 412); but others insist on the separate aims of the two sexes, perhaps scarred by experiences like women being banned from the Anti-Slavery Convention. Still, one idealist sees the "woman movement" as "consolidating the interests of the sexes, and uniting men and women in their business and in their pleasure to an extent never before approached" (*Babs*, 344).

Unlike Grand's characters, no woman in *Uncle Tom's Cabin* ever demands the right to change the law or seeks the power to do so. Yet Stowe suggests that women's and men's disparate values create their divergent attitudes toward abolition. Senator Bird tries to convince his wife they must obey the runaway slave laws. Placing virtue and human decency first, she refuses to obey a law she regards as shameful and wicked. Stowe reinforces the rightness of the woman's position by having the senator follow his heart—and his wife's guidance—when the runaways Eliza and Harry materialize.

Lacking Grand's vehemence, Stowe reveals implicit support for the women's movement. In *Uncle Tom's Cabin* she ironically but realistically notes that characters who oppose slavery see no harm in men treating their wives and children as possessions. She commends liberated characters like Harry and his mother in *My Wife and I*, who believe they must help create the ideal society. Sympathetically observing women's crusade for education and careers, Harry vows to strive so that someday no one will feel "it was a pity not to have been born a man" (125). Neither Harry nor Stowe quite approves of the significantly named Audacia Dangyereyes who smokes, visits Harry in his rooms, and seeks the vote. Yet Harry and his friend Ida realize the importance of reform: "a woman who really does accomplish a life-work is just like one that cuts the first path through a wood. She makes a way where others can walk" (248).

Alcott's personal life demonstrated the need to redefine women's potential, and her literature let her convey this message to others. She begins *Work* with the heroine's proclaiming "a new Declaration of Independence" (1). Her female characters become doctors, authors, and actors; they face the trauma of trying to earn a living; some express belief in suffrage. Her characters' persistence and her praise for them show how literature "makes a way where others can walk." Alert to the obstacles facing women, the excitement and pain that came from trying to tear down the barricades, Alcott suggests that all women struggling to alter their lives had to confront the conflict between being a "lady" and being a "woman." American women also had to cope with the belief that the archetypal American hero could not be female. Female Huck Finns—independent, experienced, individualistic—were condemned, if not impossible. Yet failing to act, no matter how painful the process, meant acceding to women's perpetual second-class position.

At the turn of the century, Grand's Beth laments that when women obediently stayed in their place, "men used to vow at their feet" they could accomplish anything; but "now that women have proved that what they choose to do they can do, men sneer at their pretensions to power, and try to depreciate them" (*Beth*, 483). Beth is correct that progress came only with immense difficulty, but it came. The narrator uses Beth's significantly-named aunt to represent the change from Old Maid to New Woman: "Aunt Victoria nowadays would have struck out for herself in a new direction," perhaps moved to the city, "joined a progressive women's club," found "work of some kind or another, and never known a dull moment" (186–7).

Some early twentieth-century writers, such as Sinclair and Wharton, continue to describe traditional women who peck in frustration at the egg-shell still confining them. Some rejoice in the reformers' many accomplishments. And others conjure up visions of an ideal world. Suffragist and popular dramatist Cicely Hamilton, with Christopher St. John, wrote a play called *How the Vote Was Won* (1910), celebrating woman suffrage just about a decade prematurely. Even stronger in its feminist ardor than this play or Bellamy's socialist novels, *Looking Backwards* and *Equality* (1897), Gilman's utopia, *Herland*, creates an all-female community.

In *The Man-Made World; or, Our Androcentric Culture*, Gilman avows that women are not a variation of a male norm; rather, there are three classifications—masculine, feminine, and human. As "woman's natural work" is motherhood, so man's is fatherhood, "but human work covers all our life outside of those specialties" (25). Women who insist on this truth meet constant rebuffs: "from her first faint struggles toward freedom and justice, to her present valiant efforts toward full economic and political equality, each step has been termed 'unfeminine,' and resented as an intrusion upon man's place and power" (24). Nonetheless, to achieve the best for themselves and all civilization, women and men must accept both their individual spheres and the common sphere. When this happens, Gilman prophesies, "distinctly fresh fields" of literature will develop, including stories about middle-aged women, relationships between women, "the long drama of personal relationship" between mother and child, and more (105).

Only one woman present at the Seneca Falls Convention lived to cast her ballot in the first presidential election after women earned the right to vote. Likewise, the dream of a new literature came true only after World War I, when writers like Woolf began to explore the kinds of themes Gilman defined, and women who wrote were no longer automatically lumped together in a distinct—that is, inferior—category. These victories came from the efforts of the early feminists. Through action, including writing, reformers changed women's lives, truly altering the whole of society. By 1900 women in real life and in literature had been freed from the myth of the Gentle Lady guided by the cult of femininity and could far more readily receive an education, marry whom they chose, obtain a divorce, raise their children, select from a wide range of job possibilities, earn a living, and keep their income. Yet divorce laws maintained the husband's supremacy, many schools and jobs failed to welcome women, and they could not vote. Women were not yet "human," in Gilman's terms, or equal under the law.

To this day, the Constitution of the United States fails to guarantee equal rights for women. English and American women earn less than men for the same or equivalent jobs, and women continue to face prejudice in the marketplace and elsewhere. The nineteenth-century reformers and writers who courageously made the transformation from femininity to feminism left to their spiritual descendants the task of striving for true equality.

Feminist or conservative, many nineteenth-century writers also left us the gift of art. Most literature, reflecting and commenting on issues of immediate concern, appeals just in its own time; it is relevant today only as a record of the past. But the best literature, outlasting that first life, has meaning for all time. Concentrating as we have on the issue of women's role in literature to some extent does a disservice to that second, greater existence. Great literature lives as long as people can read—*not* because it presents interesting views of women's changing roles, whether truthful or skewed, but because it taps into human experience. Such literature transforms life into art, and through that creative act it teaches us, arouses us, pleases us, nourishes us—all of us, male and female.

Chronology

Because the publication dates for the literature appear in the text, that information is not repeated here.

1792	Mary Wollstonecraft, *A Vindication of the Rights of Women*.
1793	Felicia Hemans born (died 1835).
1795	Rebecca Cox Jackson born (died 1871).
1797	Emily Eden born (died 1869). Mary Shelley born (died 1851). Sojourner Truth born into slavery; escaped 1827 (died 1883). Mary Wollstonecraft dies (born 1759).
1799	Catherine Gore born (died 1861).
1800	Catherine Crowe born (died 1876). Catherine Sinclair born (died 1864).
1802	Sarah Coleridge born (died 1852). Lydia Maria Child born (died 1880). Dorothea Dix born (died 1887). Harriet Martineau born (died 1876). Emma Caroline Wood born (died 1866).
1804	Rosina, Lady Bulwer-Lytton born (died 1882).
1805	Sarah Flower Adams born (died 1848).
1806	Elizabeth Barrett Browning born (died 1861). Julia H.S. Pardoe born (died 1862).
1807	Anne Manning born (died 1879).
1809	Fanny Kemble born (died 1893).
1810	Elizabeth Cleghorn Gaskell born (died 1865). Sarah Ellis born (died 1872).
1811	Fanny Fern (Worboise) born (died 1872). Harriet Beecher Stowe born (died 1896).
1814	Mrs. Henry Wood (Ellen Price) born (died 1887).
1815	Elizabeth Cady Stanton born (died 1902). Elizabeth Missing Sewell born (died 1906).

1816	Charlotte Brontë born (died 1855).
1817	Jane Austen dies (born 1775).
1818	Harriet Brent Jacobs (Lydia Brent) born into slavery; escaped to freedom 1845 (died 1896). Emily Brontë born (died 1848).
1819	Queen Victoria born. George Eliot (Mary Ann Evans Cross) born (died 1880). Julia Ward Howe born (died 1910). Susan Warner born (died 1885).
1820	Susan Brownell Anthony born (died 1906). Anne Brontë born (died 1849). Florence Nightingale born (died 1910). Anna Sewell born (died 1878).
1822	Eliza Lynn Linton born (died 1898).
1823	Ann Radcliffe dies (born 1764). Charlotte Maria Yonge born (died 1901).
1825	Frances E. W. Harper born (died 1911).
1826	Dinah Maria Mulock Craik born (died 1897). Barbara Leigh Smith (B.L. Bodichon) born (died 1891).
1827	Maria Cummins born (died 1866).
1828	Josephine Butler born (died 1906). Caroline Lamb dies (born 1785). Margaret Oliphant born (died 1897).
1830	Emily Davies born (died 1921). Emily Dickinson born (died 1886). Christina Rossetti born (died 1894).
1831	Isabella Bird (Bishop) born (died 1904). Rebecca Harding Davis born (died 1910). Amelia B. Edwards born (died 1892). Helen Hunt Jackson born (died 1885).
1832	Louisa May Alcott born (died 1888).
1836	Isabella Beeton born (died 1865). Elizabeth Garrett Anderson born (died 1917).
1837	Mount Holyoke College founded. Oberlin College begins to admit women. Sarah and Angelina Grimké lead the first National Female Anti-Slavery Society. Mary Elizabeth Braddon born (died 1915). Anne Thackeray (Lady Ritchie) born (died 1919).
1838	Florence Marryat born (died 1899).
1839	Infants' Custody Act (England). Ouida (Marie Louise de la Ramée) born (died 1908).
1840	Lucretia Mott and Elizabeth Cady Stanton are among the women delegates barred from the World Anti-Slavery Convention.
	Rhoda Broughton born (died 1920). Fanny Burney dies (born 1752). Rosa Nouchette Carey born (died 1909).
1847	Alice Meynell born (died 1922).

1848	The Seneca Falls Convention, organized by Mott and Stanton, leads to the *Declaration of Sentiments*. Married Woman's Property Act (United States). Alice James born (died 1892).
1849	Frances Hodgson Burnett born (died 1924). Sarah Orne Jewett born (died 1909). Maria Edgeworth dies (born 1767).
1850	Ella Wheeler Wilcox born (died 1919).
1850–1853	Crimean War.
1851	Suffrage movement begins in England. Kate Chopin born (died 1904). Mrs. Humphrey Ward born (died 1920).
1852	Mary E. Wilkins Freeman born (died 1930).
1855	Mary Russell Mitford dies (born 1787). Olive Schreiner born (died 1920). Dorothy Wordsworth dies (born 1771).
1856	Violet Paget born (died 1935).
1857	Matrimonial Causes Act (England).
1858	Beatrice Potter Webb born (died 1943).
1859	Carrie Chapman Catt born (died 1947). Mary Cholmondeley born (died 1925). George Egerton (Mary Chavelita Dunne Bright) born (died 1945).
1860	Charlotte Perkins Gilman born (died 1935).
1860s	Married Women's Property Acts passed in 17 American states.
1861	Mary Elizabeth Coleridge born (died 1907).
1861–1865	American Civil War.
1862	Sarah Grand (Frances McFall) born (died 1943). Edith Wharton born (died 1937).
1863	May Sinclair born (died 1946). Frances Trollope dies (born 1780).
1864	Marie Corelli (Mary MacKay) born (died 1924).
1865	Lydia Sigourney dies (born 1791). Vassar College founded.
1866	First U.S. Senate debate on woman suffrage.
1867	Catharine Sedgwick dies (born 1789).
1868	Fourteenth Amendment defines citizenship to include freed male slaves and to exclude women. Bill supporting woman suffrage introduced in the House of Representatives; introduced in the joint Congress in 1869.
1869	Fifteenth Amendment forbids denying suffrage on account of race, but excludes women. Anthony and Stanton found the National Woman Suffrage Association. Wyoming territory is the first to grant suffrage to women. John Stuart Mill, *The Subjection of Women* (written 1861).
1870	Girton College established. English Married Woman's Property Act (later amended).
1871	Newnham College founded.
1872	Anthony registers to vote, faces trial.

1873   Women's Christian Temperance Union established.

1875   Supreme Court decides that suffrage need not be granted to
            women, criminals, or the mentally deficient. Smith College
            founded. Wellesley College founded.

1877   Obscenity trial of Besant and Bradlaugh for *The Fruits of Philoso-
            phy*, a birth-control pamphlet.

1879   Radcliffe College ("Harvard Annex") founded.

1884   Oxford and Cambridge allow women to sit in selected classes.

1885   Bryn Mawr College founded.

1889   Jane Addams founds Hull House. Barnard College founded.

1890   National American Women's Suffrage Association established,
            joining the American Women's Suffrage Association with
            the more radical National Woman's Suffrage Association.
            Wyoming enters the union with a constitutional guarantee of
            suffrage for women.

1897   Queen Victoria's Golden Jubilee.

1901   Queen Victoria dies.

1914–1919   World War I.

1919   Suffrage for women passed in England.

1920   Oxford University grants women degrees. Nineteenth Amend-
            ment, granting suffrage for women, ratified in the United
            States.

Notes and References

Chapter One

1. Virginia Woolf, *A Room of One's Own* (New York: Harcourt Brace Jovanovich, 1929), 68.
2. Abigail Adams to John Adams, 31 March 1777, *Familiar Letters of John Adams and His Wife Abigail Adams, During the Revolution*, ed. Charles Francis Adams (Boston: Houghton, Mifflin, & Co., 1875), 149.
3. Eneas Sweetland Dallas, *The Gay Science* (London, 1866), 2:287, quoted in Richard Stang, *The Theory of the Novel in England, 1850–1870* (New York: Columbia University Press, 1959), xi.
4. Currer Bell [Charlotte Brontë] to G. H. Lewes, 6 November 1847, quoted in *Nineteenth-Century British Novelists on the Novel*, ed. George L. Barnett (New York: Meredith Corporation, 1971), 136.
5. *Saturday Review* (24 October 1863), 555, quoted in Stang, *Theory*, 181.
6. On the general issue of social class, see Richard Faber, *Proper Stations: Class in Victorian Fiction* (London: Faber and Faber, 1971). Good sources on the reading public and the marketplace include: Margaret Dalziel, *Popular Fiction One Hundred Years Ago: An Unexplored Tract of Literary History* (London: Cohen and West, 1957) and Richard Altick, *The English Common Reader: A Social History of the Mass Reading Public, 1800–1900* (Chicago and London: University of Chicago Press, 1957). Also useful are: Stang, *Theory*, 3–88; Guinevere L. Griest, *Mudie's Circulating Library and the Victorian Novel* (Bloomington: Indiana University Press, 1970); Amy Cruse, *The Victorians and Their Books* (London: Allen and Unwin, 1935); J. A. Sutherland, *Victorian Novelists and Publishers* (Chicago: University of Chicago Press, 1976); Richard Altick, *Victorian People and Ideas* (New York: W. W. Norton & Co., 1973); and Frank Luther Mott, *Golden Multitudes: The Story of Bestsellers in the United States* (New York: Macmillan, 1947).
7. Seymour Tremenheere, *Report on the Mining Districts* (1850), Parliamentary Papers 1850, 23:53–54; cited in E. Royston Pike, *"Golden Times": Human Documents of the Victorian Age* (New York and Washington: Frederick A. Praeger, 1967), 254–55.

Chapter Two

1. Sarah Grimké, "Marriage," in *The Female Experience: An American Documentary*, ed. Gerda Lerner (Indianapolis: Bobbs-Merrill, 1977), 89.

2. *The Report of the Registrar-General on the Census of 1851*, Parliamentary Papers 1852–53, 85: xxxv–xxxvi; as quoted in Pike, "*Golden Times*," 234.

3. Virginia Woolf, "Professions for Women," in *Collected Essays II*, ed. Leonard Woolf (London: Chatto and Windus, 1966), 284–89.

4. William Blackstone, "Of Husband and Wife," in *Commentaries on the Law of England* (1765), vol. I, chap. 15.

5. *Royal Commission on Population: Report* (1949; reprint, London: Her Majesty's Stationery Office, 1964), 10; hereafter cited as *Population: Report*. On issues related to family size, see also Neil Tranter, *Population since the Industrial Revolution: The Case of England and Wales* (New York: Barnes and Noble, 1973), 53; Michael Drake, ed., *Population in Industrialization* (London: Methuen & Co., 1969), 124; Grosvenor Talbot Griffith, *Population Problems of the Age of Malthus* (London: Frank Cass & Co., 1926; 2d ed., New York: A. M. Kelley, 1967), 28. On some of the limitations of all these reports, see M. Drake's "The Census, 1801–1891," in *Nineteenth-Century Society: Essays in the Use of Quantitative Methods for the Study of Social Data*, ed. E. A. Wrigley (Cambridge: Cambridge University Press, 1972), 7–46. The data from various sources differ in suitability and apparent accuracy.

6. Peter Laslett, *Family Life and Illicit Love in Earlier Generations* (New York: Cambridge University Press, 1977), chap. 3, esp. pp. 105, 156–57. Laslett observes that illegitimacy rates were higher in rural or country areas than in metropolitan ones.

7. C. Ansell, *On the Rate of Mortality at Early Periods of Life, the Age at Marriage, the Number of Children to a Marriage, the Length of a Generation, and Other Statistics of Families in the Upper and Professional Classes* (1874); cited by Patricia Branca, *The Silent Sisterhood: Middle Class Women in the Victorian Home* (Pittsburgh: Carnegie-Mellon University Press, 1975), 75.

8. Edward Gibbon Wakefield, *England and America: A Comparison of the Social and Political State of Both Nations* (New York: Harper and Brothers, 1834; reprint, New York: Augustus M. Kelley, 1967), 67.

9. Margaret Sanger, *An Autobiography* (New York: W. W. Norton & Co., 1938; reprint Elmsford, N.Y.: Maxwell Rpt Co., 1970).

10. Branca suggests that the persistence of a high maternal mortality rate probably added impetus for using birth control (81). On attitudes about and practices in childbirth, see John Hawkins Miller, "'Temple and Sewers': Childbirth, Prudery and Victoria Regina," in *The Victorian Family: Structure and Stresses*, ed. Anthony S. Wohl (New York: St. Martin's Press, 1978), 23–43. See also James Reed, *The Birth Control Movement and American Society: From Private Vice to Public Virtue* (Princeton: Princeton University Press, 1983).

11. Francis Place, *Some Illustrations of the Principles of Population* (1822), cited by *Population: Report*, 36. Possible effects of a rising standard of living and the women's rights movement on limiting family size are discussed respectively in J. A. Banks, *Prosperity and Parenthood: A Study of Family Planning among the Victorian Middle Class* (London: Routledge and Kegan Paul, 1954), and J. A. and Olive Banks, *Feminism and Family Planning in Victorian England* (New York: Schocken, 1964).

12. George Drysdale, *The Elements of Social Science; or, Physical, Sexual, and Natural Religion: An Exposition of the True Cause and Only Cure of the Three Primary Evils: Poverty, Prostitution, and Celibacy* (1854; 35th ed., 1905), 346–52; quoted in Pike, "*Golden Times*", 362–66.

13. *Population: Report*, 10; Tranter, *Population*, 53; Drake, *Population*, 28; Griffith, *Population*, 124.

14. *The Female Aegis; or, The Duties of Women* (1798; reprint, New York and London: Garland, 1974).

15. Charlotte Perkins Gilman, *Women and Economics* (1898; reprint, London: G. P. Putnam's Sons, 1900), 65.

16. William Acton, *Prostitution Considered in Its Moral, Social and Sanitary Aspects, in London and other Large Cities and Garrison Towns, with Proposals for the Control and Prevention of Its Attendant Evils* (1858), says that most prostitutes were transient, often married into higher social classes, and were probably healthier than middle-class mothers or working-class factory women; cited in Steven Marcus, *The Other Victorians: A Study of Sexuality and Pornography in Mid-Nineteenth-Century England*, 2d ed. (New York: Basic Books, 1974), 5–6.

17. Marcus, *Other Victorians*, 12–32. The positive response to Acton is outlined by Marcus, 12; the negative by Branca, *Silent Sisterhood*, 124–25. The most balanced analyses are: F. Barry Smith, "Sexuality in Britain, 1800–1900: Some Suggested Revisions," in *A Widening Sphere: Changing Roles of Victorian Women*, ed. Martha Vicinus, 182–98 (Bloomington: Indiana University Press, 1977); and Eric Trudgill, *Madonnas and Magdalens: The Origins and Development of Victorian Sexual Attitudes* (New York: Holmes and Meier, 1976). Trudgill defines the ideas, fears, and situations that shaped Victorian attitudes toward sexuality. Combining twentieth-century psychological theory with a wide range of nineteenth-century sources, Peter T. Cominos discusses the psychosexual nature of Victorian women in "Innocent Femina Sensualis in Unconscious Conflict," in *Suffer and Be Still: Women in the Victorian Age*, ed. Martha Vicinus (Bloomington: Indiana University Press, 1972), 155–72.

18. Elizabeth Cady Stanton, quoted in Mary P. Ryan, *Womanhood in America: From Colonial Times to the Present* (New York: New Viewpoints, 1975), 172.

19. O. R. McGregor, *Divorce in England* (London: Heinemann, 1957), 17. This is a solid historical source. On the significance of legal reform for married women, see also Lee Holcombe, "Victorian Wives and Property," in Vicinus, *Widening Sphere*, 3–28.

20. Alexander Walker, *Women Physiologically Considered as to Mind, Morals, Marriage, Matrimonial Slavery, Infidelity and Divorce* (1839; reprint, New York: J. and H. G. Langley, 1840), 221, 258; general discussion on divorce, 217–69.

21. William L. O'Neill, "Divorce as a Moral Issue: A Hundred Years of Controversy," in *"Remember the Ladies": New Perspectives on Women in American History*, ed. Carol V. R. George (Syracuse: Syracuse University Press, 1975), 127–43.

Chapter Three

1. John Henry Newman, *The Idea of a University* (1852; reprint, London: Longmans, Green & Co., 1919), 99. Future references to these lectures will appear in the text by section title.

2. On the uses and limits of the data, see B. I. Coleman, "The Incidence of Education in Mid-Century," in Wrigley, *Nineteenth-Century Society*, 397–410; and E. G. West, *Education and the Industrial Revolution* (New York: Barnes and Noble, 1975), parts 1 and 2. The contemporary view appears in the *Central Society for Education* (London: Taylor and Walton, 1837; reprint, New York: Augustus M. Kelley, 1969), 1:24–25. On the relationship of educational advances to economic, political, and social developments, see West, *Education*; and H. C. Dent, *The Educational System of England and Wales* (London: University of London Press, 1969). David Wardle, *English Popular*

Education 1780–1970 (Cambridge: Cambridge University Press, 1970) also covers government action, curricular revision, and the status of teachers.

3. See West, *Education*, 75–77, 95–99; and W. H. G. Armytage, *Four Hundred Years of English Education* (Cambridge: Cambridge University Press, 1964), 118, 202. Government intervention, spending, numbers of schools and students, teachers, and new laws are discussed in M. E. Sadler and J. W. Edwards, "Public Elementary Education in England and Wales, 1870–1895," Great Britain Board of Education, *Special Reports on Educational Subjects, 1896–7* (London: Her Majesty's Stationery Office, 1897), 1:1–71, 2:431–544. Contemporary documents may be found in Mary Sturt, *The Education of the People: A History of Primary Education in England and Wales in the Nineteenth Century* (London: Routledge and Kegan Paul, 1967); and J. Stuart Maclure, *Educational Documents: England and Wales, 1816–1963* (London: Chapman and Hall, 1966). See also H. C. Dent, *1870–1970: Century of Growth in English Education* (London: Longman, 1970); T. W. Bamford, *Rise of the Public Schools: A Study of Boys' Public Boarding Schools in England and Wales from 1837 to the Present Day* (London: Thomas Nelson Sons, 1967); Ellwood P. Cubberley, *Syllabus of Lectures on History of Education* (1902; revised, 1904; reprint, Totowa, N.J.: Rowman and Littlefield, 1971) Janet Roebuck, *The Making of Modern English Society from 1850* (New York: Charles Scribner's, 1973); and Sir James Kay-Shuttleworth, *Memorandum on Popular Education* (London: Ridgway, 1868; reprint, New York: Augustus M. Kelley, 1969).

4. Thomas Huxley, "A Liberal Education and Where to Find It," in *The Collected Essays of Thomas Henry Huxley*, vol. 3, *Science and Education* (New York: 1897), 76–100. All references to Huxley are from this essay.

5. John Stuart Mill, *Autobiography* (1873; reprint, London: Oxford University Press, 1958), chap. 1.

6. Herbert Spencer, *Education: Intellectual, Moral and Physical* (1860; reprint, New York and London: Appleton, 1914), 1–87.

7. Mrs. G. R. (Sarah) Porter, "On Infant Schools for the Upper and Middle Classes," *Central Society of Education* 2:229–42.

8. Charles Baker, "Infants' Schools," *Central Society of Education* 3:25.

9. J. Burton, *Lectures on Female Education and Manners*, 2 vols. (London: J. Johnson, J. Murray and J. Evans, 1793; reprint, New York: Source Books, 1970), 169.

10. Edward H. Clarke, *Sex in Education; or, A Fair Chance for the Girls* (Boston: James R. Osgood and Co., 1873; reprint, New York: Arno Press and the New York Times, 1972), esp. 13–18, 39, and part 3. Within a year, Julia Ward Howe published a collection of responses to Clarke's work: *Sex and Education: A Reply to Dr. E. H. Clarke's "Sex in Education"* (New York: Arno Press, 1972).

11. Hannah More, *Strictures on the Modern System of Female Education*, 2 vols. (London: T. Cadell Junior and W. Davies, 1799; reprint, New York: Garland, 1974), 55–56.

12. Emily Davies, *The Higher Education of Women* (London: Alexander Strahan, 1866; reprint, New York: AMS Press, 1973), 10–13, 36.

13. Dinah Muloch Craik, *A Woman's Thoughts about Women* (Columbus: Follett, Foster and Co., 1858), 3, xxi–xxii.

14. Lady Mildred Ellis, "The Education of Young Ladies of Small Pecuniary Resources for Other Occupations than That of Teaching," in *Second Publication* of the *Central Society of Education*, 192–97.

15. Phyllis Stock, *Better Than Rubies: A History of Women's Education* (New York: G. P. Putnam's Sons, 1978), and Josephine Kamm, *Hope Deferred: Girls' Education in English History* (London: Methuen & Co., 1965) are fine sources on secondary and higher education for women. For university education, see Stock, 179–83; Kamm, 184–98, 250–70; Rita McWilliams-Tullberg, "Women and Degrees at Cambridge University,"

in Vicinus, *Widening Sphere*, 117–45; and Vera Brittain, *The Women at Oxford: A Fragment of History* (New York: Macmillan, 1960).

16. S. A. Burstall, *English High School for Girls* (London: 1907), 13.

17. Anne Scott Firor, ed. *The American Woman: Who Was She?* (Englewood Cliffs, N.J.: Prentice-Hall, 1971), 68.

18. J. F. C. Harrison, *Learning and Living, 1790–1960: A Study in the History of the English Adult Education Movement* (Toronto: University of Toronto Press, 1961), 231.

Chapter Four

1. S. G. Checkland offers an overview of economic history in *The Rise of Industrial Society in England* (New York: St. Martin's Press, 1964), esp. 6–70. Specifically on women, see Margaret Hewitt, *Wives and Mothers in Victorian Industry* (London: Rockliff, 1958; facsimile, Ann Arbor: University Microfilms, 1975); Lee Holcombe, *Victorian Ladies at Work* (Hamden, Conn.: Shoestring Press, 1973); and Alice Kessler-Harris, *Out to Work: A History of Wage-Earning Women* (New York: Oxford University Press, 1984). Wanda F. Neff's use of fiction as a source of history calls into question the reliability of *Victorian Working Women: An Historical and Literary Study of Women in British Industries and Professions, 1832–1852* (New York: Frank Cass & Co., 1929; reprint, 1966). Penina Glazer and Miriam Slater, *Unequal Colleagues* (New Brunswick, N.J.: Rutgers University Press, 1987), identify strategies women professionals used, including "subordination" and "super-performance." Banks, *Prosperity and Parenthood*, presents data about entering professions, incomes, etc. See also B. R. Mitchell and Phyllis Deane, *Abstract of British Historical Statistics* (London: Cambridge University Press, 1962), 60f, and Charles Booth's *Life and Labour of the People in London*, 9 vols. (1892–97; reprints, 17 vols., New York and London: 1902–4; reprint, New York: AMS Press, 1970); and "Occupations of the People of the United Kingdom, 1801–1881," *Journal of the Statistical Society* (1886), 49:314–435. In conjunction with modern sociological and historical sources, Booth's work is interesting and helpful.

2. Thomas Wright, "The Journeyman Engineer," in *Our New Masters* (London: Strahan & Co., 1873; reprint, New York: Augustus M. Kelley, 1969), 4.

3. Baxter's figures, from works like *National Income* (1868) and *The Taxation of the UK* (1869), and some useful analysis appear in John Burnett, ed., *The Annals of Labour: Autobiographies of British Working Class People, 1820–1920* (Bloomington: Indiana University Press, 1974), 261f; and in Geoffrey Best, *Mid Victorian Britain: 1851–75* (New York: Schocken, 1972), 90f.

4. Henry Mayhew, *Selections from London Labour and the London Poor* (originally published in 4 vols. by Griffin, Bohn, & Co., 1861–62), introduction by John L. Bradley (London: Oxford University Press, 1965), ix, xxxiii, xxxv.

5. Miss Downing, "Work as a Necessity for Women" (Paper delivered to the Victoria Discussion Society), reported in *Victoria Magazine* (January 1872) 18:221, quoted in Banks, *Feminism and Family Planning*, 30–31.

6. Davies, *Higher Education*, 49–50, 66–67; on jobs see 80–96; on the benefits of a liberal education, 77–80; on combining a career and marriage, 96–123.

7. [Harriet Martineau], "Female Industry, *The Edinburgh Review* (April 1859), no. 222, 293–336; reprinted in *Working Conditions in the Victorian Age: Debates on the Issues from 19th Century Critical Journals*, ed. John Saville (Westmead, England: Gregg International Publishers, 1973); Author identified by Holcombe, *Victorian Ladies*, 10–12, Hereafter cited as *ER*.

8. Holcombe, *Victorian Ladies*, surveys nurses, training, working conditions, social status, and jobs (68–102). See also Booth, *Life and Labour*, 2d ser., 4:87–106.

Chapter Five

1. Susan B. Anthony, Elizabeth Cady Stanton, and Matilda Gage, *History of Woman Suffrage* (Rochester, N.Y., 1889), 1:70–73.
2. Chapter subtitle from Lucy Stone, quoted in Alice Blackwell, *Lucy Stone* (Boston: 1930), 67, as cited by Eleanor Flexner, *Century of Struggle: The Women's Rights Movement in the United States* (1959; revised, Cambridge: Belknap Press of Harvard University Press, 1975), 69.
3. Margaret Fuller, *Woman in the Nineteenth Century* (1845; reprint, New York: W. W. Norton & Co., 1971), 172.

Bibliography

Primary Sources

NOTE: The original publication date, if known to differ from that of the edition used, appears in brackets.

Literature

ADAMS, HENRY. *Democracy*. New York: New American Library, 1961 [1880].

ALCOTT, LOUISA MAY. *Eight Cousins: or, The Aunt Hill*. Boston: Little, Brown & Co., 1927 [1874].

———. *Jo's Boys, and How They Turned Out*. New York: Collier Books, 1962 [1886].

———. *Little Men*. New York: Collier Books, 1962 [1871].

———. *Little Women*. Cleveland: World, 1946 [1868].

———. *Rose in Bloom*. Boston: Little, Brown, & Co., 1919 [1876].

———. *Work: A Story of Experience*. New York: Schocken Books, 1977 [1873].

AUSTEN, JANE. *Emma*. Boston: Houghton Mifflin, 1957 [1816].

———. *Mansfield Park*. Boston: Houghton Mifflin, 1965 [1814].

———. *Northanger Abbey*. New York: New American Library, 1965 [1803].

———. *Persuasion*. Boston: Houghton Mifflin, 1965 [1818].

———. *Pride and Prejudice*. Norton Critical Edition. New York: W. W. Norton, 1966 [1813].

———. *Sense and Sensibility*. New York: Modern Library, n.d. [1811].

BARR, AMELIA E. *Jan Vedder's Wife*. New York: Dodd, Mead, & Co., 1885 [1881].

BELLAMY, CHARLES. *An Experiment in Marriage*. Albany: Weed Parsons & Co., 1899.

BELLAMY, EDWARD. *Equality*. Upper Saddle River, N.J.: Gregg Press, 1968 [1897].

———. *Looking Backwards: 2000–1887*. New York: New American Library, 1960 [1888].

BENNETT, ARNOLD. *The Old Wives' Tale*. New York: Modern Library, 1911 [1908].

BLACK, WILLIAM. *A Daughter of Heth*. New York and London: Harper and Bros., n.d. [1871].

———. *A Princess of Thule*. New York: Harper and Bros., 1873.

BLACKMORE, RICHARD. *Lorna Doone: A Romance of Exmoor*. 3 vols. New York: A. L. Burt, n.d. [1869].

BRADDON, MARY ELIZABETH. *Aurora Floyd*. New York: Garland Press, 1979 [1863].

———. *Ishmael*. New York: Garland Publishing Co., 1979 [1884].

BRADSTREET, ANNE. *The Works of Anne Bradstreet*. Edited by Jeannine Hensley. Cambridge, Mass.: Belknap Press of Harvard University Press, 1967.

BRAEME, CHARLOTTE MONICA. *See* Clay, Bertha.

BRONTË, ANNE. *Agnes Grey*. London: Oxford University Press, 1907. Reprint 1959 [1847].

———. *The Tenant of Wildfell Hall*. London: Oxford University Press, 1906. Reprint 1974 [1848].

BRONTË, CHARLOTTE. *Jane Eyre*. Boston: Houghton Mifflin, 1959 [1847].

———. *The Professor*. London: J. M. Dent and Sons, 1910. Reprint 1955 [1857].

———. [by Currer Bell] *Shirley: A Tale*. New York: Derby and Jackson, 1860 [1849].

———. *Villette*. London: J. M. Dent and Sons, 1909 [1853].

BRONTË, EMILY. *Wuthering Heights*. Boston: Houghton Mifflin, 1956 [1847].

BROUGHTON, RHODA. *Dr. Cupid*. Philadelphia: J. B. Lippincott, 1887.

———. *"Good-bye, Sweetheart!": A Tale in Three Parts*. New York: D. Appleton & Co., 1872.

———. *Miss Litton's Lovers*. New York: George Munro, 1880. (Bound with *Second Thoughts*.)

———. *Nancy: A Novel*. New York: D. Appleton & Co., 1874.

———. *Second Thoughts, A Novel*. New York: George Munro, 1880. (Bound with *Miss Litton's Lovers*.)

BROWNING, ELIZABETH BARRETT. *Complete Poems*. London: Oxford University Press, 1934.

BULWER, LADY LYTTON [*sic*]. *Cheveley: or, The Man of Honour*. Paris: Baudry's European Library, 1839.

BURNEY, FRANCES (D'ARBLAY). *Evelina*. London: Dent, 1958 [1778].

BURY, LADY CHARLOTTE SUSAN. *The Separation*. New York: J. and J. Harper, 1830.

BUTLER, SAMUEL. *Erewhon: or, Over the Range*. London: Trubner, 1872.

———. *The Way of All Flesh*. London: Richards, 1903.

CAREY, ROSA NOUCHETTE. *Aunt Diana*. New York and Boston: H. M. Caldwell, n.d. [1892].

———. *But Men Must Work*. London: MacMillan, 1906 [1892].

———. *Herb of Grace*. Philadelphia: J. B. Lippincott, 1901.

———. *Lover or Friend?* New York: Hurst & Co., n.d. [1890].

———. *The Mistress of Brae Farm*. Philadelphia: J. B. Lippincott, 1897 [1896].

———. *Mrs. Romney*. London: MacMillan, 1906 [1894].

CHOLMONDELEY, MARY. *Red Pottage*. New York and London: Harper and Bros., 1899.

CHOPIN, KATE. *The Awakening*. New York: Capricorn Books, 1964 [1899].

———. *The Complete Works of Kate Chopin*. Edited by Per Seyersted. 2 vols. Baton Rouge: Louisiana State University Press, 1969.

CLAY, BERTHA M. [CHARLOTTE BRAEME]. *Heiress of Hilldrop*. Cleveland: Arthur Westbrook Co., n.d. [1885].

———. *A Fatal Wedding*. New York: International Book Co., n.d. [1880–84].

———. *Beyond Pardon*. New York: F. M. Lupton Publishing Co., n.d. [1880–84].

CLEMENS, SAMUEL. *See* Mark Twain.

COLLINS, WILKIE. *Armadale*. New York: Dover, 1977 [1866].

———. *The Moonstone*. New York: Doubleday, 1946 [1868].

———. *The New Magdalen*. New York: Charles Scribner's Sons, 1908 [1878].

———. *Poor Miss Finch*. New York: Charles Scribner's Sons, 1909 [1872].

COOPER, JAMES FENIMORE. *The Deerslayer*. Franklin Center, Penn.: Franklin Library, 1983 [1841].

———. *The Last of the Mohicans*. New York: Scribner's, 1945 [1826].

———. *The Pioneers*. New York: Washington Square Press, 1962 [1823].

———. *The Ways of the Hour*. New York: G. P. Putnam, 1850. Reprint. Upper Saddle River, N.J.: Gregg Press, 1968.

CORELLI, MARIE [MARY MACKAY]. *Thelma*. Chicago: E. A. Weeks and Co., n.d. [1887].

———. *A Romance of Two Worlds*. London: Methuen & Co., 1896. Reprint 1963 [1896].

CRAIK, DINAH MARIA MULOCK. *John Halifax, Gentleman*. New York: Merrill and Baker, n.d. [1856].

CRANE, STEPHEN. *Maggie: A Girl of the Streets*. In *The Red Badge of Courage and Selected Prose and Poetry*, edited by William M. Gibson. New York: Holt, Rinehart and Winston, 1964 [1896].

CROWE, MRS. *Susan Hopley: or, The Adventures of a Maid Servant*. New edition. London: Routledge, Warne, and Routledge, 1861.

DEFOE, DANIEL. *Moll Flanders*. Boston: Houghton Mifflin, 1959 [1722].

DE LA RAMÉE, MARIE LOUISE. *See* Ouida.

DICKENS, CHARLES. *Bleak House*. Norton Critical Edition. New York: W. W. Norton, 1977 [1853].

———. *David Copperfield*. New York: Pocket Books, 1958 [1850].

———. *Dombey and Son*. Greenwich, Conn.: Fawcett, 1963 [1848].

———. *Great Expectations*. New York: E. P. Dutton, 1950 [1861].

———. *Hard Times*. New York: Harper and Row, 1958 [1854].

———. *Little Dorrit*. New York: Dodd, Mead, & Co., 1951 [1857].

———. *Martin Chuzzlewit*. London: MacMillan, 1910 [1892].

———. *Nicholas Nickleby*. Middlesex: Penguin, 1978 [1839].

———. *The Old Curiosity Shop*. New York: Coward-McCann, 1950 [1841].

———. *Oliver Twist*. New York: Dodd, Mead, & Co., 1979 [1841].

———. *The Posthumous Papers of the Pickwick Club*. Garden City, New York: International Collectors Library, 1944 [1837].

———. *Our Mutual Friend*. New York: New American Library, 1964 [1865].

DICKINSON, EMILY. *The Complete Poems of Emily Dickinson*. Edited by Thomas H. Johnson. Boston: Little, Brown & Co., 1960.

DISRAELI, BENJAMIN. *Coningsby: or, The New Generation*. London: Dent, 1911. Reprint 1963 [1844].

———. *Sybil: or, The Two Nations*. London: MacMillan, 1895 [1845].

———. *Tancred; or, The New Crusade*. New York: Collier, n.d. [1847].

———. *Vivian Grey*. London: Longmans, Green, & Co., 1906 [1825–26].

DU MAURIER, GEORGE. *Trilby*. New York: Harper and Bros., 1894 [1893].

DUNNE, MARY CHAVELITA BRIGHT. *See* Egerton, George.

EDEN, EMILY. *The Semi-Attached Couple*. Boston: Houghton Mifflin, 1947 [1860].

———. *The Semi-Detached House*. Boston: Houghton Mifflin, 1948 [1859].

EDGEWORTH, MARIA. *Helen*. London: Pandora Press, 1987 [1834].

————. *Patronage*. London: Pandora Press, 1986 [1814].

EDWARDS, MRS. ANNIE. *A Ballroom Repentance*. London: Richard Bentley and Son, 1883 [1882].

————. *A Girton Girl*. New York: John W. Lovell, 1885.

————. *Susan Fielding: A Love Story*. New York: G. W. Carleton & Co., 1883 [1864].

EGAN, PIERCE. *The Flower of the Flock*. London: W. S. Johnson & Co., n.d. [1859].

EGERTON, GEORGE [MARY CHAVELITA DUNNE BRIGHT]. *Keynotes*. London: E. Mathews and J. Lane, 1893.

ELIOT, GEORGE [MARY ANNE EVANS]. *Adam Bede*. New York: Dodd, Mead, & Co., 1947 [1859].

————. *Daniel Deronda*. Middlesex: Penguin, 1967 [1876].

————. *Felix Holt, the Radical*. London: M. M. Dent and Sons, 1901 [1866].

————. *Middlemarch: A Study of Provincial Life*. Boston: Houghton Mifflin, 1956 [1871].

————. *The Mill on the Floss*. Boston: Houghton Mifflin, 1961 [1860].

————. *Scenes of Clerical Life*. Boston: Small, Maynard, & Co., n.d. [1858]. (Contains three stories: *The Sad Fortunes of the Reverend Amos Barton*, *Janet's Repentance*, and *Mr. Gilfil's Love Story*.)

EVANS, MARY ANNE. *See* Eliot, George.

FARRAR, FREDERIC WILLIAM. *Eric; or, Little by Little: A Tale of Roslyn School*. London: A. and C. Black, 1892. Reprint. New York: Garland Publishing Co., 1977 [1858].

FERN, FANNY. *See* Willis, Sara Payson (Parton).

FIELDING, HENRY. *Joseph Andrews*. Boston: Houghton Mifflin, 1961 [1742].

————. *The History of Tom Jones*. New York: W. W. Norton & Co., 1973 [1749].

FORSTER, E. M. *Howards End*. New York: Random House, 1921 [1910].

————. *A Room with a View*. New York: Random House, n.d. [1908].

————. *Where Angels Fear to Tread*. New York: Random House, 1920 [1905].

FREDERIC, HAROLD. *The Damnation of Theron Ware*. New York: Fawcett, 1962 [1896].

FREEMAN, MARY E. WILKINS. *A New England Nun and Other Stories*. New York: Harper, 1891.

GALSWORTHY, JOHN. *In Chancery*. New York: Charles Scribner's Sons, 1931 [1920].

————. *The Man of Property*. New York: Charles Scribner's Sons, 1931 [1906].

GASKELL, ELIZABETH. *Cousin Phillis*. London: George Bell and Sons, 1930 [1865].

————. *Cranford*. London: J. M. Dent and Sons, 1906. Reprint 1948 [1853].

————. *Mary Barton*. New York: Norton, 1958 [1848].

————. *North and South*. London: Oxford University Press, 1973 [1855].

————. *Ruth*. New York: G. P. Putnam's Sons, 1906 [1853].

————. *Sylvia's Lovers*. World's Classics. London: Oxford University Press, 1901. Reprint 1974 [1863].

————. *Wives and Daughters: An Every-day Story*. Baltimore: Penguin, 1969 [1866].

GILBERT, SANDRA M., AND SUSAN GUBAR, eds. *The Norton Anthology of Literature by Women*. New York: W. W. Norton & Co., 1985.

GILMAN, CHARLOTTE PERKINS. *Herland*. New York: Pantheon Books, 1979 [1915].

————. *The Yellow Wallpaper*. Boston: Small, Maynard, 1899. Reprinted. New York: Feminist Press, 1973 [1892].

GISSING, GEORGE. *The Emancipated*. Rutherford, N.J.: Fairleigh Dickinson University Press, 1977 [1890].

————. *The Odd Women*. New York: Norton, 1971 [1892].

GORE, CATHERINE (MOODY). *Mothers and Daughters*, 2 vols. 1st American ed. Philadelphia: E. L. Carey and A. Hart; Boston: Allen and Ticknor, 1834 [1830].

————. *Progress and Prejudice*. 2 vols. Leipzig: Bernhard Tauchnitz, 1854.

————. *Women as They Are; or, The Manners of the Day*. 2 vols. London: Richard Bentley, 1854 [1830].

GRAND, SARAH [FRANCES ELIZABETH CLARKE MCFALL]. *Babs the Impossible*. New York: Harper and Bros., 1901.

————. *The Beth Book*. New York: Dial Press, 1980 [1897].

————. *Ideala*. New York: Optimus Printing Co., n.d. [1888].

————. *The Heavenly Twins*. New York: Cassell Publishing Co., 1893.

GUYTON, EMMA JANE. *See* Worboise, Emma Jane.

HAMILTON, CICELY, AND CHRISTOPER ST. JOHN [CHRISTABEL MARSHALL]. *How the Vote Was Won*. Chicago: Dramatic Publishing Co., 1910.

HARDY, THOMAS. *Far from the Madding Crowd*. London: MacMillan, 1957 [1874].

————. *Jude the Obscure*. London: Orgood, Mclvaine & Co., 1896. Reprint. Garden City: Doubleday & Co., n.d. [1894].

————. *The Mayor of Casterbridge*. New York: W. W. Norton & Co., 1977 [1886].

————. *The Return of the Native*. London: MacMillan, 1958 [1878].

————. *Tess of the D'Urbervilles: A Pure Woman Faithfully Presented*. New York: Harper and Bros., n.d. [1891].

HAWTHORNE, NATHANIEL. *The Blithedale Romance*. Boston: Houghton, Mifflin, 1884 [1852].

————. *The House of the Seven Gables*. Boston: Houghton Mifflin, 1964 [1851].

————. *The Marble Faun*. Indianapolis: Bobbs-Merrill, 1971 [1860].

————. *The Scarlet Letter*. New York: Washington Square, 1972 [1859].

HELME, ELIZABETH. *The Farmer of Inglewood Forest; or, An Affecting Portrait of Virtue and Vice*. 7th ed. London: George Virtue, n.d. [1825].

HOFLAND, MRS. *The Daughter of a Genius: A Tale for Youth*. Boston: Munroe and Francis, 1824.

————. *Patience: A Tale*. New York: W. B. Gilley, 1825.

HOLMES, OLIVER WENDELL. *Elsie Venner*. Boston: Houghton Mifflin, 1891 [1861].

HOOK, THOMAS. *Sayings and Doings: First Series*. London: Henry Colburn, 1836. (Contains three stories: *Danvers*, *The Friend of the Family*, and *Merton*.)

HOWELLS, WILLIAM DEAN. *Dr. Breen's Practice*. Boston: Houghton Mifflin, 1881.

————. *The Landlord at Lion's Head*. New York: New American Library, 1964 [1897].

————. *A Modern Instance*. Boston: James R. Osgood & Co., 1882 [1881].

————. *The Rise of Silas Lapham*. New York: Harper and Row, 1965 [1885].

————. *The Undiscovered Country*. Boston: Houghton Mifflin, 1880.

HUGHES, THOMAS. *Tom Brown's Schooldays—By an Old Boy*. London: J. M. Dent and Sons, 1949. Reprint. 1969 [1857].

HUNGERFORD, MARGARET. *Molly Bawn*. London: Smith, Elder, and Co., 1895.

JACKSON, HELEN MARIA HUNT. *Ramona*. New York: New American Library, 1988 [1884].

JAMES, HENRY. *The Ambassadors*. New York: Dell, 1964 [1903].

————. *The American*: W. W. Norton & Co., 1978 [1877].

————. *The Bostonians*. New York: Random House, 1956 [1886].

————. *Daisy Miller.* In *Daisy Miller and Other Stories.* New York: Airmont, 1969 [1879].

————. *The Golden Bowl.* New York: Dell, 1963 [1904].

————. *The Portrait of a Lady.* New York: Modern Library, 1966 [1881].

————. *Washington Square.* New York: Thomas Y. Crowell, 1970 [1880].

————. *What Maisie Knew.* Garden City: Doubleday & Co., 1954 [1897].

————. *The Wings of the Dove.* New York: Dell, 1965 [1902; revised 1909].

JEWETT, SARAH ORNE. *The Country of the Pointed Firs and Other Stories.* Garden City: Doubleday & Co., 1956 [1896].

KINGSLEY, CHARLES. *Two Years Ago.* New York: American Publishers Corp., n.d. [1857].

KINGSLEY, HENRY. *The Hillyars and the Burtons.* Boston: Ticknor and Fields, 1865. Reprint. Sydney: Sydney University Press, 1973 [1865].

LAWRENCE, D. H. *The Rainbow.* New York: Viking, 1971 [1915].

————. *Sons and Lovers.* New York: Viking, 1958 [1913].

————. *Women in Love.* New York: Viking, 1967 [1920].

LEVER, CHARLES. *Our Mess: Jack Hinton, The Guardsman.* Dublin: William Curry, Jun. & Co., 1843.

————. *St. Patrick's Eve.* London: Chapman and Hall, 1845.

LINTON, ELIZA LYNN. *The Autobiography of Christopher Kirkland.* 3 vols. London: R. Bentley, 1885. Reprint. New York and London: Garland Publishing, 1976.

————. *The True History of Joshua Davidson.* London: Strabham, 1872. Reprint. New York and London: Garland Publishing, Inc., 1975.

LISTER, THOMAS H. *Granby.* 2 vols. New York: J. and J. Harper, 1826.

MACDONALD, GEORGE. *David Elginbrod.* London: Hurst and Blackett, 1863. Reprint. New York and London: Garland Publishing, 1975.

MCFALL, FRANCES ELIZABETH CLARKE. *See* Grand, Sarah.

MARRYATT, FLORENCE [MRS. ROSE CHURCH]. *Too Good for Him.* London: Frederick Warne and Co., 1868 [1865].

MARTINEAU, HARRIET. *Deerbrook.* New York: Doubleday & Co., 1984 [1839].

MAUGHAM, W. SOMERSET. *Of Human Bondage.* Middlesex: Penguin, 1966 [1915].

MELVILLE, HERMAN. *Pierre; or, The Ambiguities.* New York: Grove Press, 1957 [1852].

MEREDITH, GEORGE. *Beauchamp's Career.* London and New York: Oxford University Press, 1950 [1876].

————. *Diana of the Crossways.* New York: Modern Library, n.d. [1885].

————. *The Egoist.* New York: Norton, 1979 [1879; revised 1897].

————. *Evan Harrington.* New York: Charles Scribner's Sons, 1923 [1860].

————. *The Ordeal of Richard Feverel.* New York: New American Library, 1961 [1859].

————. *Rhoda Fleming.* In *The Works of George Meredith,* vols. 9 and 10. Westminster: A. Constable and Co., 1897 [1865].

MILLER, THOMAS. *Gideon Giles, the Roper.* London: W. Nicholson and Sons, n.d. [1841].

MITFORD, MARY RUSSELL. *Atherton.* In *Atherton, and Other Tales.* Boston: Ticknor and Fields, 1854.

————. *Our Village.* 5 vols. London: MacMillan, 1893 [1824–32].

MOORE, GEORGE. *Esther Waters: An English Story.* New York: Liveright Publishing Corp, 1932 [1894].

————. *A Mummer's Wife.* New York: Brentano's, 1925 [1888].

————. *Sister Teresa.* New York: Brentano's, 1920 [1901].

MULOCK, MISS. *See* Craik, Dinah Maria Mulock.

OLIPHANT, MARGARET. *Agnes*. Leipzig: Bernhard Tauchnitz, 1865.

―――. *The Doctor's Family*. In *The Rector* and *The Doctor's Family*. Edinburgh: W. Blackwood, 1863. Reprint. New York: Garland Publishing, 1975.

―――. *Heart and Cross*. New York: James G. Gregory, 1863.

―――. *Miss Marjoribanks*. Edinburgh: W. Blackwood, 1866. Reprint. New York: Garland Publishing, 1976.

―――. *Oliver's Bride*. New York: George Munro, 1885. (Bound with *Mrs. Smith of Longman's.*)

―――. *The Perpetual Curate*. Edinburgh: W. Blackwood, 1864. Reprint. New York: Garland Publishing, 1975.

―――. *The Rector*. In *The Rector* and *The Doctor's Family*. Edinburgh: W. Blackwood, 1863. Reprint. New York: Garland Publishing, 1975.

―――. *Salem Chapel*. Edinburgh: W. Blackwood, 1863. Reprint. New York: Garland Publishing, 1976.

OUIDA [MARIE LOUISE DE LA RAMÉE]. *Moths*. Philadelphia: J. B. Lippincott, 1901 [1880].

PARTON, SARA. *See* Willis, Sara Payson (Parton).

PATMORE, COVENTRY K. D. *The Angel in the House*. London: G. Bell, 1892.

PHELPS, ELIZABETH STUART (WARD). *Beyond the Gates*. Boston: Houghton Mifflin, 1883.

―――. *The Story of Avis*. Rev. ed. New York: Arno Press, 1977. reprint of 1879 edition, Boston: Houghton, Osgood. [1877; revised 1879].

―――. *Dr. Zay*. Boston: Houghton Mifflin, 1882.

―――. *The Gates Ajar*. Boston: Fields, Osgood, 1868.

―――. *The Gates Between*. Boston: Houghton Mifflin, 1887.

―――. *Hedged In*. Boston: Fields, Osgood, 1870.

―――. *The Silent Partner*. Boston: James R. Osgood, 1871.

REYNOLDS, GEORGE W. M. *The Soldier's Wife*. London: John Dicks, n.d. [1852].

ROSSETTI, CHRISTINA GEORGINA. *Complete Poems of Christina Rossetti*, edited by Rebecca W. Crump. Baton Rouge: Louisiana State University Press, 1979.

ROSSETTI, DANTE GABRIEL. *Collected Works*. Edited by W. M. Rossetti. London: 1911.

SCHREINER, OLIVE. *The Story of an African Farm*. New York: Schocken Books, 1976 [1883].

SCOTT, SIR WALTER. *Waverley: or, 'Tis Sixty Years Since*. 12 vols. Philadelphia: J. B. Lippincott, 1856 [1814f].

SEWELL, ELIZABETH. *Amy Herbert*. 2 vols. Leipzig: Bernhard Tauchnitz, 1857 [1844].

SHELLEY, MARY WOLLSTONECRAFT (GODWIN). *Frankenstein: or The Modern Prometheus*. London: J. M. Dent and Sons, 1963 [1818].

SINCLAIR, CATHERINE. *Holiday House*. Edinburgh: W. Whyte, 1839. Reprint. New York: Garland Publishing, 1976.

SINCLAIR, MAY. *The Three Sisters*. New York: Dial Press, 1985 [1914].

STERNE, LAURENCE. *The Life and Opinions of Tristram Shandy, Gentleman*. New York: Odyssey Press, 1970 [1767].

STOWE, HARRIET BEECHER. *Dred: A Tale of the Great Dismal Swamp*. New York: AMS Press, 1970 [1856].

―――. *My Wife and I; or, Harry Henderson's History*. New York: AMS Press, 1967 [1871].

―――. *The Minister's Wooing*. New York: AMS Press, 1967 [1859].

————. *Uncle Tom's Cabin; or, Life among the Lowly*. 2 vols. New York: AMS Press, 1967 [1852].

SURTEES, ROBERT SMITH. *Jorrock's Jaunts and Jollities*. London: J. M. Dent and Sons, 1941 [1838].

THACKERAY, WILLIAM MAKEPEACE. *The Newcomes*. New York: E. P. Dutton, 1913 [1855].

————. *Pendennis*. 2 vols. London: Dent, 1910. Reprint 1965 [1850].

————. *Vanity Fair*. New York: Holt, Rinehart, Winston, 1961 [1848].

TROLLOPE, ANTHONY. *Barchester Towers*. New York: Doubleday & Co., 1945 [1857].

————. *Dr. Thorne*. London: Zodiac Press, 1951 [1858].

————. *Framley Parsonage*. London: Oxford University Press, 1926 [1861].

————. *The Last Chronicle of Barset*. London: Zodiac Press, 1949 [1867].

————. *Orley Farm*. New York: Alfred A. Knopf, 1950 [1862].

————. *The Three Clerks*. London: Oxford University Press, 1907. Reprint 1952 [1858].

————. *The Warden*. New York: Washington Square Press, 1962 [1855].

TWAIN, MARK. [SAMUEL CLEMENS]. *The Adventures of Huckleberry Finn*. Boston: Houghton Mifflin, 1958 [1884].

————. *The Adventures of Tom Sawyer*. Berkeley: University of California Press, 1980 [1875].

WARD, MRS. HUMPHREY. *Lady Rose's Daughter*. London: Smith, Elder, & Co., 1903.

————. *Marriage a la Mode*. New York: Doubleday, Page, & Co., 1909 [1908].

————. *The Testing of Diana Mallory*. New York and London: Harper and Bros., 1907.

WELLS, H. G. *Ann Veronica*. New York: Modern Library, n.d. [1909].

————. *Tono-Bungay*. New York: New American Library, 1961 [1909].

WHARTON, EDITH. *The Age of Innocence*. New York: New American Library, 1962 [1920].

————. *The House of Mirth*. New York: Charles Scribner's Sons, 1933 [1905].

WILLIS, SARA PAYSON (PARTON) [FANNY FERN]. *Ruth Hall and Other Writings*. New Brunswick, N.J.: Rutgers Univ. Press, 1986 [1854].

WOOD, MRS. HENRY (ELLEN PRICE). *East Lynne; or, The Earl's Daughter*. New York: A. L. Burt, n.d. [1866].

WOOLF, VIRGINIA. *Night and Day*. New York: Harcourt Brace Jovanovich, 1948 [1919].

————. *The Voyage Out*. New York: Harcourt, Brace, and World, 1948 [1915].

WORBOISE, EMMA JANE (MRS. GUYTON). *Married Life; or, The Story of Philip and Edith*. London: James Clarke & Co., 1872 [1863].

YONGE, CHARLOTTE. *The Daisy Chain: or, Aspirations: A Family Chronicle*. London: MacMillan, 1868. Reprint. New York: Garland Publishing, 1977 [1856].

————. *The Heir of Redclyffe*. London: Gerald Duckworth & Co., 1964 [1853].

Nonfiction

NOTE: Material appearing in Notes and References is generally not repeated here.

ADDAMS, JANE. *Twenty Years at Hull House*. New York: Macmillan, 1910.

BEECHER, CATHARINE E. *A Treatise on Domestic Economy for the Use of Young Ladies at Home and at School*. 3d ed. New York: Harper and Bros., 1855 [1842].

BENNETT, JOHN. *Strictures on Female Education*. London: Ishaiah Thomas, Jr., 1795. Reprint. New York: Source Book, 1971.

BIRD, ISABELLA L. *Six Months in the Sandwich Islands*. 7th ed. Rutland, Vt.: Charles E. Tuttle Co., 1974 [1875].

BURNETT, JOHN, ed. *The Annals of Labour: Autobiographies of British Working Class People, 1820–1920*. Bloomington: Indiana University Press, 1974.

CATT, CARRIE CHAPMAN, AND NETTIE ROGERS SHULER. *Woman Suffrage and Politics*. New York: Charles Scribner's Sons, 1923.

GASKELL, P. *Artisans and Machinery*. London: John W. Parker, 1836. Reprint. New York: Augustus M. Kelley, 1968.

GILMAN, CHARLOTTE PERKINS. *The Man-Made World: or, Our Androcentric Culture*. New York: Charlton Co., 1911. Reprint. New York: Johnson Reprint Co., 1971.

HALE, SARAH J. *Manners: or, Happy Homes and Good Society All the Year Round*. New York: Arno Press, 1972 [1867].

JAMES, ALICE. *The Diary of Alice James*. Edited by Leon Edel. New York: Dodd, Mead & Co., 1934.

MARTINEAU, HARRIET. *Harriet Martineau on Women*. Edited by Gayle Graham Yates. New Brunswick, N.J.: Rutgers University Press, 1985.

MILL, JOHN STUART. *The Subjection of Women*. 2nd ed. London: Longmans, Green, Reader, and Dyer, 1869.

NATION, CARRY A. *The Use and Need of the Life of Carry A. Nation*. Topeka, Kans.: F. M. Steves, 1908.

PRUETTE, LORINE. *Women and Leisure: A Study of Social Waste*. New York: E. P. Dutton & Co., 1924. Reprint. New York: Arno Press, 1972.

SAVILLE, JOHN, ed. *Working Conditions in the Victorian Age: Debates on the Issue from 19th Century Critical Journals*. Westmead, England: Greeg International Publishers, 1973.

SCHREINER, OLIVE. *Woman and Labour*. New York: Frederick A. Stokes, 1911.

STANTON, ELIZABETH CADY. *Eighty Years and More: Reminiscences 1815–1879*. New York: Schocken Books, 1971.

———. *The Woman's Bible*. New York: European Publishing Co., 1895, 1898.

STANTON, ELIZABETH CADY, SUSAN B. ANTHONY, MATILDA JOSLYN GAGE, AND IDA HUSTED HARPER, eds. *History of Woman Suffrage*. 6. vols. Rochester: Susan B. Anthony, 1881–1886. Reprint. New York: Source Book Press, 1970.

STEVENS, DORIS. *Jailed for Freedom: The Story of the American Suffragist Movement*. New York: Boni and Liveright, 1920. Reprint. New York: Schocken Books, 1976.

THORNWELL, EMILY. *The Lady's Guide to Perfect Gentility in Manners, Dress, and Conversation*. New York: Derby and Jackson, 1856.

VEBLEN, THORSTEIN. *The Theory of the Leisure Class: An Economic Study of Institutions*. New York: Modern Library, 1961 [1899, revised 1912].

WARWICK, FRANCES EVELYN MAYNARD, ed. *Progress in Women's Education in the British Empire, Being the Report of the Education Section, Victorian Era Exhibition*. New York: Longman's, Green, 1898.

WOLLSTONECRAFT, MARY. *A Vindication of the Rights of Woman*. Edited by Carol H. Poston. New York: W. W. Norton & Co., 1975 [1792].

Secondary Sources

Collections and Reference Guides

BAXANDALL, ROSALYN, LINDA GORDON, AND SUSAN REVERBY. *America's Working Women: A Documentary History, 1600 to the Present.* New York: Vintage, 1976. Excerpts from many important and interesting early sources.

FAUST, LYNNE LANGDON, editor. *American Women Writers: A Critical Reference Guide from Colonial Times to the Present.* 4 vols. New York: Frederick Ungar Publishing Co., 1979. A handy guide with over 1,000 brief essays of biography and criticism (400 in the abridged edition), discussing both well-known and neglected authors.

KRADITOR, AILEEN. *Up from the Pedestal: Selected Writings in the History of American Feminism.* Chicago: Quadrangle Books, 1968. Documents on women's "sphere," education, religion, fashion, family life, and the reform and suffrage movements.

LERNER, GERDA, ed. *The Female Experience: An American Documentary.* Indianapolis: Bobbs-Merrill Co., 1977. Ninety excerpts from the 1600s through the 1970s on daily life, childhood, marriage, old age, education, laws, and work.

PIKE, E. ROYSTON. *"Busy Times": Human Documents of the Age of the Forsytes.* New York and Washington: Praeger, 1970. Numerous excerpts providing background on social life.

———. *"Golden Times": Human Documents of the Victorian Age.* New York and Washington: Frederick A. Praeger, 1967. Numerous excerpts providing background on social life.

———. *"Hard Times": Human Documents of the Industrial Revolution.* New York and Washington: Praeger, 1966. Reprint. 1969. Numerous excerpts providing background on social life.

SCHNEIR, MIRIAM, ed. *Feminism: The Essential Historical Writings.* New York: Random House, 1972. Good collection of basic readings.

SCOTT, ANNE FIROR, ed. *The American Woman: Who Was She?* Englewood Cliffs: Prentice-Hall, 1971. Extensive anthology of documents showing changes in education, work, family, and reform since the Civil War.

Studies of Society and History

BANNER, LOIS W. *American Beauty.* New York: Alfred A. Knopf, 1983. Shows how fashion interacts with social, psychological, and economic factors to create a varying ideal of beauty.

BRANCA, PATRICIA. *The Silent Sisterhood: Middle Class Women in the Victorian Home.* Pittsburgh: Carnegie-Mellon University Press, 1975. Accurate and detailed analysis, using many contemporary sources.

COGAN, FRANCES B. *All American Girl: The Ideal of Real Womanhood in Mid-Nineteenth Century America.* Athens, Ga.: University of Georgia Press, 1989. Offers a counterideal to the cult of femininity, in emphasis on physical and spiritual health, education, and economic self-reliance.

COTT, NANCY F. *The Grounding of Modern Feminism.* New Haven: Yale University Press, 1987. Considers how the time leading up to and after the granting of the vote lay the groundwork for the rebirth of the women's movement.

Douglas, Ann. *The Feminization of American Culture*. New York: Alfred A. Knopf, 1977. Traces the development of sentimentalism and mass culture through the influence of middle-class women and the clergy.

Flexner, Eleanor. *Century of Struggle: The Woman's Rights Movement in the United States*. Cambridge: Harvard University Press, 1965. Superb historical background in a detailed, readable volume.

George, Carol V. R., editor. *"Remember the Ladies": New Perspectives on Women in American History*. Syracuse: Syracuse University Press, 1975. Ten articles on social change, including influences on and perceptions of women's roles from 1600 to the present.

Gurko, Miriam. *The Ladies of Seneca Falls: The Birth of the Woman's Rights Movement*. New York: Macmillan, 1974. Discusses the feminist movements of the eighteenth and nineteenth centuries, with a focus on Stanton and Anthony.

Rosenberg, Rosalind. *Beyond Separate Spheres: Intellectual Roots of Modern Feminism*. New York: Yale University Press, 1982. Describes the early modern reevaluation of the Victorian understanding of women's roles and gender differences.

Ryan, Mary P. *Womanhood in America: From Colonial Times to the Present*. New York: New Viewpoints, 1975. Studies how American society kept women subservient, from the agrarian beginnings to the present.

Showalter, Elaine. *The Female Malady: Women, Madness, and English Culture, 1830–1980*. New York: Pantheon Books, 1985. Examines how cultural ideas about women's behavior shape the definition and treatment of female insanity.

Vicinus, Martha, ed. *Suffer and Be Still: Women in the Victorian Age*. Bloomington: Indiana University Press, 1973. Ten articles on British women's lives, including sexuality, stereotypes, and jobs; detailed bibliography.

———. *A Widening Sphere: Changing Roles of Victorian Women*. Bloomington: Indiana University Press, 1977. Ten articles on British women's lives, including laws, sex, emigration, family magazines, and education; detailed bibliography.

Studies of the Literature

Bardes, Barbara, and Suzanne Gossett. *Declarations of Independence: Women and Political Power in Nineteenth-Century American Fiction*. New Brunswick, N.J.: Rutgers University Press, 1990. Analyzes fiction's presentation of the politics of women's struggle for power and rights.

Basch, Françoise. *Relative Creatures: Victorian Women in Society and the Novel*. New York: Schocken Books, 1974. Surveys social roles by examining the "anemic" heroine from 1837 to 1867.

Bennett, Paula. *My Life a Loaded Gun: Female Creativity and Feminist Poetics*. Boston: Beacon Press, 1986. Argues that social restrictions, tradition, and private inhibitions prevented earlier women poets from truly expressing themselves.

Calder, Jenni. *Women and Marriage in Victorian Fiction*. New York: Oxford University Press, 1976. Covers many variations of the central themes of marriage and courtship during a time of changing attitudes.

Cornillon, Susan Koppelman, editor. *Images of Women in Fiction: Feminist Perspectives*. Bowling Green: Bowling Green University Popular Press, 1972. Twenty-four essays on topics including heroines, feminist aesthetics, nineteenth- and twentieth-century writers.

FLEISCHMANN, FRITZ, editor. *American Novelists Revisited: Essays in Feminist Criticism.* Boston: G. K. Hall and Co., 1982. Eighteen essays on Cooper, Hawthorne, Stowe, Melville, Twain, Howells, James, Wharton, Crane, and others, reevaluated from various feminist perspectives.

FOSTER, SHIRLEY. *Victorian Women's Fiction: Marriage, Freedom and the Individual.* Totowa, N.J.: Barnes and Noble Books, 1985. Close studies of the works of Craik, Charlotte Brontë, Sewell, Gaskell, and Eliot, in the historical context.

FRYER, JUDITH. *The Faces of Eve: Woman in the Nineteenth-Century American Novel.* New York: Oxford University Press, 1976. Examines the American Eve, compared to the American Adam, in the works of male and female novelists.

GILBERT, SANDRA, and SUSAN GUBAR. *The Madwoman in the Attic: The Woman Writer and the Nineteenth-Century Literary Imagination.* New Haven: Yale University Press, 1979. Excellent background in history and discussion of lesser-known writers inform this study of women in literature.

HUF, LINDA. *A Portrait of the Artist as a Young Woman: The Writer as Heroine in American Literature.* New York: Ungar, 1983. Considers how society and culture affected women writers and how women created their own literary tradition.

KELLY, MARY. *Private Women, Public Stage: Literary Domesticity in Nineteenth-Century America.* New York: Oxford University Press, 1984. The lives and writings of Gilman, Stowe, and ten less famous female authors like Cummins and Sedgwick.

MEWS, HAZEL. *Frail Vessels: Woman's Role in Women's Novels from Fanny Burney to George Eliot.* London: University of London Press, 1969. Analyzes women novelists' presentation of women in relationships and in independent lives.

SHOWALTER, ELAINE. *A Literature of Their Own: British Women Novelists from Brontë to Lessing.* Princeton: Princeton University Press, 1977. Identifies three periods of writing: in the "feminine," women work within the dominant male culture; in the "feminist," they protest; in the "female," they define themselves.

WALKER, CHERYL. *The Nightingale's Burden: Women Poets and American Culture before 1900.* Bloomington: Indiana University Press, 1982. Establishes the tradition of women's poetry and discusses Bradstreet, Dickinson, and less well known authors.

WATT, GEORGE. *The Fallen Woman in the Nineteenth-Century English Novel.* Totowa, N.J.: Barnes and Noble Books, 1984. Demonstrates the development of a sympathetic view of "fallen women" in England in half a dozen novels.

Index

About the Author

Susan Rubinow Gorsky is a dean and English teacher at the Punahou School in Honolulu. After graduating from Smith College and earning her Ph.D. from Case Western Reserve University, she served as an associate professor of English at Cleveland State University and as teacher and dean at the Harrisburg Academy.

She is the author of *Virginia Woolf* (Twayne, 1978; revised 1989) and the monograph *March to Equality: Women in Pennsylvania's 300 Year History* (Harrisburg: Pennsylvania Commission for Women, 1982). She and her husband, Benjamin H. Gorsky, coauthored *An Introduction to Medical Hypnosis* (Medical Examination Publishing Co., 1981). Her articles on women in literature and society have appeared in publications such as *Modern Fiction Studies, Journal of Popular Culture, Journal of Women's Studies in Literature,* and *Images of Women in Fiction: Feminist Perspectives* (Susan Koppelman Cornillon, editor).

About the Editor

Kinley E. Roby is Professor of English at Northeastern University. He is the 20th-Century Field Editor of the Twayne English Author Series, Series Editor of Twayne's Critical History of British Drama, and General Editor of Twayne's Women And Literature Series. He has written books on Arnold Bennett, Edward VII, and Joyce Cary and edited a collection of essays on T. S. Eliot. He makes his home in Sudbury, Massachusetts.